Positive Parenting with a Plan

(Grades K – 12): FAMILY Rules

By
Matthew A. Johnson, Psy.D.

Intermedia Publishing Group

Positive Parenting with a Plan
(Grades K-12): FAMILY Rules

Published by:
Intermedia Publishing Group, Inc.
P.O. Box 2825
Peoria, Arizona 85380
www.intermediapub.com

ISBN 978-0-9819682-7-8

"*Children today are tyrants. They contradict their parents, gobble their food, and tyrannize their teachers.*"

Socrates
Greek Philosopher from Athens
(469 BC - 399 BC)

"I spend a great deal of time working with "AT RISK" children and their families. I have observed that organization and structure helps to greatly improve the family environment. Dr. Johnson's book, Positive Parenting with a Plan, helps parents to restore responsibility and respect in their homes. Children and adolescents learn to obey their parents and other authority figures at school, church, and in their community. Everyone learns to communicate their expectations and friendships develop as a result. The whole family wins with FAMILY Rules!"

Mark Eaton, Former NBA All-Star Center, Utah Jazz

"Raising healthy, responsible, contented children is a challenge! Most parents grew up with little experience in child rearing, then suddenly find themselves responsible for the 24-hour care of a precious little one who eats, sleeps, breathes, and acts in ways which alternately delight and frustrate. In a simple, direct, light-hearted, and principled way, Dr. Johnson's book, FAMILY Rules, provides a practical instruction manual for helpfully dealing with the inevitable challenges of parenting."

Rodger K. Bufford, Ph.D.,
Professor and Director of Integration, Graduate School of Clinical Psychology, George Fox University

"Dr. Johnson's book, FAMILY Rules, provides the best way to run a family whether you think you've got it together or not. Applying concepts of FAMILY Rules in our family was a major key to our successful journey from chaos and rebellion to a place of family wholeness and peace. Most importantly, applying FAMILY Rules in our family got dad and mom on the same sheet of music, clarified our family priorities, and gave us the structure we needed to succeed. Thanks, "Dr. J." for showing the world again, that you don't want to live outside of FAMILY's rules!"

James M. Dorman, Lt. Col., USAF

"Dr. Johnson's FAMILY Rules is the best parenting program out there. It's simple, kids love it, and parents love it even more. However, what I like about it is that it works well across all cultures. I work with a lot of African-American families. They love FAMILY Rules because it creates and maintains what parents won't compromise on... R-E-S-P-E-C-T!

Alduan Tartt, Ph.D.,
Licensed Psychologist in Georgia
Serves on the Board of Directors for the 100 Black Men of DeKalb
Author of "The Ring Formula: How to Marry Mr. Right"

Table of Contents

Foreword..i

Acknowledgments...iii

I Had The Meanest Mother In The World................................v

Introduction..vii

Part 1   Understanding the Basics of FAMILY

1   Where's the Instruction Manual on Parenting? 3

2   The Philosophical Underpinnings of FAMILY Rules 15

3   The Struggles of Parenting 35

4   The Seven Bad Habits of Parenting.......................................45

5   Reasons FAMILY Rules Could Fail in Your Home.................51

6   Tactics Used by Children to Manipulate Authority 57

7   Childhood Struggles that Might Interfere with
    Compliance...67

Part 2   The Mechanics of the FAMILY System

8   The FAMILY Rules Parenting System....................................87

9   Introducing FAMILY Rules in Your Home 107

10 Rats and Cockroaches 115

11 Community Parenting 123

Part 3   Anecdotal and Research Information

12 The Successes of FAMILY Rules With Parents and
    Professionals..133

Part 4   Questions about FAMILY Rules

13 Questions and Answers..183

Part 5   Appendices

Appendix A   How to Become a "Counselor Who Uses
                FAMILY Rules"...203

Appendix B-1   An Adolescent's Perspective about
                Residential Treatment 205

Appendix B-2   An Adolescent's Perspective About Being
                Escorted to Residential Treatment....................207

Appendix C   A Sample List of FAMILY Rules..........................209

Appendix D   A Sample List of Good Habit Cards 213

Appendix E   A Sample List of Chores.......................................217

Appendix F   A Sample List of Rewards 219

Appendix G   "P3" Preferred Treatment Programs....................221

Appendix H   Great Resources to Help Find Therapeutic
                Boarding Schools, Group Homes, and
                Long-Term Residential Treatment Facilities,
                and Therapeutic Wilderness Programs...............225

Appendix I   Funding Options for Therapeutic Treatment
                Away from Home..233

Appendix J   Finding Low Cost Therapeutic Treatment
                Options and Social Services 237

Appendix K   Information about Possible Tax Deductions..........241

Appendix L   Professionals Who Help Transport Children to
                Treatment..243

Appendix M   How to Schedule a FAMILY Rules Seminar..........245

Appendix N   The FAMILY FUNctions Parenting Tool Kit 247

Appendix O   Dr. Matthew A. Johnson's Private Practice 249

Appendix P   "Mad Matt's Mashed Potato Salad".....................251

About the Author 255

Foreword

An absence of structure afflicts a vast number of contemporary American families. There are many sources of this dreadful phenomenon including substance abuse, mental illness, divorce, illegitimacy, financial pressures, and moral inadequacy, to name just a few. Whatever the primary sources of the lack of family structure may be, the absence of structure itself invariably leads the family further down the spiral of despair, dysfunction, disease and delinquency.

Dr. Matthew A. Johnson ("Dr. J.") and his FAMILY Rules parenting system offer a powerful alternative to family chaos. FAMILY Rules presents a solid and coherent structure for families in need. In this book, he first presents a philosophical and intellectual framework for FAMILY Rules and then presents the system itself in an absolutely clear and straightforward manner.

FAMILY Rules is a product of who and what "Dr. J." himself is, a child of a family with problems, an outstanding competitive athlete, a dedicated and highly trained professional, and a man of strong conviction who practices what he believes.

While FAMILY Rules is highly structured, it is not rigid. Within the structure is plenty of room for individuality and creativity just as the rules of basketball leave room for the individuality and creativity of a Michael Jordan or a Dr. J. Families who understand and correctly and consistently implement FAMILY Rules will be protected from many of the most pernicious ills of our time. I am pleased to recommend FAMILY Rules.

Hillel I. Swiller, MD, FAPA, FAGPA
Clinical Professor of Psychiatry
Mount Sinai School of Medicine
New York, New York

Acknowledgements

The writing of any book is a major endeavor. A book cannot be written without encouragement, support, and assistance from many individuals. First, I would like thank my wife, Amanda, who is always there for me no matter what. She's my best friend and my rock. I would like to thank my four children: Levi, Hannah, Micah, and Grady. They are loving and patient guinea pigs as we implement FAMILY Rules in our home. They are blessings from above as well as bona fide keepers.

I am indebted to my parents for their love and support throughout my life. Although we have had more than our fair share of dysfunctional times together, they always tried their best to teach me sound morals and values. They also taught me to be confident with who I am and why I am on this planet. I am also indebted to L.D. and Darlene Mattson, along with their son, Scott, who have always been a second family to me. They taught me the importance of personal commitment to faith, hope, and love. The greatest of these is love.

I owe much to several friends for their generosity, love, and ongoing encouragement they have extended to my family over the years. Also, I really appreciate the ongoing love and support from my dear friends, Kevin and Karen Elliott, Andy and Brenda Ridgeway, Tracy Deacon, Michelle Farmer, Wendy Gutierrez, Eric and Jennifer DuPree, Dan and Stefanie Aldrich, Denise Greenhalgh, Barbara Polonsky, and my sister, Kristine Dhabolt.

I thank Janice Cocklereece for her transcription work which made writing this book much easier. I would much rather dictate than type. Many thanks to Wendy Gutierrez, Jeni Taylor, Dr. David Jenkins, Dr. Andy Sapp (Even though he's an Oregon State University Beavers fan - Go University of Oregon Ducks!!!), Matt Crosby, Gage Young, and Jeff Wheaton who provided their expertise while editing my rough draft. Their feedback was very direct but gentle and kind. I thank all the schools, churches, agencies, universities, and civic groups who have sponsored FAMILY Rules seminars. They have helped to spread the good news: "Every home needs a FAMILY."

I am particularly grateful to all of the families I have worked with in various treatment facilities, in my private practice, and via my FAMILY Rules seminars. Their feedback in helping to tweak, tune, adjust, and modify the FAMILY Rules parenting system has been invaluable. Some of their stories are used as examples in this book to help further explain the philosophical underpinnings of the FAMILY Rules parenting system and the importance of implementing this parenting program in every home. Names, situations, and settings have been changed to protect confidentiality.

Finally, I would like to thank all of the children, parents, and professionals who took the time to share their stories and research information in Chapter Twelve of my revised book. It is one thing to read the words of a biased author, me, but it's another thing to read about the undeniable successes and effectiveness of FAMILY Rules parenting program from those who are using it in their own homes or with their clients. I believe you will find their anecdotal and research information to be very encouraging as you seek to implement this program in your own home or with the clients you are working with.

I Had The Meanest Mother In The World

I had the meanest mother in the world. While other kids had candy for breakfast, I had to eat cereal, eggs, and toast. While other kids had cake and candy for lunch, I had a sandwich. As you can guess, my dinner was different from other kids' dinners too. My mother insisted on knowing where we were at all times. She had to know who our friends were and what we were doing.

I was ashamed to admit it, but she actually had the nerve to break the child labor law. She made us work. We had to wash dishes, make the beds, and learn how to cook. That woman must have stayed awake nights thinking up things for us kids to do. And she insisted we tell the truth, the whole truth, and nothing but the truth.

By the time we became teenagers, she was much wiser and our life became more unbearable. None of this honking the car horn for us to come running. She embarrassed us to no end by insisting that our friends come to the door to get us.

I forgot to mention that most of our friends were allowed to date at the mature age of 12 or 13, but our old fashioned mother refused to let us date until we were 15. She really raised a bunch of squares. None of us were ever arrested for shoplifting or busted for pot. And who do we have to thank for this? You're right, our mean mother.

I am trying to raise my children to stand a little straighter and taller and I am secretly tickled to pieces when my children call me mean. I thank God for giving me the meanest mother in the world. The world needs more mean mothers like mine.

Author Unknown

Introduction

I have written and rewritten this book at least one-hundred times in my mind. I'm sure I'll rewrite it one-hundred more times in my mind after the first revision. Positive Parenting with a Plan (Grades K-12): FAMILY-Rules, referred to as FAMILY Rules throughout the remainder of the book, is the summation of working in the mental health field since 1982 with children, adolescents, and parents. FAMILY Rules is based on three basic principles: (1) More often than not, mothers are the primary caregivers and disciplinarians in the home. This parenting system honors that fact, (2) Kids need rules, and the FAMILY Rules parenting system provides them, and (3) Discipline in the home is essential to a healthy home. FAMILY Rules gives organization and structure for discipline, more than any other parenting systems available. It's also very simple to implement. Therefore, this specific parenting discipline system is the MOTHER of all parenting discipline systems. In summary, mothers rule, FAMILY has rules, and FAMILY rules.

I have "begged, borrowed, and stolen" (only a figure of speech) the principles of FAMILY Rules from my work in residential treatment facilities, group homes, inpatient treatment settings, and youth groups. I have taught FAMILY Rules to over 10,000 families via my private practice and FAMILY Rules seminars. I have also taught FAMILY Rules to over 50,000 professionals across the USA, Canada, and Europe. These professionals have chosen to use FAMILY Rules with the parents and children they work with in their agencies, group homes, residential treatment facilities, juvenile justice systems, divorce courts, adoption agencies, foster care agencies, child protective services agencies, college and university classrooms, schools, churches, and synagogues. You will read more about their use of my parenting program with their clients in Chapter Twelve of this book.

Before developing FAMILY Rules, I was frustrated to see so many young patients make tremendous progress through their work in various mental health settings, only to regress shortly after returning home. We as mental health professionals would work hard to stabilize a child's out of control behaviors and attitudes via a consistently implemented behavior modification program. It never made any sense to me that both counselor and patient put out so much effort, only to send the child back home to his or her parents, who were usually as dysfunctional as their child. In addition, these parents rarely had any consistent structure and organization in their home. Eventually the child would return to his or her inappropriate behaviors and the parents would call us up, yelling and complaining. One day it dawned on me. Why not teach parents the strategies that we, as mental health professionals, implement in group homes, residential treatment facilities, and acute care facilities for children? Parents could then continue the same process at home. As a result, FAMILY Rules was conceived in my mind and birthed in Anchorage, Alaska - A melting pot of cultural diversity.

Since the conception of FAMILY Rules, it has been tweaked, tuned, adjusted, and modified over time thanks to ongoing feedback from the parents and children who learned the system. There is, however, one consistent piece of feedback from parents I have been ignoring for many years: "You should write a FAMILY Rules book and make it available nationally and internationally so more families can benefit from the system." Also, many parents said to me, "You should teach FAMILY Rules seminars around the world." Parents and professionals have told me they have tried other parenting approaches with far less success. Most parenting books and parenting seminars teach very important parenting principles as well as some useful tools for disciplinary interventions. However, most other parenting books lack a complete system of organization and structure to assist parents with intervention tools for discipline in the home. FAMILY Rules, on the other hand, is a complete system. Also, it's written at an eighth grade reading level with a whole lot of humor so even professionals, like me, can understand it.

Over the years, I have used two excuses to ignore writing a book about FAMILY Rules: (1) "I don't have the time to write a book because I'm overwhelmed by the time it takes to be a father, advisory board member, coach, and psychologist in private practice;" and (2) "I don't have enough professional experience under my belt to present a credible and unique intervention strategy to assist parents and their children in their homes." Well, much time has passed, and now I have no excuse. Don't worry, I'm still a husband and father. After teaching FAMILY Rules to over 50,000 professionals and 10,000 families with much success, and incorporating their feedback, I now believe I can offer a credible and unique behavior modification system to other families for use in their homes. I now feel compelled to write as well as revise this book.

Part 1

Understanding The Basics Of FAMILY Rules

.

~Chapter One~

Where's the Instruction Manual on Parenting?

"They didn't give us an instruction manual on parenting when we brought our child home from the hospital!" "They didn't give us a warranty either!" These are commonly stated phrases among parents I have worked with over the years. Most parents can relate to both statements. The "how to" questions of parenting never end. First, we have often wondered "where do the batteries go" in all four of my children? What about other "troubleshooting" problems such as when the talking, crying, screaming, fighting and laughing buttons get stuck in the "on" position? Where's the Prozac button so everyone is happy? Where's the Kaopectate button so the brown mushy stuff firms up? Finally, where's the psychostimulant button so they can focus and slow down?

Second, there have been times when dads have wanted to return the apparent defective product directly to the production plant; however, wives raised strong objections to this idea. It's one thing to watch the birth video in reverse, it's another thing to … well, you get the picture. So, I guess we all are kind of stuck with the little "Rug Rats," "Curtain Climbers," "Carpet Crawlers," "Teeny Boppers," "Crumb Crunchers," and "Adult Wannabes." Besides, no other kids are as smart and as good looking as our children. Right? Right!

Problems arise around the age of two when our cute little toddlers start to say, "No!" In our case, with Grady, it was "No! No! No! No!" Okay, I confess, it is cute and sometimes funny at first. It is also developmentally necessary for our children to start the process of becoming their own individual selves—separate from mom and dad. However, as our toddlers pass through the "terrible-two's," become children, and inevitably teenagers, they say "No!" much louder and with more frequency, determination, and defiance.

The challenge of parenting is to balance our children's developmental needs, such as autonomy, individuation, and identity with plain old common sense. We want them to take responsibility for their choices and to develop a healthy respect for authority. Therefore, the issues that parents want addressed in an "instruction manual for parenting" are the following: (1) help to better organize and structure their families, (2) practical parenting tools which will assist them in teaching the proper morals and values to their children, (3) assistance in clearly communicating expectations to their children while giving them reasonable rewards and consequences for their choices, and (4) an alternative to going insane or slowly torturing their kids to death. Just kidding! Please do not try this at home!

Let's face it, parents have a challenging task and they want to do it right the first time. Most parents desire to see their child grow up to become a successful contributing member of society rather than an inmate in the county jail or state correctional institution. Please take notice of the fact that I used the word "most" and not "all" when referring to parental desires for their children. Some parents don't appear to care at all as to how their children grow up. The truth is parental action or inaction speaks louder than words.

We are living in troubled times when you consider how children and adolescents are behaving today. The terrible lethal tragedies at Columbine High School in Littleton, Colorado and the Virginia Tech massacre in Blacksburg, Virginia confirm this harsh reality. This fact is true no matter where I travel in the United States or around the world. While in Western Samoa, I spoke with a parent from Australia and another parent from New Zealand who expressed their concerns about the poor choices adolescents are making in their countries as well as the disrespect they continually convey toward adult authority figures. After explaining FAMILY Rules to them, they expressed an urgent desire to see FAMILY Rules published and distributed in their countries, too. A look beneath the surface reveals that many parents are concerned, but don't know what to do. In most cases, parental action and/or inaction has contributed to their children's inappropriate behaviors.

Parental Action

Some examples of parental actions that contribute to a child's inappropriate, acting out behaviors are verbal, physical, and/or sexual abuse in the home, role-modeling poor attitudes about authority, poor diet, lack of exercise, and low self-esteem. Essentially, this is about parents not walking their talk or practicing what they preach. Quite frankly, consistency is a major challenge for all of us. From a personal perspective, it is an ongoing challenge for me to **Correctly** and **Consistently** implement FAMILY Rules in my own home because I am a creature of habit just like everyone else (i.e., "The two 'C' words"). I like the comfort of daily routines even if those routines are self-serving, counterproductive to my goals for raising my children and counterproductive to my own health. For me, the path of least resistance is the most comfortable path as well as the most nonproductive one. It took a public service reminder from a supportive friend to practice **Correct** and **Consistent** implementation of FAMILY Rules in my own home—and I'm the author of the system! Imagine that! Consistent parenting helped my children behave better.

I once worked with a family in Oregon. Martha, a very tall mother, took great pride in butting heads with school board members, teachers, and city officials. She talked openly in front of her children about the incompetence of various authorities. These authorities were always wrong and Martha was always right. Also, Martha always verbalized self-put downs concerning her height to her children. She viewed her height as a handicap and didn't wish this curse on anyone, especially her children.

Martha was shocked when I had the gall to suggest the possibility that her parental role-modeling contributed to her very tall son's defiance toward the authority of school officials, as well as his low self-esteem concerning his own height. You see, Martha brought her son, Warren, into therapy because her son's defiance toward authority at school started to infiltrate her own home. Warren was telling her "no" more frequently and defiantly. What goes around comes around. She didn't like the idea that her actions contributed to her son's problem behaviors. I taught FAMILY Rules to Martha and her husband and they reluctantly chose to implement it in their home with their son. They were reluctant because they were required to walk the talk. Martha wasn't allowed to violate her own rules for her son. She couldn't talk negatively about authority figures, she couldn't swear, and she had to talk positively about her own height. Through counseling and the implementation of FAMILY Rules in their home, her family was turned right side up. During the following year, I ran into Martha at the state fair. She shared with me that Warren was doing much better. He was no longer getting into trouble at school and he actually appreciated his height. She acknowledged her initial reluctance to implement FAMILY Rules, but was glad she did. She was also glad I confronted her about low self-esteem issues concerning her own height which eventually affected her very tall son. The cognitive intervention strategies via counseling were also helpful in turning her thinking around in a more positive direction.

I could relate to Martha and her son, Warren, concerning their issues surrounding being very tall. I'm six feet nine inches tall and have been taller than my peers my whole life. While in grade school, I would often come home crying. Taking the time to uncover the reason why I was so sad, my mother discovered my peers were making fun of me because I was much taller than they were. They called me many names and excluded me from their games on the playground during recess. My mother is tall. She talked about her height and my own height with great pride. She taught me to think about my height in many positive ways. As a result, I have used my height to open doors for me socially, academically (via a full-ride college basketball scholarship), in the area of employment, and in the arena of public speaking. My height and humor go a long way when speaking to a group of people. Having a Doctorate in Psychology helps as well. Finally, knowing and trusting in God is the icing on the cake that opens doors for success.

Another example of parental actions that contributed to their child's problems is in the case of Todd, Kris, and David. They were referred to my office in New Jersey because David was caught at school with marijuana, a marijuana pipe, and mushrooms. I was confused during the diagnostic interview as to why Todd and Kris, the parents, only verbalized concern about David's possession of mushrooms and not marijuana. After all, this was David's third offense involving the possession of marijuana while on school property. What parents in their right mind wouldn't be incensed by now?

I later put one and one together in the subsequent counseling sessions. Todd and Kris verbalized an ideology that society as a whole is wrong about narcotics and that all drugs should be legalized, especially marijuana. They openly espoused their ideology in front of David, and yet, they were surprised that he was busted for a third time on school grounds for possession of drugs. Duh! When I raised the possibility that their personal ideology was contributing to the delinquency of their minor, they genuinely looked puzzled. Although they thought the drug laws were wrong, they thought their son had enough common sense not to bring drugs to school. In their minds, the problem was their son's lack of common sense—not their ideology. They refused to learn FAMILY Rules. Needless to say, in spite of all the wonderful counseling I had to offer, their son remains at high risk for using drugs and getting busted again for possession on school grounds. When the inevitable happens, I'm sure they'll blame their son's lack of common sense or my counseling—not their ideology nor their own parental actions. After all, they're right and it's the rest of us who are wrong.

Parental Inaction

Some examples of parental inaction that contribute to childhood problems and defiance consist of neglect, abandonment, absences due to a workaholic attitude and/or the lack of taking disciplinary action. Parents are often afraid to act, fearing that their child may run away, become violent, withdraw, never talk to them again, or commit an act of self-harm, including the possibility of suicide.

While living in Alaska, I once worked with a single parent named, Connie, who had an adolescent son, Ed, and an adolescent daughter, Teresa. Ed and Teresa slapped, punched, kicked, and cussed at their mother with a sailor's vocabulary. They often slammed her against the wall and threatened her life. Connie experienced constant verbal and physical abuse by Ed and Teresa when they were home. They came and went as they pleased and defied school authority as well. Connie feared putting her foot down with her children because she didn't want to be physically abused more frequently than she already was. They also threatened her with the possibility that they would leave and go live with their father in the "Lower 48 States" if she didn't let them do what they wanted to do when they wanted to do it.

I helped Connie to rebuild her self-esteem after several counseling sessions. She needed to see herself as having a parental backbone of steel rather than a wet spaghetti noodle. Then I taught her FAMILY Rules and helped explain it to her children. I never heard so much swearing in my life and I used to play college basketball (i.e., my teammates were not missionaries in the locker room). Connie put her foot down in one session and told Ed and Teresa that they were going to follow FAMILY Rules in their home or they could go live with their father.

Connie also told them that she would send them away if they ever physically abused her again. Connie took the wind out of Ed and Teresa's sails as they never really wanted to go live with their father. They were merely using the threat of leaving their mother as a means of control over her. Once I convinced Connie that Ed and Theresa were bluffing her like a hustler in a Las Vegas poker game, she called their bluff. They were no longer king of the hill and went tumbling down the hill while their mother ascended to the throne. Their family was turned right side up. As a result, their behaviors improved greatly at home and at school.

Approximately two years later, Connie returned to my office at her children's insistence. They all informed me that their family life was taking a turn for the worse again. Ed and Theresa were not happy campers. Apparently, Connie was dropping the ball concerning correct and consistent implementation of FAMILY Rules in their home. Remember "the two 'C' words?" Correct and consistent implementation. Surprisingly, Ed and Teresa were demanding the reinstitution of FAMILY Rules in their home. They were tired of their mother's yelling and inconsistent implementation of rewards and consequences. It takes a great amount of effort to maintain a consistent bedtime when the sun is still high up in the sky at midnight in Alaska. Connie fell victim to the Alaska summer – "The land of the midnight sun." It was easier to let her kids run free than correctly and consistently implement FAMILY Rules.

Connie also disregarded the doctor's orders, or in this case, the psychologist's orders. Whenever I teach FAMILY Rules to parents and children, I tell them to take FAMILY Rules until it is all gone. Usually, the family members will look at me with weird expressions on their faces and ask, "What do you mean by 'until it's all gone'?" At that point, I provide a little education utilizing an analogy about physicians instructing their patients to take their medication as prescribed until it's all gone. Often, physicians warn their patients about discontinuing their medication simply because they are starting to feel better. Some people will save the remainder of their medication so they will have it available the next time they are sick because they don't want to have to endure the inconvenience and expense of seeing their physician again. However, because they choose not to listen to their physician, and finish their medication, the illness comes back and hits them with a double strength whammy upside the head. These patients end up going back to their physician, eventually spending more time and money getting over their illness. They would have gotten better sooner if had they just followed their physician's orders.

In the same manner, parents and children need to take FAMILY Rules until it's all gone. In other words, FAMILY Rules should be implemented in the home until the last child has turned eighteen, graduated from high school, and has moved out. Connie's parental inaction led to her own chastisement by her son and daughter, who used to verbally and physically abuse her. Connie thought their home life was going much better so she backed off of the correct and consistent implementation of FAMILY Rules in their home. Ed and Teresa wanted consistent structure and order in their home and turned their mom in to the FAMILY Rules police. That would be me or any other counselor who uses FAMILY Rules. (See Appendix A for more information.)

Finally, parental inaction can be clearly seen in the case of Jason and Cathy concerning their adopted son, Carl. For many years, Carl seemed like the perfect kid; however, he slowly began to change for the worse as his adoption issues and other issues began to surface. He began to hang out with the wrong crowd, smoke, and use drugs. Eventually, he dropped out of school. He threatened to beat up his mother and father whenever they attempted to confront him about his problems. They were legitimately afraid to take action because Carl had recently beaten up his older brother, Keith, with a baseball bat. Their parental paralysis, caused by fear of Carl's threats, was contributing to his demise.

Jason and Cathy are humble, gracious, God-loving people. They decided to give Carl space and love him back into being a good boy, but his problems worsened. Unknowingly, they were loving him to death. They sought out my counseling and psychological testing services to help them deal with Carl. After meeting with Carl and his parents for a couple of sessions, I had to inform Jason and Cathy that Carl was in need of long-term residential treatment to address his conduct disorder. Carl's attitudes and behaviors were greatly out of control. He had no respect for his parents, other authority figures, or for himself. He was headed down the proverbial slippery slide to incarceration or a premature death. He needed intensive long-term residential treatment immediately or it would be "Hasta-la-bye-bye" for him one way or another.

Needless to say, my recommendation was a real challenge for Jason and Cathy to accept. They did not want to send Carl away again. At the age of ten, they had sent him to a therapeutic snow boarding school in the "Lower 48 States" and saw no improvement. Also, because Jason and Cathy sent him away for treatment, Carl claimed abandonment issues related to his adoption. Carl knew how to push their guilt buttons. I assured them that the treatment program they were considering had a fantastic success rate. I gave them names and phone numbers of other parents who had sent their children to this program so they could talk with them for encouragement. I also told them about a support group for parents with troubled teens that met at the local hospital in their community every other Sunday. Jason and Cathy understandably hesitated. They needed time to think and pray.

As time passed, Carl's behaviors worsened. He made it clear that he was his own boss and that he was not going to obey his parents or any other adult authority figures. The occasional resurfacing of Carl's nice qualities kept his parents hanging on to a thin thread of hope that he would ultimately change and they would not need to intervene. The sun went down on their hope and Jason and Cathy eventually realized and accepted the fact that Carl needed residential treatment as soon as possible. He was almost seventeen so they only had one year left to effect positive change in his life. They were finally willing to put their foot down and implement the "teeth" FAMILY Rules provides and encourages as a last resort option. Thus, I provided Carl's parents with professional escort options. They chose to have me escort him to a residential treatment program in the South Pacific. I'll provide more details on Carl's story later in the book. Stay tuned.

Children Have Free Will

Although parental actions or inactions speak louder than words and greatly influence the family, please don't forget that children and adolescents also have free will. They can choose to obey or disobey in spite of parental influences to the contrary.

I have worked with almost perfect parents who appeared to have a D.C. sniper or international terrorist for a child. They walk the talk, love their children unconditionally, provide them with correct and consistent structure, and their children still choose to jump off into the deep end of the cesspool of defiance and disobedience. Also, I have worked with "parents from the pits of hell," who have children on the honor roll, participating in school sports and clubs, and they don't drink, smoke, or chew and they don't hang out with kids who do. Go figure?

While attending graduate school in Oregon, I worked with a gentleman named Allen. He was a nice man who was overwhelmed by much emotional pain and anger rooted in his past. Allen grew up in a home with parents who loved him very much. They poured their time and resources into correcting his developmental problems (e.g., feet, hearing, speech, and orthodontic problems) and they invested themselves into his athletic development. This investment eventually led to his obtaining a full-ride scholarship to play collegiate basketball. However, in spite of their love and devotion, they also had problems in their family. Allen's mom's alcoholism kicked in right around the time he entered the ninth grade. His father always had an anger management problem and the stress of his job didn't help matters. Allen's parents would occasionally take turns verbally and physically abusing their kids - his mom, during her drunken states, and his dad, during his anger episodes.

Once, when Allen was a senior in high school, his mom came into his bedroom in the early morning hours. Allen was sound asleep. His mom was drunk. She proceeded to slap Allen out of his sleep and told him what a lousy son he was. Her tirade went on for a few minutes while Allen laid there in shock. He was very confused by her words because he was receiving very good grades, active in sports, participating in the school choir, active in the youth group at church, and he never drank alcohol or used drugs. Allen's mom ended her tirade by stating, "I wish you were never born!" She left his room. Allen laid in his bed, crying, staring up at his ceiling in the darkness. Although he loved his parents, Allen was hurt and angry at God. While lying there crying in his dark bedroom, he asked God, "Why did you stick me in a family like this?"

For as long as Allen could remember, his parents seldom ever got along. He remembered being a very frightened three-year-old, lying in his upstairs bedroom, while his parents were downstairs yelling and screaming at each other. This went on just about every night. In spite of this, Allen sometimes felt safe because he was in his bed, in his room, with his blanket. Now, fifteen years later, their anger had finally invaded the refuge of Allen's bedroom. Allen's mom returned to his bedroom five minutes later crying, still very drunk, wanting to apologize for what she had said. She wanted Allen to forgive her and she wasn't going to leave his bedroom until he gave her a hug and a kiss. Needless to say, Allen did not want to touch her. Her breath smelled like a brewery. If someone lit a match at that moment in time, they probably would have lost the backside of their house. Allen was hurt, angry, and wanted to vomit due to the stench. The thought of her hugging and kissing him was more than he could handle.

At that time in Allen's life, during his senior year, he was quite tall for his age (i.e., he was 6 feet 9 inches tall). Being a rather tall basketball player, he could have picked up his mom and thrown her out of his room; however, Allen loved her and respected her. Allen chose to honor her with his behaviors rather than to use her alcoholism and verbal and physical abuse as an excuse to hurt her back. Allen eventually gave his mom a hug and a kiss just to get her out of his bedroom. She left his room feeling better. Allen still lay in his bed, crying, staring up at the ceiling, asking God, "Why?!!" The next morning, Allen's mom acted like nothing happened the night before. He was very hurt. Years later, Allen learned that his mom was experiencing an alcoholic blackout. She had damaged brain cells from her drinking. Alcohol had damaged her brain cells so much she could not remember what happened that night in Allen's bedroom.

In spite of the occasionally abusive environment that Allen grew up in as a child and adolescent, he still knew the difference between right and wrong and he chose to do what was right. Allen did not use his parents' shortcomings and mistakes as an excuse to behave in the same inappropriate ways. Thanks to the positive influence of Allen's youth pastor, his goal as an adolescent was to honor his dad and mom no matter what. Allen never got drunk, high, nor did he ever assault anyone. Yet, it is amazing to me how many times I encounter adolescents in my private practice who use their dysfunctional family environments as an excuse to behave like Mike Tyson or Marv Albert. They are constantly 'biting' the hands that feed them. Although parents can influence their children for better or worse, never forget that a child's "free will" is always an important variable that is mixed into the stew pot of life. A child can choose to behave right even though raised wrong. Another child can choose to behave wrong even though raised right. This can be very perplexing at times. Nevertheless, children should be held accountable for their choices. Sometimes parents opt not to hold their children accountable because of their own guilt from past parental mistakes. This parental inaction only leads to the creation of monsters in their home.

As I was previously saying, children have free will. FAMILY Rules is not a "let's blame the parents" book. Rather, it's a "let's help the parents increase the odds of raising emotionally healthy and obedient children" book. Raising perfect children is not the goal of FAMILY Rules. Increased compliance with and respect for adult authority is the goal of FAMILY Rules via positive parenting and positive parental role modeling. "Honor your father and mother" is not a bad virtue for children to learn. Most parents would not argue with this goal, but surprisingly, some parents do. Imagine that. I will comment in more detail concerning this sad truth in the next chapter.

~Chapter Two~

The Philosophical Underpinnings of FAMILY Rules

All existing systems of parenting have philosophical underpinnings as their foundation. This is the driving force behind what makes any parenting system work - if it works. Likewise, FAMILY Rules has philosophical underpinnings that make the parenting discipline system work in the home. Many parents lack any kind of a parenting philosophy in their home other than relying on thoughts and feelings once experienced in childhood: "When I'm a parent, I'm not going to raise my kids the way my parents raised me!" Unlike most other parenting systems, FAMILY Rules provides you with more than just philosophical underpinnings for raising your children in the real world. Instead, FAMILY Rules also provides parents with specific steps to implement the philosophy while still allowing parents the opportunity to incorporate their own unique values and morals. The remainder of this chapter will identify and explain the philosophical underpinnings of FAMILY Rules.

1. The "real world" is ordered and structured and the lack of order and structure results in chaos.

You will find some form of order and structure most everywhere you go on the earth. These important variables make the world turn. Without order and structure, we wouldn't know where to go or what to do next. How would we prioritize our goals without knowing the objectives and mission statement? How are decisions to be made? We all can't be the head. Someone has to be the arms, hands, legs, and feet. Someone has to clean the mess at the bottom and take out the trash. All positions are equally important in making order and structure work. Whether we are talking about various international organizations such as the United Nations, NATO or OPEC; or national governments such as the United States, Russia, or China; or

State governments such as New York, Texas, or California; or local governments such as the city assembly, mayor's office, or the school board; or grass roots groups such as MADD, Guardian Angels, or NAACP; or private groups such as churches, synagogues, the Rotary Club, or Boy Scouts, organization and structure are the bones that hold everything together. Without order and structure, we would all be like lost sheep without a shepherd. We would all be wandering around in the wilderness without purpose or direction. As a result, chaos would ensue like in Cambodia, Somalia, Bosnia, Kosovo, East Timor, and New Orleans, Louisiana after hurricane Katrina hit.

Can you imagine being lucky enough to win two front row tickets on the fifty yard line to watch the Super Bowl? The top two NFL teams are playing for the championship. You arrive at the stadium with your child and there are no lines, just masses of people swarming around the entire sports complex trying to get inside. You see people pushing and shoving while others are yelling obscenities at the gatekeepers. It takes several hours just to get inside. You are a little troubled by the lack of organization at the gates, but you'll manage, because you are at the Super Bowl for free and you have the best seats in the house! You walk down toward your seats and stop in your tracks as you observe two individuals attempting to obtain their seats next to where your seats are located. There is an intoxicated mob of strong men, World Wrestling Federation material, with painted faces that grab the two individuals and throw them over the railing to the ground below. You contact the stadium security to inform them about what you just witnessed as well as your desire to obtain your prized seats. The stadium chief security officer laughs at you. He says, "It's first come first served, Mac! Go find some empty seats!" Suddenly, you realize that you won't be watching the game from the best two seats in the stadium.

You're finally seated in the last two open seats at the top of the stadium behind one of the goal posts, when the coin toss occurs. The captains of the team calling the coin toss didn't guess right and decide to beat up the officials. The sidelines clear and a brawl ensues. It takes an hour to get both teams back to their sidelines, and the injured players off the field. While waiting, you talk with the one-eyed guy in the seat next to yours. You know, the guy with a patch over his eye and a scar across the front of his neck. After some discussion, you learn that he acquired his ticket for this game from an old lady he beat up outside the stadium. He also explains how he lost his eye and got the scar at the last two Super Bowls.

The team finally kicks off and the other team receives the ball. You notice that there are no officials on the field and the clock is not running. The players are throwing the ball back and forth and running anywhere they want to, on and off the field. No one is listening to their coach. After ten more minutes of observation, you quietly exit the stadium because you and your child want to leave alive and unharmed. You have had enough of chaos. Organization and structure would have made your Super Bowl experience much more enjoyable. Fortunately for football fans, the Super Bowl is run with a high degree of professionalism, organization and structure. Most of us have noticed this fact over the years from the best seats in the house - on the couch at home, strategically located near the kitchen and bathroom. These seats are cheap and we won't miss the Super Bowl commercials.

2. A hierarchy of authority and a healthy respect for it is a vital part of making order and structure work effectively.

Once again, everywhere you go on the earth, you will find evidence of the necessity of order and structure. As previously stated, someone has to be the head. Too many chefs in the kitchen can ruin a good meal. Every church has a pastor or priest. Every synagogue has a rabbi. Every school has a principal. Every city has a mayor. Every state has a governor. Every country has a prime minister, king, president or dictator. A healthy respect for those in authority is definitely a vital part of making order and structure work effectively.

Now imagine your child attending a middle school or high school where the students lack a healthy respect for and compliance to their teachers' and principal's authority. The students attend class when they want, fight in the hallways, bring weapons to school, buy and sell drugs on campus, curse at the teachers, and dress offensively without much, if any, consideration for the consequences. Imagine that you want your child to learn in a safe, organized and structured environment, but the school authorities fear implementing consequences. They fear being sued by litigious, irresponsible parents who are more interested in gaining a quick dollar than they are in having their children learn anything at all, especially respect and responsibility. You also learn that the school authorities fear taking a stance because their own school board may not back them up due to the very same fear of possible litigation. As a result, imagine yourself placing your child in a private school or charter school setting where the tolerance level for inappropriate behaviors is much lower and the teachers are supported by their administrators and parents. A civil suit is the last thing on their mind. Teaching children "the three R's" is the primary focus. Finally, everyone knows that the child will receive consequences at school and at home for breaking the rules, especially for being disrespectful toward authority figures. Imagine that! Parents, teachers and administrators working together, clearly communicating, can foster a healthy respect for authority in the students at home, school and the community.

Please do not mistake the above paragraph as an endorsement of private or charter schools over public schools. I bee edjumakated en dee publik skoolz. I am very happy with the public education I received at Morningside Elementary School, Leslie Middle School, and South Salem High School in Salem, Oregon. I'm pleased with the public education I received at the University of Alaska at Anchorage as well as at Rutgers University in New Jersey. Finally, I'm pleased with the private education I received at George Fox University in Newberg, Oregon. My oldest son has attended both private and public schools. I have been pleased with both learning environments. At present, all four of my children attend public schools and universities. There are pros and cons to both settings. Nevertheless, regardless of the setting, if students lack a healthy respect for authority at school, none of us as parents will be pleased with their learning environment. Most parents would perceive such a disorderly school setting as being poorly structured and ineffective in addressing our children's educational needs. We can all work together to improve our children's respect for the authority, organization, and structure in both public and private educational settings.

3. Authority flows downward; however, without checks, balances, and feedback there is an increased risk of developing an absolute dictatorship (i.e., Absolute power corrupts - ask Adolph Hitler).

The vice-president doesn't tell the president what to do. The employee doesn't tell the employer what to do. The defendant doesn't tell the judge what to do. Finally, a child does not tell a parent what to do. It is a well known fact around the world that authority flows downward. Our own forefathers knew the risk they were taking when they defied the King of England and his Redcoats army. The Confederates knew the risk they were taking when they took on President Abraham Lincoln and the Yankee soldiers. There is power behind authority. Right or wrong, it is this power that makes authority effective. However, absolute power corrupts. It is important for people in positions of authority to be open to feedback from those lower on the totem pole of hierarchy. Otherwise, they will become an absolute dictatorship and develop major blind spots to the error of their ways.

Adolph Hitler was destined for leadership. Initially, he wanted to study in seminary and become a man of the cloth. He had a strong desire to lead others down what he perceived to be a righteous path. Unfortunately, instead of seminary, the doors for the military, and eventually politics, opened up. He was not open to feedback from those serving directly underneath him. His absolute power, his self-perceived righteousness, and his unwillingness to listen to those serving below him eventually corrupted his own heart and mind in addition to the many Germans who blindly followed him. As a result, some of Hitler's own soldiers tried to assassinate him without success (i.e., Operation Valkyrie). He was bound and determined to demonstrate the dominance of a white Aryan nation. Fortunately,

Jessie Owens, an African-American, rained on Hitler's racist parade during the Olympics in Munich, Germany. Jessie Owens outran Hitler's best athletes and took the gold medals back to the United States. Unfortunately, Hitler's leadership abilities were used to murder millions of men, women, and children. You know how the story ends. The Americans and Russians closed in on Berlin and Hitler's defeat was imminent. He ended up murdering his wife, Eva Braun, and killing himself. Absolute power corrupts and leads to very disappointing conclusions that affect many lives.

Imagine a parent who becomes an absolute dictator in the home. The parental dictator believes he or she knows what is best for the family. The spouse and children are out to lunch. The spouse greatly desires to co-parent, making decisions together, but is forbidden the opportunity to do so because of a lack of cooperation, apathy, insults, abuse, or threats of divorce often used by parental dictators. Imagine the children becoming angry, depressed, and possibly dabbling in inappropriate activities as an act of rebellion against the dominant tyrant in the home. Imagine the spouse of the dictator retreating into his or her own world in order to cope with the harsh reality of living behind the iron curtain where the fear of being shot discourages scaling the wall to escape. This is not an environment that anyone would want to live in whether it is a communist country or an extremely dysfunctional family. Finally, imagine watching another movie on TV about some kid that shoots his father because of a history of physical abuse toward himself and his mother. How about a TV show depicting an abused woman who sets her husband's bed on fire as a desperate act to escape. Unfortunately these events have happened and, as previously mentioned, absolute power corrupts and leads to very disappointing conclusions. There is a better way. Keep on reading.

4. Families need to be ordered, structured and have a hierarchy of authority. Authority flows downward within families - not upward (i.e., Children must learn to respect authority - parents, teachers, police, clergy, etc.).

Without repeating the obvious, I will assume that you have thoroughly read the proceeding philosophical underpinnings. I was taught in some of my social work and psychology classes that the ideal family system is a democratic one (i.e., King Arthur's round table). Everyone has an equal say and equal vote. The philosophy of democratic parenting was also promoted in some treatment environments where I worked. I was young and idealistic when I first entered the mental health profession. My instructors certainly knew better than what my parents demonstrated for me while I was growing up. Therefore, I attempted to help families learn and practice the democratic model of parenting. There was only one problem. It never worked. Parents quickly became frustrated because common sense told them they should have authority and power in the home, but these so called educated clinicians, including myself, were telling them to parent differently. I remember parents yelling at me about how their kids were going to get away with murder if they actually practiced this model of democratic parenting. They would tell me, "You're undermining our parental authority!" I would look at them with a patronizing smile and gently encourage them to defy common sense and practice democratic parenting. Again, it never worked. At this time, I would like to extend a thousand apologies to those families, as should any clinician that promotes the democratic model of parenting. Elevating personal ideology over the practical realities of life and good behavioral science is self-serving and morally reprehensible.

Fortunately, I was exposed to working in other therapeutic treatment environments where democratic parenting was not practiced. Instead, parents were encouraged to take control of their home by becoming benevolent dictators – not absolute dictators. In other words, parents were encouraged to lovingly assert their authority and seek compliance from their children concerning their parental values and morals. Although parents were directed to listen to their child's thoughts and feelings concerning various issues with a sensitive ear, ultimately, the parents had the final say. There were only two votes – dad's and mom's. Children were taught that their parents were in charge and they needed to learn how to submit to their parents' authority, as well as submitting to the authority of other adults at school, church, synagogue, and in the community. I began to see the benefits of behavior modification and how its techniques were used successfully to gain compliance from children toward parents and other authority figures.

Eventually, I began to "beg, borrow, and steal" various concepts of behavior modification from my experiences working in different therapeutic settings and from behavioral research. As a result, FAMILY Rules was born. Occasionally, I'll have parents in my office who want help getting their adolescent's attitudes and behaviors under control, but they want me to teach them the model of democratic parenting. I flat out refuse to teach them this model and offer FAMILY Rules as a successful alternative. Sometimes, I have to refer these passive parents to another counselor who will coddle them as they stroll down their unsuccessful ideological path. However, most other parents will reluctantly try to learn and implement FAMILY Rules in their home. Some parents have heard success stories from their friends about FAMILY Rules and become eagerly willing to try it in their own home. Sometimes, I'll receive a letter or a phone call from these reluctant parents extending appreciation for my sticking to my guns and refusing to teach them the democratic model of parenting. They often share many examples of positive changes in their family due to the correct and consistent implementation of FAMILY Rules (i.e., "the two 'C' words"). You will read about some of their stories later in Chapter 12.

5. *A parent's primary responsibility is to prepare their child(ren) for the "real world" which is ordered, structured and requires a healthy respect for authority.*

If the real world is ordered, structured and requires a healthy respect for authority, then why on earth would parents want to teach their children that these realities don't matter? These kinds of parents are doing their children and the community a great disservice. They are setting their children up for a lifetime of hardship and failure. Parents must take the time, and it does take time, to teach their children correctly and consistently that the real world has rules, regulations, laws, policies, and procedures. These rules need to be obeyed because breaking them can result in unemployment, prison, divorce, or death. Parents are doing their children and community a great service when they teach their children a healthy respect for authority. This is adequate preparation for the real world. This is how you train up a child in the way they should go.

Unfortunately, some adults are unwilling to change their own bad habits or take the necessary time to correctly and consistently discipline their children. I have worked with some parents who fear taking the reigns of control away from their children because of possible resulting tension, conflict, and rebellion. I try to help them understand that they should fear what will happen to their children if they don't put their foot down now. Their child may wind up strung out on drugs, living on the streets, selling their bodies, incarcerated in a youth facility, or dead. Fear of the unknown can be paralyzing for many parents.

Speaking of fear, a healthy respect for authority requires reverent fear. Some therapists, especially those utilizing the democratic model of parenting, will argue against parents utilizing reverent fear as one of their parenting intervention strategies. However, fear is not always a bad thing. Reverent fear of consequences for bad or dangerous choices is good. There is an Old Testament verse that goes something like this, "The fear of God is the beginning of wisdom and only a fool despises discipline." I believe this verse conveys the truth that only a Silly Billy would tell God and his commandments to take a hike. On the other hand, those who are wise will listen to and obey God. They fear God's consequences if they don't obey. There is a verse in the New Testament that goes something like this, "Perfect love casts out fear." I believe this verse conveys the truth that eventually an individual will want to listen to and obey God. Over time, he or she eventually realizes that God's commandments were given as an act of love. God's commandments protect us from harm rather than act as a list of divine rules to ruin our day. In the same way, children who are correctly and consistently disciplined by their parents eventually realize that their parents' discipline is an act of love - not as an attempt to ruin their children's lives. Finally, there's a verse in the New Testament that goes something like this, "We love Him because He first loved us." In the same way, children eventually mature from a reverent fear-based model of decision making to a love-based model of decision making (i.e., "Our children love us because we first loved them by taking the necessary steps to teach them and to keep them safe"). However, if you're under the belief that children can pop out of the chute and naturally begin their life's journey from a love-based model without you taking the time to train them up in the way they should go (i.e., utilizing rewards and consequences) so when they're older, they won't depart from it, then you're just being a Silly Billy.

An example of reverent fear being good would be teaching your toddlers not to run around in the parking lot at the grocery store. If they do, they might have an appointment with the time-out chair, or worse yet, they might become a parking lot pancake. Another example would involve teaching your adolescent children that they are not going to curse at their teachers, get into fights at school, or go to parties and get drunk or high. If they do, they will endure consequences at home they will live to regret. These consequences do not involve physical abuse and/ or prolonged torture. Children who respect and reverently fear authority at home will respect and reverently fear authority away from home.

The bottom line is, regardless of what some well-intended mental health professionals think, fear is a part of life and helps to make the world go round. Without fear, we would be in a heap of trouble. Years ago, when a friend and I were walking along a path adjacent to the Russian River in Alaska, we rounded a corner and ran right into a grizzly bear. The bear was only five feet away from us. The grizzly bear's face looked shocked and I'm pretty sure our faces looked the same too. I guarantee it! The grizzly bear turned around and ran about fifty feet and so did we in the opposite direction. Then the bear stood on it's hind legs to look over the brush to see what we were doing. We waved our hands up high in the air and yelled and screamed. We were hoping to scare the bear away. Unfortunately, this grizzly bear had an attitude problem. He growled, dropped down on all four legs, and charged right at us. We were armed only with our fishing poles.

My friend started to run and I grabbed his shoulder and told him, "Walk fast but don't run! You'll kick in the bear's instinct to chase it's prey!" I followed behind my friend, maintaining a brisk pace, while the grizzly bear followed behind me down the path. Fear is good! Every time I looked over my shoulder to see if the grizzly bear was still behind us, he would growl and charge at me. I prayed like I never prayed before. Fear is good! We continued our brisk pace back to the trailhead that originally brought us down to the river. I looked over my shoulder again. The grizzly bear growled and charged again. I prayed. Fear is good! Finally, we reached the bottom of the hill. The grizzly bear was gone. Now, I was really scared. Where was the bear now? Fear is really good! We ran up the hill to my truck and climbed in back of it. Our hearts were pounding and we both were thanking God that we went to the bathroom before we walked down that trail to the Russian River.

Two days later, while eating breakfast, I read in the **Anchorage Daily News** that the Fish and Game officers had to shoot the same grizzly bear because he was charging other fishermen. The grizzly bear was trying to intimidate the fishermen in order to get them to drop their fish. He wanted an easy free meal. Unfortunately for the grizzly bear, he lost his fear of man. He was starting to physically bump into them to increase his intimidation. Therefore, he had to be shot. Fear is good! Fear makes the world go round. If we lose our fear, we get into big trouble. Parents need to teach this reality to their children. Today, unfortunately, many children and adolescents lack reverent fear of parents, teachers, police, clergy, and God.

6. Written rules help to clarify expectations which ultimately increases compliance and decreases inappropriate behaviors for most individuals.

Let's face it. Everywhere we go on the planet, rules, laws, regulations, treaties, policies and procedures are written down. They help us know how to behave with one another. Written rules act as a legal, ethical, and/or social contract between individuals, institutions, and governments. If these written standards are not complied with, then people lose their jobs, go to prison, pay penalties and interest, or work off community service hours. Nations might even go to war if a treaty is broken. The rules are written down at schools, churches, synagogues, work, clubs, governments, bars, and even on airplanes.

Every institution on the planet has taken the time to develop and post written rules, except the most important institution in the world - the family. In the family, most parents have the rules listed in their minds only. Mom has a list of rules floating around inside her head and dad has a list of rules floating around inside his head. Some of these rules overlap in agreement; however, mom has rules that dad doesn't know about, or he does know about them and he doesn't like them. Likewise, dad has a list of rules floating around inside his head that mom doesn't know about, or she does know about them and she doesn't like them either. This common scenario in most homes leads to great tension and conflict between spouses as well as between parents and their children.

The fact that most parents don't write down their rules for the family often causes their children to conduct Vulcan mind-melds to obtain the rules from their parents' brains. In other words, many children have to guess at what will or won't please their parents each day. Whether or not certain rules will be enforced may depend on one or both parent's mood and energy levels. How confusing for the kids! Parents are supposed to prepare their children for living in the real world. Doesn't it make sense that the rules at home should be written down just like everywhere else on the planet? Who can argue against plain old common sense? Oops! I spoke too soon.

I once talked with a therapist who I will refer to as Clyde. He did not see the value in writing down the rules in the home. Clyde wanted to see the research to back up my philosophical statement: "Written rules help to clarify expectations which ultimately increases compliance and decreases inappropriate behaviors for most individuals." Well, first things first. I informed Clyde that a former psychology instructor of mine once stated during a statistics lecture, "Good research often confirms common sense to be true" or "What everyone pretty much already knew to be true is actually true." Secondly, I reminded Clyde that everywhere we go on the planet, important rules, laws, regulations, treaties, policies and procedures are written down. It is a way of life for all institutions, micro and macro, to help clarify expectations via appropriate communication. In other words, written rules help all of us to stay on the same page.

Finally, I informed the skeptical therapist, Clyde, that if writing down the rules was good enough for the State Division of Occupational Licensing (SDOL) as well as God, then it was good enough for me. Clyde responded, "What do you mean by that?" I responded, "If the SDOL thought it was important enough to specifically spell out in a handbook what it takes to obtain or lose a license to work in the mental health field, then it is good enough for me. Also, if God thought it was important enough to have the Old and New Testaments recorded, including the Ten Commandments, in order to clarify His expectations for the human race and to increase our compliance with His standards, then it is good enough for me today. I'll use the same method with my children in our home." It's amazing how I see parents and professionals alike scramble in their minds while they try to deny the reality of this simple truth. But wait, there's more.

I explored further why Clyde was being so apprehensive about something that made absolute common sense. He shared his personal preference to "fly by the seat of my pants" without having to adhere to much order and structure. Clyde wasn't used to imposed boundaries and accountability and often, unknowingly, violated the boundaries of others. When boundaries were clarified for Clyde, he would become angry and oppositional. I wonder why Clyde was skeptical? Perhaps some unresolved issues were interfering there, huh? Clyde didn't want to be confused by the reality of common sense. The scary thing is that there are therapists like Clyde out there who unknowingly mess up your kids. I meant "work" with your kids. Although they truly mean well, they're only throwing fuel on the fire of adolescent rebellion via their own errant ideology.

Before I explain how the parenting system works to children and adolescents, I often share the following analogy with them in my private practice or at my FAMILY Rules seminars. I ask them to imagine how they would think and feel if they woke up the next morning and read in the newspaper, watched on TV or heard on the radio that the governor of their state had stepped down from office. In addition, the state legislature had suspended itself and all state law. There were no more local, county, or state police, the military bases were closed, and everyone was released from jail and prison. Most kids look shocked and tell me that they would feel very afraid of what others might do to them and their families. Naturally, there are always a few oppositional kids that say something like, "Cool!" I always respond by saying, "Cool, huh? So it would be cool if Joe Schmoe comes by your house, blows your dad away, slices your mothers throat, rapes and tortures you before burning you alive in your home, after, of course, looting your home for all the money and valuables they can find?"

Even the most oppositional children are eventually willing to concede that written rules help to protect all of us from others as well as ourselves. Defiant children are used to living by a double standard and they don't like having it pointed out to them. They want to have everyone else follow the rules, but they don't want to live under the same obligation. Oppositional children want their parents to care for them by providing food, clothing, shelter, education, and medical attention. However, they also want to come and go as they please, drink alcohol and use illicit drugs, smoke, skip school, cheat, steal, have sex, and have the right to treat others rudely. They want to be masters of their own destiny and live by their own set of rules, even if their rules violate the rules in their home, school, church, synagogue, and/or community. Basically, they want their cake and the freedom to eat it, too. Well, I'm sorry, but that's not going to happen as long as "Dr. J" is alive and well. That would be me. I work with parents to clarify their expectations through written rules. In the long run, my experience has been that written rules help to increase compliance with parental expectations. This is especially true when the written rules and subsequent rewards and consequences are implemented correctly and consistently (i.e., "the two 'C' words").

Now that you have finished reading through the six philosophical underpinnings of FAMILY, let's quickly review the six statements in bold italic print:

1. The "real world" is ordered and structured and the lack of order and structure results in chaos.

2. A hierarchy of authority and a healthy respect for it is a vital part of making order and structure work effectively.

3. Authority flows downward; however, without checks, balances, and feedback there is an increased risk of developing an absolute dictatorship (i.e., Absolute power corrupts - ask Adolph Hitler).

4. Families need to be ordered, structured and have a hierarchy of authority. Authority flows downward within families - not upward (i.e., Children must learn to respect authority - parents, teachers, police, clergy, etc.).

5. A parent's primary responsibility is to prepare their child(ren) for the "real world" which is ordered, structured and requires a healthy respect for authority.

6. Written rules help to clarify expectations which ultimately increases compliance and decreases inappropriate behaviors for most individuals.

If you agree with the philosophical underpinnings of FAMILY Rules, please continue to read this book. If you don't agree with the philosophical underpinnings of FAMILY Rules, please read through them again. If after reading this section for a second time, you still don't agree with the philosophical underpinnings of FAMILY Rules, please give this book to someone else who will benefit from reading it. This is America and you have the freedom to raise your children the way you want to. However, please ask them not to run for the office of the President of the United States. We need respectful leaders who understand the way the real world works.

Important Definitions in order to Understand FAMILY Rules

Throughout the years, I occasionally hear parents say something like, "This FAMILY Rules system of yours sure sounds awfully rigid to me. I'm not sure if something like this will help us with our family problems." Although they were correct in implying that rigidity would not help their family through troubled times, they were incorrect in their assumptions that FAMILY Rules is a rigid system. FAMILY Rules is a flexible system. It is a living and breathing document. The rules are not chiseled in stone. The list of rules can be added to, deleted from, or modified at anytime. I'll explain more about this later in chapter eight. FAMILY Rules provides order and structure for parents pertaining to their already existing rules and disciplinarian intervention strategies. FAMILY Rules doesn't offer much of anything new. Instead, it helps to organize and structure what parents are already trying to do, but in a much more effective way.

Let's take a closer look at a few key definitions that contribute to the philosophical underpinnings of FAMILY:

Order - 1. A condition of logical or coherent arrangement among the individual elements of a group. 2. A. A condition of standard or prescribed arrangement among component parts, such that proper functioning or appearance is achieved. B. Systematic arrangement and design. 3. A. The established organization or structure of society. B. The rule of law and custom or the observance of prescribed procedure (Merriam-Webster's Collegiate Dictionary, 2008).

Simply put, FAMILY Rules offers parents a logical arrangement for their family. It helps facilitate clear expectations and standards in order to achieve proper family functioning and appearance. FAMILY Rules, by design, is systematic in its arrangement. FAMILY Rules helps prepare children for the established organization and structure of society. Children learn the rule of law and custom and how to observe prescribed procedures at home, school, church, synagogue, and in their community. Order is good. Order is not rigid. FAMILY Rules is ordered - not rigid.

Let's take a look at another key definition that is a significant building block in the philosophical underpinnings of FAMILY Rules:

Structure - 1. Something made up of a number of parts held or put together in a specific way. 2. The manner in which parts are arranged or combined to form a whole. 3. Interrelation of parts in a complex entity. 4. Relatively intricate or extensive organization. 5. To give form or arrangement to. (Merriam-Webster's Collegiate Dictionary, 2008).

FAMILY Rules assists parents by organizing their values and morals (i.e., expectations) in a specific way that forms a whole system of family structure. The system gives form or arrangement to what is often identified as "flying by the seat of their pants" (i.e., "parenting by ear"). Quite often, parents cross their fingers and pray that their children will survive adolescence. With FAMILY Rules, parents can take a proactive positive approach instead of "parenting by ear." FAMILY Rules helps them organize and structure their approach to parenting. No more "flying by the seat of your pants" or "playing it by ear."

Just for the fun of it, let's take a peek at the definition for rigid/rigidity. Since some parents think there is a possibility that FAMILY

Rules might be too rigid for them, they should at least try and understand what rigid really means. The definition is as follows:

Rigid/Rigidity - 1. Not bending: INFLEXIBLE. 2. Not moving: Stationary. 3. Difficult. Synonyms: stiff, unbending, unyielding. Core meaning: not changing shape or bending (rigid iron bars). (Merriam-Webster's Collegiate Dictionary, 2008).

FAMILY Rules is anything but rigid. If you haven't figured it out by now while reading up to this point in my book, then you will have it figured out by the end of the book. As previously stated, FAMILY Rules is flexible and is a living and breathing document. It is not chiseled in stone. As long as both parents are in agreement, they can add rules, delete rules, and/or modify existing rules anytime they want to.

Once again, order and structure are not the same as rigid/rigidity. FAMILY Rules provides order and structure but it is not rigid. FAMILY Rules is a living and breathing document that can change over time. It bends, it's flexible, it moves, it's easy, and it changes shape as needed. If you're still thinking that FAMILY Rules is rigid, it is because you lack a proper understanding of the previous definitions and how they differ from one another. Structure and order are healthy and necessary to make the "real world" and families run smoothly. If you still can't see this, there is a serious possibility that you may have unresolved issues from your past with authority, structure and discipline that are interfering with your present ability to rationally perceive what I'm trying to convey. Consider addressing these issues in therapy before implementing any kind of parenting program.

Now, before we move on to the next chapter, we need to take a quick peek at a couple more definitions. FAMILY Rules utilizes consequences for bad behaviors (e.g., Good Habit Cards), as well as rewards for good behaviors (e.g., Daily Tokens and RAK chips). Every once in awhile, I have a parent say the following concerning the rewards aspect of the system: "You're asking me to bribe my kid to behave. I shouldn't have to bribe my kid to do the right thing!" I couldn't agree more with the concerned parent. The very definition of the word, "bribe," means something completely different than the understanding the concerned parent is conveying. Bribe is defined as follows:

Bribe - 1. Something, as money or a favor, offered or given to someone in a position of trust to induce him or her to act dishonestly (Merriam-Webster's Collegiate Dictionary, 2008).

The FAMILY Rules parenting system would never encourage parents to offer money or a favor to their children to induce them to act dishonestly. Quite the contrary, FAMILY Rules encourages honest behaviors and seeks to move children in a positive direction toward conforming to their parents' values and morals (i.e., expectations). I would never ask a parent to bribe their child. Reward their child, yes. Bribe their child - absolutely not! Since the "R" word was brought up (i.e., reward), maybe we should take a quick peek at what the definition truly means:

Reward - 1. Something, as money given or offered especially for a special service [i.e., involving honest behavior]. 2. A satisfying result (Merriam-Webster's Collegiate Dictionary, 2008).

Clearly, FAMILY Rules encourages parents to reward, not bribe, their children for their good behaviors which bring about satisfying results for everyone involved. Happy children make for happy parents. Happy parents make for happy children. It's a never ending circle of familial bliss which is certainly better than the other conflictual option which many families experience.

In summary, compensating your children for good behaviors is not bribery. Adults are rewarded in their jobs by receiving paychecks, bonuses, awards, trips, raises, tips, promotions, recognition by the company, the coveted parking space near the front door, and other possible benefits. Likewise, children are rewarded for good behaviors by their parents. This is appropriate preparation for the real world.

You'll never ever insist that your employer stop rewarding you for your good hard efforts on the job. Likewise, go therefore to your domicile and bless the buns of the fruit of your loins or womb (i.e., reward your children when they do well).

~Chapter Three~

The Struggles of Parenting

The biggest challenge for parents is balancing the roles of disciplinarian and friend. Unfortunately, many parents favor one role over the other. Dads usually lean in the direction of disciplinarian and may or may not invest time and energy in the role of friend. Moms, on the other hand, tend to lean in the direction of friend while sacrificing the role of disciplinarian. How most parents choose to parent often depends on what was role modeled for them while growing up. Some parents like what they experienced growing up and try to repeat it with their own children. Conversely, other parents consciously attempt to raise their children in the opposite manner in which they themselves were raised.

Both roles, disciplinarian and friend, are important and must be utilized by both parents in the home. Although some parents don't like to hear this, the role of disciplinarian is primary while the role of friend is a very close second. Unfortunately, too many parents have a misconception as to what the role of disciplinarian really means. Some parents experienced abuse while being disciplined and automatically think that any form of disciplinary action should be avoided. In a sense, they are choosing to throw the proverbial "baby out with the bath water." I believe that they are understandably overreacting emotionally to past abuses and they do not understand the definition of disciplinarian which is defined as follows:

Discipline - Training expected to produce a specific type or pattern of behavior, especially training that produces moral or mental improvement; A systematic method to obtain obedience; A state of order based on submission to rules and authority (Merriam-Webster's Collegiate Dictionary, 2008).

In spite of the past abuses I experienced while being punished, I clearly understand that the definition of disciplinarian does not involve the beating of a child with a belt, shoe, bat, fist, or 2x4, nor does it involve the pulling of hair, ears or lips, cigarette burns, cold water in a bathtub, or the verbal assault of the child. Rather, the word discipline comes from the root word, "disciple." To disciple a child means to guide, teach and instruct them in a manner which will help them stay on the straight and narrow path in life. Parents need to teach their children to stay between the lines on the road of life. The lines represent the rules they are to follow. Occasionally, parents need to be the guardrails for their children when they are nearing the dangerous curves in their early lives. Like most driving instructors, as parents, you hope that your child remembers to slow down for those dangerous curves along life's path after they are grown and leave your care.

A parent must be a disciplinarian first before being a friend. If the roles are reversed and the parent uses the democratic model of parenting (i.e., King Arthur's round table), taking on the lower role of a sibling, the parent is undermining his or her own parental authority. Inevitably, the parent will have to put his or her foot down or draw a line in the sand. Sadly, the child will laugh at the parent and continue to disobey. After all, the child doesn't have to listen to the parent; he or she is just another sibling. They're just another friend. However, the parent who is a disciplinarian first and, secondly, a very close friend, will have the respect of their children during the difficult moments in life. This type of parent is more apt to experience the desired outcome from the child during trying times because the child knows that their parent means business. The child knows, without a doubt, that he or she will pay the piper for disobedient behavior. The fear of dad and mom is the beginning of wisdom. Fear is good. Reverent fear of authority figures is a must and it begins in the home.

For those of you who struggle with prioritizing these two roles, let's take a look at the definition of a friend:

Friend - A person whom one knows, likes, and trusts; A person with whom one is allied in a struggle or cause; A supporter or sympathizer; Worthy of a friend; Warm and comforting; One fighting on or favorable to one's own side (Merriam-Webster's Collegiate Dictionary, 2008).

For those parents who struggle with the concept of friendship with their children, especially fathers, it really isn't that difficult to do. Being a friend just takes spending consistent time with your children. Just for the record, spending time with your children means doing what they want to do. This does not mean running errands with you. In other words, dad, inviting your children to go with you to the hardware store or auto parts store is probably not their idea of having a good time. Investigate how your children would like to spend time with you. This might include coloring, putting puzzles together, playing with toys, bike riding, surfing the Internet, going to a movie, fishing, shooting baskets, shopping, or going out for a hamburger. The point is, it takes consistent time to develop a friendship with your children and they need to know that you are willing to meet with them on their turf. You just might have to stretch yourself a little. Time spent with your children is time well invested; however, don't forget your primary role of being a disciplinarian.

If parents are really going to be friends to their children, they will admit they need to be a disciplinarian first and foremost. Children need to trust their parents to be allied with them in their developmental struggles in life. Children need to know their parents are fighting on their side in a supporting and sympathizing manner. Most important of all, children need to know that if their parents see them walking toward a cliff, their parents won't just stand there, smile, and wave goodbye. Rather, children truly want their parents to provide boundaries for them (i.e., order and structure with appropriate rewards and consequences). A primary disciplinarian becomes a true friend, one that is dependable and safe. What's that? Are you laughing at what I just wrote? So you don't believe that children want structure, huh? That's "eh" for you Canadian readers. Do you want an example? Just read the letter to the editor found in the **Daily News Miner** published in Fairbanks, Alaska:

I'm Sorry - December 18, 1996

To the editor:

Today I turn 17. My cellmate wished me a happy birthday, but my outlook is still considerably less than jovial. Not only am I sad because I'll probably be spending the next 30 years of my life in prison, but I am ashamed of all the evil, rotten, and downright horrible things I have done to people. I ripped off countless upstanding citizens, vandalized cars, garages and yards, and shot probably the finest member of the Alaska State Troopers.

I will say that I'm sorry to all those who I wronged. I will take responsibility for my actions. I will take this opportunity to make a public apology to Sergeant Roberts and his family who went through a terrible ordeal because of my stupidity and cruelty. I will say that I am not proud of anything that I have done, and that I never brag to any of the sick inmates here who commend me for my "bravery." Finally, I will get down on my knees every night for the rest of my life and thank God that I didn't kill that man.

That is all I can do. If that doesn't make anyone feel better, maybe the knowledge that the best years of my life belong to the state of Alaska will console them. I don't know. What I do know is that something must be done about juvenile crime. There is probably one stoned kid in every classroom at West Valley [High School] during any given period. (I know, I was one of them.) Vandalism is out of control. Kids love to brag about how much damage they caused and theft and burglary have become more and more common. More police would help. Stiffer penalties for first-time offenders are a must; extra youth activities might do some good, but the most important thing is families. Talk to your kids. Find out where they are going and what they are doing. Do anything but please don't let them end up like me. Please.

David J. Knutson
Fairbanks Correctional Center

This young man's letter is crying out for order and structure. He is encouraging parents to recognize the fact that the family unit is the most important institution on the planet. David encourages parents to talk with their children, find out where they are going and what they are doing, and to do anything to prevent them from getting into trouble so they don't end up like him and become incarcerated. David Knutson was sentenced to prison for thirty years due to his actions which almost cost the life of Alaska State Trooper, Sergeant J.R. Roberts.

What? Okay, I get it. You're still unconvinced that children want their parents to provide them with order and structure even if they appear to be stating the opposite. Well, here goes another attempt at winning you over. I will discuss another example of parental inaction in the following paragraphs.

A former client in New Jersey, Linda, was a very popular girl in high school. She enjoyed the social scene like other teens at school. As a result, she ended up succumbing to various forms of peer pressure and engaged in experimentation with alcohol, marijuana, and sexual promiscuity. Linda was angry at her parents' unwillingness to set limits for her or confront her about her inappropriate behaviors. One time, Linda wrote a letter to her parents about the frustration she felt and left it by her bed, knowing her parents would find it. They found it, read it, and didn't do a thing about it. According to Linda, her parents were too afraid of how she might respond to their confrontation so they did nothing. "Parental paralysis" in action.

Linda continued with her anger and inappropriate behaviors. Eventually, while in college, she chose a different path. However, it took many years for her to get over her anger toward her parents' inaction. You're still not convinced that children want their parents to put their foot down? Didn't you read about Ed and Theresa in chapter one? Remember what they did? They brought their mom to see me due to her lack of consistency in implementing FAMILY Rules. Okay, I recognize the fact that you need a little more convincing.

Even if your child is looking you in the face and screaming, "I hate you! I'll never talk to you again," at the top of their lungs, they still want you to put your foot down and set limits for them. This will be my last attempt to convince you. Otherwise, I'll allow you to choose your path which will ultimately lead to your having to put up or shut up concerning your children's inappropriate behaviors because you're unwilling to do anything about it. Inaction is never productive or healthy.

Remember Carl in chapter one? Well let's take another look at his story. The saga continues. After his parents, Jason and Cathy, finally decided to send him to long-term residential treatment, they asked me to transport their son, and they made arrangements for his admission into a residential treatment program on a South Pacific island. I met Carl's parents to discuss the intervention strategies. I arrived at their home on a Sunday evening around 9:00 P.M. and went into the living room to talk with Carl. He was understandably surprised by my appearance. I talked with him about the fact that his parents love him and have tried everything under the sun to help him without success. I reminded Carl that he continually violated their expectations of him and that he was out of control. I informed him, that because of those choices, his parents had decided to admit him into a long-term residential treatment program in the South Pacific.

Immediately, Carl became understandably upset and went into a tirade. He took physically aggressive steps toward his father, Jason, with raised closed fists. I was left with no other choice but to restrain Carl to the floor to help keep him and his parents safe. Carl immediately began to cry with deep sobs. Jason immediately got down on the floor with Carl and cried too, with his loving arms wrapped around him. This moment was truly difficult for all involved. I could tell that it was tearing Carl's parents' apart to put their foot down. I spent the night at Carl's home making sure that he didn't try to run away or harm himself. His mother, Cathy, called the Alaska State Troopers to inform them of our escort plans just in case they went sour. Fortunately, Carl got the point that I was following him around his home like a shadow, all night long, and that he wasn't going to have a chance to flee on foot.

Therefore, Carl began to lobby his parents during the early morning hours to rescind their decision. He was not successful with his mother so he went into Jason's bedroom to emotionally twist his arm to no avail. At 5:00 A.M., Carl's pastor and a deacon from his church arrived. As we were leaving, Carl made one last attempt to get his parents to change their mind. He screamed, while crying, and told them he hated them. He told them that what they were doing was wrong and that he would never talk with them or see them again. His words were like a sharp dagger piercing his parents' hearts. Carl's parents are to be admired and applauded for the love they demonstrated that day for the welfare of their son. They were willing to take the risk and put their foot down regardless of the threats. Carl's parents stayed at home while the pastor, deacon, and I escorted him to the Fairbanks airport. We were met by the airport police and a friend of mine. At this point in time, Carl clearly understood he was headed for residential treatment. There was no turning back.

When we landed in Seattle, Carl told me about all the fun things he was going to do with his father once he returned to Fairbanks, Alaska. He was looking forward to going up the river on their boat with his father to help him on the family cabin. He said, "My dad is getting older and he needs my help." He told me several times how he needs to take care of his father and mother because no one else will. We were greeted by the Seattle airport police and escorted to a waiting room until our plane departed. Carl and I had a great talk about his behaviors and attitudes. He was willing to admit, for the first time, that he was out of control. When we landed in Los Angeles, Carl was crying and stated, "Will you please call my parents and tell them thank you because I think they just saved my life." While Carl was sitting in a waiting room at the LA airport with a police officer, I called Cathy and informed her about Carl's statements. Cathy cried tears of joy and couldn't wait to tell Jason. I shed some tears too. When we arrived in Honolulu, Carl couldn't stop talking about the residential treatment facility and what it would be like; however, he made it clear to me that he was going to miss his snowboarding back home in Alaska. When we arrived to the South Pacific Island, Carl wanted to tour the island for a day and then go to the treatment center. Carl's words had changed from intense hatred, threatening never to see his parents again, to those of appreciation. For his personal well-being, Carl's parents were willing to put their foot down.

Approximately eight months later, I provided another professional escort service for a fifteen year old boy from Fairbanks, Alaska to the same facility in the South Pacific. Escorting Michael provided me with an opportunity to personally check up on how Carl was doing. After Michael's admission to the residential treatment facility was completed, I asked to meet with Carl. I waited with emotional reservation trying to anticipate how Carl would respond when he saw me. Carl walked through the administrative office door. His eyes opened wide and he ran across the room toward me with a big smile. He slapped a big bear hug on me and almost picked me up off the floor. He gave the biggest and longest hug of my life. He ended the hug with an affectionate rubbing of the hair on my head. I was overwhelmed with joy and blown away by the look of mature serenity on his face.

While on the South Pacific Island, I was able to take Carl off grounds twice and spend time with him. He talked nonstop about everything he was learning about himself and his family while receiving treatment at the residential treatment facility. Occasionally, he would shed tears of remorse when he would recall how he treated his family and how he treated himself. He thanked me numerous times for bringing him to the island. Most important of all, Carl never stopped talking about his love for his parents and his appreciation for the great deal of love it must have taken them to send him all the way to the South Pacific Island for treatment. He stated, "You guys saved my life. Thanks!"

Although I left the South Pacific Island feeling good about Carl's undeniable growth and progress, I couldn't help but feel the hurt and anger Michael was feeling by my leaving him behind for treatment. However, I am confident beyond a shadow of a doubt that Michael will also one day see the error of his choices and ultimately thank his parents and me for what needed to be done on his behalf. Nevertheless, even if they deny it up front, children are always eventually grateful when parents provide structure for them. Parents who spare discipline ultimately harm their children because sparing discipline is neglect. Neglect is abuse. This makes a child feel unloved and very sad. This leads to anger and rebellion in an attempt to get their parents to provide order and structure so they feel safe and loved.

~Chapter Four~
The Seven Bad Habits of Parenting

As you have learned in Chapter Three, and most likely have experienced, it is difficult to balance the two roles of disciplinarian and friend. Since I'm on a roll in challenging your thinking about parenting, let's explore the seven bad habits of parenting. You know, the seven guaranteed ways to undermine your own parental authority. The seven quick steps of assuring that you will lose the respect and control of your children; consequently, you end up living in misery for the next two decades of your life until your children are grown and gone.

1. Talking Too Much (i.e nagging, lecturing, etc.).

Have you ever watched a Charlie Brown cartoon? Do you remember the classroom scenes where the teacher talks nonstop? "Wha wha wha, wha wha wha wha. Wha wha wha wha, wha wha wha wha." As the teacher goes on and on and on and on and on, the Peanuts characters tune her out. Her lesson is going in one ear and out the other. Sound familiar?

It is absolutely amazing how quickly we, as parents, forget the important lessons from our own childhood experiences. Whenever one of my parents went into a lecture mode, within two minutes, I would tune them out. I figured, like most kids, that most of the important stuff was said already and the rest of the words were emotional filler material so they could feel better. Now look at us! Here we are, taking the same silly approach with our children that our parents used with us, and their parents used with them, and their grandparents used with their parents. It's a never-ending vicious cycle. A trans-generational curse. Stop the merry-go-round and let me off!

You can break free of the curse. You can decide right here and now to say what you need to say in only two or three sentences. Two paragraphs at the most. If your mouth can't stop talking, go see someone for help. Your children are intelligent and can quickly understand what you are trying to convey. Treat them as such. Expect as much. You will be surprised at the compliance you will gain from your children by stopping your tour on the lecture circuit. They will be more apt to listen to you the next time you have something to say to them.

2. Tirades and Temper Tantrums.

When was the last time you were the recipient of someone's tirade? I mean a good, old fashioned, in your face, red skinned, bulging jugular veins, bugged out eyes, ear drum piercing tirade, all just for your listening pleasure. Didn't you just love it? Secretly wishing you could experience a similar tirade on a daily basis? Didn't it make you feel loved unconditionally? No!!! It didn't!!! So why are you doing it with your children? What do you think you're going to accomplish by these angry outbursts besides having your children disrespect you, fear your presence, and think and see less of you when they are adults? While disciplining your child, never ever yell, scream, belittle, or cuss at them. You just simply don't do it.

When I was growing up, my father tried to teach me how to repair car engines and how to build various projects in the backyard. Initially, I liked being with my father. What kid doesn't? The demands of being an Oregon State Trooper kept my father away from home, so when he was home, I loved spending time with him. However, I quickly grew tired of trying to be his student because he would get mad so easily about insignificant issues. Accidentally, I would hand him the wrong tool from time to time. He would yell, "If your head wasn't screwed on, you'd lose it!" Sometimes he would say, "If you had brains, you'd be dangerous!" Of course, there were the customary swear words and other put downs that always made those learning times memorable. Please don't get me wrong, I love my father and I still love to spend time with him; however, he now realizes that what he did with his anger toward us kids while we were growing up was way out of line.

He has since apologized profusely. I accepted his apologies, forgave him, and our relationship is healed.

When you are disciplining your child, you ought to treat the situation as if you are conducting business. Pretend you are a Wal-Mart cashier standing behind a counter and Mr. Rude of America comes up to you and let's you have it verbally. As much as you probably want to, you don't punch him between the eyes or rip out his heart quick enough so he has a chance to watch it pump before he falls on the floor. Instead, you calmly listen to the customer and try to remedy the situation. Once again, when you are disciplining your child, pretend they are the customer and you are the Wal-Mart cashier. Treat them politely and with respect. Get your point across without demeaning them and use as few words as possible.

I'm serious about this: if you can't get a handle on controlling your anger, then maybe you need to see a counselor in your community for anger management. Perhaps you need to be evaluated by a psychologist or psychiatrist for depression or a bipolar disorder (i.e., manic depressive disorder) or adult ADHD. Don't be too proud. If you have tried and tried to manage your own impulsive anger without success, then seek professional help. You are worth it, your spouse is worth it, and so are your children. It's better to work on resolving your problems now than to wait to say you're sorry later. How you treat your children today will have a strong impact on how they treat your grandchildren in the future.

3. Tears (i.e., sadness and guilt trips).

I'm not trying to be a sexist here, but the reality is that moms usually transgress in this department more often than dads do. When you feel like you have tried everything under the sun to get your children to cooperate and succeed in life, it's easy to become frustrated with them. Sometimes the frustration can feel so overwhelming that it can lead a parent to tears. While crying, and sometimes emotionally despondent, some mothers attempt to guilt trip their children into compliance. As a result, your children perceive you as weak and ineffective. They will not obey a whiny sniveling sibling. You just successfully undermined your own parental authority. Never ever let your children see you as a broken down victim of their manipulation and disobedience. Rather, muster up enough strength, courage, and wisdom to save your tears for a private moment or leave your home and visit with a friend, counselor, or clergy person. Like Connie, the single parent, in Chapter One, you must develop a parental backbone of steel instead of a wet spaghetti noodle. "I can't do it," is unacceptable. If Connie could do it, any mom can. You may need the assistance of a counselor or friend.

4. Terror (i.e., threats of violence).

When I was a young adolescent, my father more or less reminded me that he was an Oregon State Trooper and that if I ever did anything illegal, he would kill me and throw my rotting corpse in jail. This was the same Oregon State Trooper and father who arrested Santa Claus for trespassing and shot Rudolph the Red Nosed Reindeer on Christmas Eve in 1965. He told me that when I was four years old and I believed him. The stern look on his face when he warned me as an adolescent convinced me to never drink, do drugs, smoke, chew, or hang with those kids who do. Nevertheless, although his threats of violence were effective, they were also very inappropriate. There is a major difference between firm discipline with appropriate consequences versus physically threatening your child. Don't ever physically threaten your child. It's definitely not good for their psychological well being or good for relationship building.

5. Inconsistency (i.e., within and between parents).

Remember "the two 'C' words" mentioned in the beginning of this book (i.e., "correct and consistent" implementation of FAMILY Rules)? Consistency is the crucial ingredient in being a successful parent. If you are unwilling to be consistent as a parent, hang it up. In reality, most of us would like to hang it up occasionally. We love our kids. We could just use an occasional vacation from them every now and then.

Parents need to consistently implement discipline in their home regardless of their mood or energy level. I don't care how hard your day was at work, if your child needs discipline, then do your job. I don't care how emotionally or physically exhausted you are, if your child needs discipline then do your job. However, never discipline in anger. If necessary, take a time out so you can discipline with a calm and rational approach.

All adults prefer consistently fair treatment from their employers. In return, do unto others as you would have others do unto you. Be consistent with your kids. Consistently give them rewards when they choose to do right and consistently nail them to the proverbial wall when they choose to do wrong. Children really appreciate consistency and structure.

Dads and moms, it's very important that you are consistent not only within yourself but also between one another, even if you're divorced. You can't have dad saying, "No", while mom is saying, "Yes." You can't have dad restricting a child from the TV for a day, while mom grounds the child for a week for the same offense. This creates confusion for the children and conflict between the parents. It also sets dad and mom up to be manipulated by their kids. Under these circumstances, children learn to go to dad for some things, and to mom for other things. A house divided will not stand.

According to all the parents I have talked to who choose to implement FAMILY Rules in a correct and consistent manner in and outside of their home, the conflict of division between dad and mom has been eliminated. The conflict is eliminated because the rules, chores, rewards, and consequences are predetermined and written down by both parents. If FAMILY Rules is correctly and consistently implemented by both parents, there will be nothing to argue about concerning discipline. Parents really like it but some children are disappointed because they can't manipulate their parents anymore. Too bad, so sad.

6. Disagreeing about Discipline in front of the Children.

You must never allow your children to see you and your spouse openly disagree about how to discipline them. These discussions are reserved for private settings only (i.e., the parents' bedroom, a long walk or drive, etc.). When you have one parent displaying open disrespect for the other parent's authority in front of the kids, you might as well declare open season on that parent. Like sharks, the children will smell the blood in the water and move in for the kill every time. The good news is that FAMILY Rules helps to eliminate this problem and you will learn how in Part II of this book.

7. Treating your Children like They are Slaves (i.e., lack of reciprocity).

Lack of reciprocity in parent-child relationships creates major resentments among children. When parents demand much, but give little, insurrections can occur. Parents who are insensitive to their children's perception of fairness and credibility are asking for trouble. Although respect comes with the position of being a parent, you must behave appropriately to preserve the respect you desire from your children.

An example of this is the office of the President of the United States of America. In the minds of most U.S. citizens, respect for the office of the President is automatic. The office of the President is a national institution. If the President wants continued respect, he or she must continue to behave in a respectful manner. Otherwise, disgrace is brought to the office of the President, whether he or she is a Republican or Democrat.

A good parent learns to lead by serving. A successful parent is sensitive to the needs of their children and seeks to meet them. As a result, the parent will reap what is sown. This will greatly increase the odds of raising children who are also sensitive to the needs of others. The acorn doesn't fall far from the tree. Parents with a humble servant's heart raise children who eventually realize the fact that the world is not centered around them. There are other people on the planet with needs, too.

~Chapter Five~

Reasons FAMILY Rules Could Fail in Your Home

I have taught FAMILY Rules to physicians, attorneys, teachers, military officers, licensed mental health professionals, pastors, entrepreneurs, janitors, and plain old everyday All-American parents such as you and me. FAMILY Rules was initially developed with feedback from two-hundred volunteer guinea pig families in Anchorage, Alaska – a melting pot of cultural diversity with people from all over the world. Additional feedback was sought from subsequent families in New Jersey, California, Oregon, and Washington. These families represent most religious, socioeconomic, ethnic, regional, and cultural populations found in the United States. FAMILY Rules has been well tested before reaching your home. If you are wondering whether or not you should try a variation or deviate from the way I am teaching you this system, please don't. Most likely, I have already been down that path with the previous thousands of families. We have already been there, done that, and got the T-shirt. I waited to write this book, after teaching FAMILY Rules to a multitude of families. I wanted to make sure the system worked before writing a book about it, which would allow you to implement it in your own home. FAMILY Rules works the way it is presented to you in this book, so please don't tinker with it or deviate from it. It works if you work it "correctly and consistently" (i.e., "the two 'C' words").

I have seen FAMILY Rules transform some of the most abusive home situations into a family environment where parents and children communicate and respect one another. Most recently, I taught FAMILY Rules to a pastor and his family because they were having difficulty with an adolescent child. The children were not thrilled about the changes that were going to occur in their home once FAMILY Rules was implemented. I warned them that life as they once knew it would cease to exist. I warned the family that changes were coming down the pike which would require an adjustment for everyone. Finally, based on my experience with multitudes of other families, I informed the children they were eventually going to be happy with the changes in their home and everyone would get along much better.

Approximately ten months after I implemented the system with the pastor's family, I drove up to a window at a fast food restaurant in the community. While I was ordering edible substances to clog my arteries, the adolescent at the window stated, "I know you. You're the guy who implemented that FAMILY Rules system with my family." I asked the adolescent, "So how is FAMILY Rules working in your home?" The adolescent stated, "It's working really well. I had my doubts at first, but we are all getting along much better, just like you said. My parents are finally listening to me and I am finally listening to them. They are starting to let me do the things I want to do, because I'm finally following the rules. They trust me more than they did a while ago." As I drove away, I was very happy because I heard another success story about FAMILY Rules and because I actually got everything in my bag that I ordered. Miracles never cease.

If you implement FAMILY Rules "correctly and consistently" in your home (i.e., "the two 'C' words"), it will work; however, if you deviate from the way FAMILY Rules is taught in this book, it will fail. In the spirit of beating a dead horse and recognizing that repetition is the best teacher, please read and reread this book to make sure you thoroughly understand the FAMILY Rules parenting system. You must implement the system correctly and, most important of all, consistently. If you don't implement FAMILY Rules "correctly and consistently," then it will fail in your home. Over the years, I have seen other reasons why FAMILY Rules has failed in the home. I point these out in an attempt to help FAMILY Rules succeed in your home. Please remember, "correct and consistent" implementation are essential ingredients for successful results.

1. See The Seven Bad Habits of Parenting (Chapter 4).

2. Parents are unwilling to put forth the time and energy necessary to implement FAMILY Rules.

Parents truly expend much more time and energy trying to haphazardly manage the chaos in their home via "flying by the seat of their pants" than they would if they "correctly and consistently" implemented FAMILY Rules in their home. Bad habits die hard. Some parents are plain old lazy when it comes to disciplining their children and simply don't want to change. They would rather remain apathetic, inconsistent, or bark out commands from their armchair, while reading the paper and watching TV at the same time. In short, they'd rather not change their own lives, let alone involve themselves personally in changing the lives of their children.

The initial implementation of FAMILY Rules in your home is very similar to pushing a stalled car out of a busy intersection. You know you need to move fast in order to avoid an accident; however, it takes a lot of energy at the beginning to get the car moving from a stand still. You lean your shoulder into the rear of the car, dig your feet into the ground and push with everything you have. Slowly, the car begins to move. The more you push it, the faster it begins to move. Eventually, you find yourself not having to expend so much energy to keep the car moving. The same is true concerning the implementation of FAMILY Rules in your home. Stay committed to "the two 'C' words" and your parenting job will be much easier down the road. If you give up and go back to "flying by the seat of your pants," you will create monsters and you will expend much more time and energy in the long run.

3. Parents are unwilling to practice what they preach (i.e., "Do as I say and not as I do.").

Life experiences, you would think, should stick in the memory banks of most adults concerning what they experienced as children growing up; however, they usually don't. I never liked it when my parents' actions clearly conveyed the message, "Do as we say - not as we do." I would ask myself, "If mom and dad say that it's not okay to cuss, then why do they cuss at others or us kids when they get mad?" The one word that came to my mind when I saw my parents behave this way is the same word that comes to the minds of most children when they see their parents provide this kind of role modeling – Hypocrite. I can really see the parents' minds spinning inside their heads when I ask them to stop swearing if they expect the same from their children. Most parents agree with the wisdom of consistent role modeling for their children; however, I remember one parent in the military who argued that his mother was a "good American citizen," even though she cussed like a trucker. No offense intended, truckers. But this principle isn't about being a "good American citizen." It's about being a consistent parental role model. It's about walking the talk and practicing what you preach.

4. Parents have unresolved issues from their childhood concerning authority (e.g., past abuses, growing up with an anti-establishment attitude, etc.).

While teaching parents how to provide discipline to their children, major roadblocks sometimes block the path to successful parenting. One married mother, Lisa, had great difficulty saying "no" to her children or holding her kids accountable for their behaviors and attitudes. After asking Lisa many questions about her past, she was willing to admit to growing up in a rigid and abusive environment with a father who never let her do what she wanted to do. She made a commitment to herself to protect her own children from a similar experience. However, Lisa created other problems for her children as a result of being overly permissive. In fact, she was always running interference to protect her children from her father. Oops! I really meant to protect them from her husband (must have been a Freudian slip). You get the picture don't you? Lisa was treating her husband as if he were her father. Believe me; this interferes with parenting as well as a marriage.

Don't forget about Todd and Kris in chapter one. They were the couple from the late 1960s and early 1970s anti-establishment era, who believed in the pursuit of alcohol, drugs, rock 'n roll, free love, and government protest. Living out these inappropriate philosophies of life as adults interfered with their ability to effectively parent their son, David. Yet, they were blind to this truth and were unwilling to admit that they were contributing to David's academic demise. Denial is another obstacle to successful parenting.

5. Parents are engaged in a power struggle with one another and don't want to give up their illusion of control (i.e. they don't want to share authority, there is marital discord, etc.).

Monkey see, monkey do. Children who witness their parents fighting while growing up learn to do likewise as married adults. Some parents don't know how to involve themselves in a marital relationship without conflict. They engage in a dance of anger and control with one another. One treats the other as a child or as being mentally deficient. Of course no one knows any better than this individual how to run the home and raise the kids. As a result, verbal and/or physical abuse sometimes occurs. In many situations, the abuse trickles down to the children as well. Marital and family counseling is needed in these situations.

If your spouse is physically abusing you, please contact a professional counselor in your community immediately. Perhaps a crisis shelter. Most importantly, contact the police and press assault charges. Don't let your spouse talk you out of it. Acquire support from loved ones, church, synagogue, and your community. Don't let the abuse continue!

Sometimes, in the midst of power struggles, one parent may become apathetic and aloof over time. This parent may withdraw from both the spouse and children. It may take professional assistance to involve the aloof parent and to stabilize the marriage.

6. Parents misuse FAMILY Rules to promote their own rigid agenda and then, when it blows up in their faces, they accuse FAMILY Rules of being rigid rather than owning their own issues.

Rigid parents promote rigid discipline. Guns don't kill people, people kill people. Rigid parents who desire to control others will use any means possible to promote their own rigid agenda. They will contaminate, twist or distort anything in order to promote their own desires. FAMILY Rules is not exempt from this reality. If you have a spouse who is behaving this way, please put FAMILY Rules on hold and seek the assistance of a professional counselor - preferably a counselor who uses FAMILY Rules (please see Appendix A).

7. Parents are struggling with their own unresolved mental health issues which interfere with their ability to correctly and consistently implement the system (e.g., depression, generalized anxiety, adult ADHD, alcohol and drug abuse, spiritual immaturity, marital problems, etc.).

The issues identified above are pretty self-explanatory. Parents are people, too. They struggle with a variety of physical, spiritual, and mental health problems that can interfere with their ability to parent successfully. You know who you are. If not, listen to your spouse, he or she will let you know. Get help if you need it. Denial for a while is understandable. Denial forever is unacceptable.

Although I can write several chapters on unresolved mental health issues for parents, for the sake of brevity, I'll address the one issue that concerns me the most: anger management for fathers. In a nutshell, there are many fathers out there who think it's okay to yell, hit, and break things when they are angry at their spouse and/or children. These fathers may have had poor role modeling while growing up and, therefore, never learned how to express their hurt and anger appropriately. These fathers may also have a major depressive disorder, a bipolar disorder, or ADHD with serious impulsivity problems. These fathers need professional help. You know who you are. Please seek professional help before you lose your wife, children, and/or career. Stop blaming your wife. Start taking responsibility for your actions before it's too late. Please get some help now. Just do it!

~Chapter Six~

Tactics Used By Children to Manipulate Authority

I have worked with children, adolescents and their families since 1982. They have taught me a lot over the years. I have learned the ins and the outs of manipulating adult authority. I was an adolescent once and utilized my own developed tactics during that time of my life. Like many of you reading this book, I personally got away with a few devious deeds in my past. I am sure my parents would drop dead if they ever learned the truth about their role model child. Naturally, as our parents once had to do when we were younger, we are now faced with raising children and adolescents of our own. We love and want the best for our children, just as our parents wanted the best for us. Now it is our turn to carry the baton of wisdom and experience.

Here is the problem: wisdom comes from experience and we don't have any previous experiences. Raising children is just as new for us as it was for our parents when we were born. It is wise to consult with our parents about what they did to raise us; however, their well-meaning advice doesn't always fit the needs of the changing times. Rest assured, there are foundational truths that transcend each new generation of children and adolescents. It is an undeniable fact of life, as certain as death and taxes, that children will manipulate adult authority to achieve their goals whether or not they are moral, ethical, legal, or safe. The following are tactics used by children and adolescents to manipulate adult authority.

1. Guilt Trips.

The first tactic that children and adolescents will use to manipulate their parents and other adult authority figures is guilt. Guilt is like a hot knife that quickly cuts through the butter of our better judgment without resistance. We all love our children and we want them to know that. It is tough when they start comparing us to Attila the Hun, Adolph Hitler, Joseph Stalin, or Sadam Hussein. Most parents desire to do a good job while raising their children and are curious about how they compare with other parents. Parents often question whether they are being too strict or too lenient. Unfortunately, parents don't always have ways of connecting with other parents. When they do connect with other parents, it is often over sports activities, church or synagogue events, community activities, or other activities that normally bring the community together. During these community events, the focal point of discussion is not based on whether or not parents are being too strict or lenient as compared to other parents; rather the discussion is focused on the specific event that brought everyone together.

Fortunately, there are parent support groups developing around the country so the focal point of the discussion can be on how to parent one's child. If you do not have a local parent support group, why not start one at your local school, church, synagogue, hospital, or community library? You can also join the free parent listserv via my website at www.Family-Rules.com and converse with parents from all over the world. Although it helps to know how you fit in with other parents in your community, ultimately, you are the ones who decide what your children may or may not do. If the majority of parents in your community believe it's okay for their children to be out until 3:00 A.M., but you would rather have yours home by 10:00 P.M., then your children will be home by 10:00 P.M. Don't allow your children to push your guilt buttons to cause you to go against your better judgment. Also, don't forget, your primary role as a parent is that of disciplinarian.

First, you must paint the lines on the road of life and act as the guard rails on the dangerous curves, and second, you are a close friend. Don't let your children guilt-trip you out of your primary role of disciplinarian. When children and adolescents want something really bad, they will try to get you to be their friend first and disciplinarian second. This is a fatal mistake and you must not let it happen. No! No! No!

Remember Carl from chapter one? He was very good at manipulating his parents and he definitely knew how to push their guilt buttons. When his parents were talking with him in therapy about the possibility of sending him to a long-term residential treatment facility, he would automatically raise abandonment issues. In the past, they sent him to a therapeutic snow boarding school in the "Lower 48 States" without much success. In my humble opinion, the program did not sound very structured, nor did it sound very thorough in it's approach to treating children with emotional issues and behavioral problems. Carl would also raise issues of abandonment related to adoption. I observed his mother's body language and facial expressions as she would back off from her stance. I saw Carl and his mother cycle in and out of this dance of guilt in my office on a few occasions. It wasn't until Carl crossed the line, one too many times, with his mother that she finally decided, along with her husband, to send Carl off to a long-term residential treatment facility. She was no longer going to allow Carl to push her guilt buttons and prevent her from doing what she knew she had to do to save his life. While on the South Pacific Island, during my third escort, I had a chance to spend more time with Carl again. He openly admitted to me with remorse about how he would push his mother's guilt buttons to avoid being sent away. Carl was glad that his mother finally put her foot down and took care of business. Carl believes that his mother and father saved his life.

2. Divide Authority and Conquer.

In 1861, President Abraham Lincoln made the very difficult decision to go to war against the southern Confederate states. He stated, "A house divided will not stand." The Civil War was not just about the emancipation of the slaves in the United States of America. Fortunately for all of us, President Lincoln saw the bigger picture concerning world economics, possible future world events, as well as potential foreign threats to our national security.

All of these issues were in his mind when he made his decision to fight for freedom and unity. He understood that if the United States became the Divided States, permanently separated into two sovereign nations, we would become very vulnerable fish food to other global powers such as England, France, or Spain. Could you imagine how the outcome of World War I or World War II might have been without the United States of America there to help fight for freedom? If instead, we were the Divided States, two separate sovereign nations, both countries might have ended up with Swastikas flying on all of our flag poles today. Because President Lincoln made the difficult decision back then to fight for maintaining the existence of the United States of America, all of us are free today. Finally, his decision ultimately led to our first elected African American as President – Barack Obama.

Unfortunately, I have worked with families where children have successfully divided their parents. As years pass, certain relational patterns develop where both mom and dad believe that one parent is the good guy, while the other parent is the bad guy. Naturally, it is the other parent who is the bad guy. The problem with this approach to parenting is the fact that the house is divided and it will not stand. Therefore, the children get to sneak out the back door and get away with murder, while mom and dad are verbally assaulting one another. Divorced parents are at high risk for being vulnerable to this tactic of manipulation. For some parents, the divorce and the reasons leading up to it have already convinced them in their own minds that the other parent is indeed, the bad guy. It doesn't take much convincing via a child's manipulation to confirm in one's own mind that their divorced spouse is always the problem. The sad truth is that some children of divorced parents know this and will use this tactic as many times as necessary to get their own way.

Jim and Cheryl divorced many years ago. Their son, Steve, lived with his mother for many years. As Steve grew older, he hooked up with a group of negative peers. His mother and new stepfather began to make more rules around the home to contain his inappropriate behaviors. Steve was not pleased with his mother's strictness, so he emotionally manipulated his father, Jim, and his new stepmother, so he could go live with them. Steve stayed with his father and new stepmother for almost one year until he burned his bridges with them too. By the end of the year, his mother, Cheryl, had forgotten all the negative manipulations that Steve did in her home, and was convinced by Steve that her ex-husband, Jim, was indeed the bad guy. Therefore, Cheryl rescued Steve and brought him back home to live with her. Everything went fine for a few weeks until the honeymoon period was over. Back to square one again.

One day, Steve's new stepfather found his credit cards in Steve's pocket. Steve was going to use the credit cards to obtain cash advances in order get money for drugs. Cheryl and her new husband called up Jim and told him that he would have to take Steve back into his home. Jim and his new wife contacted me and set up an appointment to help them with the transition. Jim and his wife along with Cheryl and her husband came into my office for an appointment. Cheryl and her new husband made it clear that they did not want Steve back in their home. They were willing to give their one-hundred percent cooperation to Jim and his wife. They signed a contract supporting Steve's presence in Jim's home and their willingness not to interfere with any therapeutic recommendations made by myself. Cheryl and her new husband also agreed that if Steve came running back to them, whining and complaining about how Jim was a bad guy, they would direct him to go back to Jim's home and work it out. They were no longer going to enable Steve with his manipulations.

I had managed to help Jim and Cheryl paint their son, Steve, into a corner that he could not get out of. Steve was left with only two options: Follow the rules at home and school and enjoy an abundant life, or disobey the rules at home and school and go away to a long-term residential treatment facility. When confronted in my office by Jim and myself, Steve chose to obey the rules at home and at school. Unfortunately, it only took approximately four weeks for Jim and me to realize that Steve's commitment to following the rules was merely lip service. As a result, Steve chose to go to long-term residential treatment. As Steve was leaving my office, he told me that he was glad he was going because he felt like his life was out of control. He wanted help in getting a handle on his life and getting his feet back on the ground. I told you so! Children and adolescents really do want organization, structure, and discipline. They want their parents to be united and to keep them safe no matter what.

3. Anger.

If guilt trips or dividing authority does not work, then children will turn up the heat by utilizing the tactic of anger to manipulate their parents. If I received a penny for every time I heard about how a child has attempted to manipulate their parents with anger, I would be a wealthy man. Children and adolescents will slam doors, break things, stomp their feet, punch, kick, scratch, bite, shove, or scream at the top of their lungs with a red face and bulging eyes as they walk towards you with clenched fists. Anger can be a very intimidating emotion, especially when you have been the victim of verbal and/or physical abuse in the past.

What is a mother to do when she is confronted with the anger of an adolescent son who is taller and heavier than she is? Sure, dad comes home and tries to intimidate the adolescent son with his anger and the possibility of his physical confrontation. Eventually mom is left to fend for herself when dad is not around the home. Many mothers live in fear of their adolescent child's anger. Some mothers may attempt to counter their child's anger with their own anger and overreact in order to regain control in their home.

I recall attempting to utilize the tactic of anger with my own mom when I was in my early teens. She slapped me, grabbed my hair, dragged me up the stairs, threw me in my bedroom, and slammed the door shut behind me. She did what she thought she needed to do to get control over the situation. Today, that would be considered child abuse. It is important not to allow your children's anger to intimidate or manipulate you.

Don't let them use anger to get their own way. It is also inappropriate for any parent to attempt to intimidate their children back and engage in physical abuse to regain control of the situation. You want to avoid the intervention of the Child Protective Services agency if at all possible. If they enter your world, they'll be like a wart on your foot that you can't get rid of to save your life. However, the Child Protective Services agency is a necessary evil. Who else will protect and advocate for the abused and neglected children in our communities?

Sherry was out of control and a very angry adolescent. She intimidated her parents often into getting her own way. No matter how many times I attempted to persuade her parents to put their foot down and no longer tolerate Sherry's outbursts, they feared drawing a line in the sand. I warned them on numerous occasions that her anger and manipulations were going to cost them greatly, one way or another, if they did not put their foot down immediately. One night, Sherry's parents had a confrontation with her about her desire to go out with some friends on a school night. Sherry was mad because her parents were going to go out on a date to celebrate their anniversary while she had to stay home and do her homework. Sherry tried to use anger, but to no avail. When her parents came home later that night, they found their living room and dining room furniture smashed to pieces. Sherry had caused approximately ten thousand dollars worth of destruction in their home. Her parents called me in a crisis and decided it was time to send Sherry to a long-term residential treatment facility. Her behaviors were obviously out of control and they needed more help than they were able to get in an outpatient treatment setting. This was obviously a "Pop-Fly" and very deserving of an immediate admission into a long-term residential treatment center. You will read about "Pop-Flies" in chapter eight. Sherry was put on a plane and transported out of Alaska down to the "Lower 48 States" by her father for treatment. Anger can be a very destructive emotion if left unchecked. Parents must never allow their children to intimidate them with anger in order to get their own way. Parents must also not confront anger with anger; otherwise, they will merely escalate the situation by adding fuel to the fire. If necessary, take a time-out, calm down, and then discipline your child.

4. Fear.

When all else fails, children and adolescents will pull out the thermonuclear warheads. The conventional warfare tactics of guilt, dividing authority, and anger have been unfruitful. Therefore, children and adolescents are now prepared to totally annihilate the enemy. Kids will attempt to intimidate their parents through fear by threatening to beat them up, kill them, hurt themselves, kill themselves, withdraw their love, run away from home, or go to school and shoot their peers. Parents must take all these threats very seriously and respond accordingly. For example, if your child threatens to harm themselves or someone else, you must immediately take them to your local psychiatric hospital or emergency room at your general hospital for a psychiatric evaluation. If your child refuses to cooperate by going to such a facility, you do have the option of contacting your local police department. Request that they send a police officer to come over to your house and perform a safety check to make sure your child is not a danger to self or others. If necessary, the police should be able to transport your child to the appropriate mental health facility for safety and a psychiatric evaluation.

By taking all threats seriously and responding accordingly, your child will quickly learn that you care. You are not willing to allow him or her to commit harm to self or anyone else. Do not stop with your goal of getting your child evaluated, even if while on the way to a local psychiatric hospital, the child admits that he or she was only trying to manipulate you. Send a message to your child(ren) that you will take each threat seriously and respond accordingly. This will make your child(ren) think twice in the future before they ever make a threatening statement again.

I cannot over state the importance of taking each threat seriously. I can recall parents who did not take their daughter's threat of suicide seriously. They thought she just wanted attention. Sadly enough, one day her mother came home from work and found her dead due to an overdose of medication. I don't have any doubt there are kids who will use threats of suicide as an act of attention-seeking and manipulation; however, you never know if your child will be the one individual who really meant what was said. Therefore, once again, take all threats of harm to self and harm to others seriously and act accordingly. Take a child to the hospital and if you do not have their cooperation, call the police for a safety check. You must keep your child safe and send a message that you will not be manipulated with such tactics.

Fear of harm to self or harm to others is a very effective tool used by children to manipulate authority figures. During my junior year of high school, we had just completed our basketball season in the State playoffs. Our season record was twenty-five wins and only one loss. We took third in the state and had a very successful season. However, that wasn't the way I thought or felt about it. As a matter of fact, I was very depressed as a result of losing the one game during the state playoffs, which cost us the opportunity to play for the state championship. Third place wasn't good enough for me. In my mind, third place really meant second place loser. At that point in my life, having been raised in a dysfunctional family, my role was one of an over-achiever. Well, we lost. Losing was not achieving. In my mind, I let down my family, school, and community of Salem, Oregon. In order to cope with my dysfunctional family environment, in my mind, I became basketball. I lost; therefore, I became very depressed. I was unworthy of their love and respect.

After the Oregon State basketball playoffs in March of 1979, I did not want to go back to school and face my peers and teachers. Now in reality, I am sure my peers and teachers didn't really care about whether or not we played in the championship game. After all, the fact that we made it to the state playoffs allowed my peers to miss many days of school and they were able to travel to Portland, to support us while we played our games. Nevertheless, in my dysfunctional narcissistic adolescent mind, I was a loser and let them all down.

As a result of my stinking thinking, I told my parents I needed time to get away and think. I informed them that I was depressed and I didn't know what I would do if I didn't have time to get away and think. Did you catch the subtle manipulation using the threat of fear? Well, mom and dad swallowed the bait, hook, line, and sinker. I got to miss school for a week.

My parents allowed me to drive to Seaside, Oregon and spend a week with our family friends. I drove the two-hour trip in approximately an hour and twenty minutes. Along the way, I almost killed myself by attempting to drive my parents' Pinto station wagon into the pillar of an overpass bridge. Fortunately, by God's grace, I did not do it. I pulled out of it at the last second. My parents did not take my threat seriously, nor act accordingly. What they should have done was take me to a therapist or a psychiatric hospital for a psychiatric evaluation. During that brief period in my life, I was very depressed and suicidal. As a result of their unwillingness to act accordingly to my threat, they almost had the unfortunate experience of having an Oregon State Trooper come to their front door to inform them of a fatal auto accident involving their son. I am sure they thought they were doing the best thing by letting me go, but the best choice would have been to have me evaluated by a mental health professional. Rest assured, I am much more emotionally stable today. I would no longer consider killing myself over losing a game of basketball or for any other reason.

~Chapter Seven~

Childhood Struggles That Might Interfere With Compliance

Sometimes, a child's lack of compliance with adult authority at home and at school is not solely due to willful disobedience. A child might be struggling with other issues in life that, when combined with willful disobedience, may make compliance with authority seem almost impossible. When a child has a disability, impairment, or disorder, it is not uncommon for parents to attribute all of the child's problems to a negative attitude problem. Sometimes parents may even conclude that these problems have their roots in spiritual matters.

I remember one day when Oprah brought her niece, Gayle, into my office for counseling. She had moved her niece up to Alaska from a large urban environment in the "Lower 48 States." Oprah wanted to remove her from the influence of gangs. While Gayle was under her Aunt Oprah's care in Alaska, they began to butt heads over different issues. Oprah brought Gayle into my office and requested that I exorcise the demon from her niece. I told her that if those were the services she desired, she would be better off pursuing an exorcism with the guidance of her pastor. I also explained to her that insurance companies don't reimburse for exorcisms performed by a psychologist.

Oprah was upset with me and demanded once again that I exorcise the demon from her niece. I utilized the initial one-hour diagnostic interview to ask her questions as to why she thought her niece, Gayle, was possessed by a demon. She began to explain many of her behaviors and symptoms to me. At the end of our session, I suggested that we proceed with psychological testing to rule out possible learning disabilities, attention deficit/hyperactivity disorder, and possible neuropsychological impairment. She stormed out of my office with

Gayle in hand. Oprah was mad at me because I refused to exorcise the demon from her niece.

Two weeks later, Gayle and Oprah had a major blow out. Oprah admitted Gayle into the psychiatric hospital where I frequently performed psychological evaluations on adolescent patients. I was able to administer the psychological tests to Gayle that I had recommended earlier. The testing results indicated Gayle had a severe attention deficit disorder to auditory stimuli. She also had a moderate level of inattention problems to visual stimuli. In addition to these struggles, Gayle was also mildly mentally retarded, and she had some neuro-psychological problems in the frontal lobe of her brain. This part of the brain manages abstract reasoning, problem solving, goal setting, and emotional regulation.

After I wrote up my report, I sat down with Gayle's aunt, Oprah, and explained to her what she was really dealing with. I shared with her how she could help Gayle compensate for her disabilities. I gave Oprah new ideas for parental interventions, such as writing down her directives, because nothing she said to Gayle ever stuck in her brain. The words Oprah spoke to Gayle in the past went in one ear and out the other due to her inability to pay attention to auditory stimuli. The psychiatrist also placed Gayle on Ritalin. A few weeks later, after Gayle's discharge from the hospital, Oprah called me and thanked me for the psychological evaluation and the parenting intervention tips. She stated that she and Gayle were getting along better now and that she did not appear to have a demon in her after all. I think Oprah finally caught on to the fact sometimes people are so heavenly minded, they are of no earthly good. Although I believe in the spiritual realm, I also believe most of the problems that we face from day to day are the results of our own emotional, psychological, physical, and relational dysfunctions.

The following childhood struggles which might interfere with compliance to authority are provided to help you screen for possible "red flags." If your child has one or more of these problems, please have them assessed by a licensed mental health professional such as a psychiatrist, psychologist, or clinical social worker.

1. Learning Disabilities.

Most parents want to believe that their child is the best looking and smartest kid on the planet. We want to believe this is a fact of life and that our parental biases have nothing to do with our conclusions. However, seventy percent of all children fit somewhere within the average range - between the low end of the average range and the upper-end of the average range. Nevertheless, average is average. There are children who exceed the average range and excel above their peers. These children are either the valedictorians at high school graduation or troublemakers in the principal's office because they're so bored with school they don't know what else to do with their time.

Unfortunately, there are children at the other end of the spectrum who struggle with learning from day to day. Sometimes, these children are not always easy to spot. Children may excel in some subjects at school and struggle in other subjects. They may study for many more hours than their peers just to bring home a "C" grade. Some children sincerely put forth a lot of effort and manage only to bring home a "D" or an "F" grade.

Once again, as I mentioned earlier, some parents will attribute negative motivations or reasons for why a child brings home a "D" or an "F" grade. In some cases they are right. In other cases they are wrong. There is such a thing as a Mathematics Learning Disability or a Disorder of Written Expression. Let's face it, the public school system is overwhelmed by the sheer number of students. Unless your child's academic struggles stick out like a sore thumb, you will need to advocate on his or her behalf with your school district. If you have any reason to suspect that your child is struggling with an academic learning disability, then you will need to approach your school to have your child evaluated. Please remember that the squeaky wheel gets the oil. Don't accept "no" for an answer. The school district should be able to provide an Academic Achievement Test to rule out one or more possible learning disabilities. If you have advocated strongly for your child and the school district is still unwilling to test him or her, then contact a local psychologist in your community and ask if he or she is trained to administer an Academic Achievement Test to your child. If a local psychologist identifies one or more learning disabilities via the appropriate testing, then you can go back to your school district armed with the necessary testing data and force them to test your child as you previously requested.

2. Intellectual Impairment.

There is a lot of controversy over whether or not an intelligence quotient (IQ) really exists. Well, let's settle this controversy once and for all. There is such a thing as an IQ. Just talk to Dr. Albert Einstein or Dr. Stephen Hawking. Then talk to your uncle, Bubba. See what I mean? My experience over the years tells me that it is important to have an understanding of what your child's IQ is really like. One thing is certain, I really doubt that any individual can accurately guess what someone's IQ score is. I recall working in a psychiatric hospital with a psychiatrist who wanted me to administer an IQ test to an adolescent female. He estimated that her IQ was in the below average range and wanted a confirmation of this fact. I tested her as he requested and her IQ score turned out to be in the superior range. The psychiatrist was flabbergasted and couldn't understand how she obtained such a high score. After all, in his mind, this adolescent female had made nothing but one stupid mistake after another to get herself admitted into the hospital. He was certain that her IQ score was in the below average range and felt threatened that the IQ test pointed out otherwise. How in the world could he be wrong? After all, he was a medical doctor and a psychiatrist on top of that.

To be fair to the psychiatrist, in spite of the fact that I have administered many IQ tests, I too will occasionally try to guess, in my mind, what someone's IQ score might be before I administer the test; however, I learn that in most cases I am not right at all. I always chuckle when I read a report from another professional in the community who adds an estimate of an individual's IQ. I know from my own experience that there is no way on earth their estimate is an accurate one. Nevertheless, I do believe in the value of IQ testing and the data that it provides for the parents and educators. If we know a child's true IQ score, rather than just an inaccurate educated guess, we can adjust our expectations accordingly.

3. Attention Deficit/Hyperactivity Disorder (ADHD) and Attention Deficit Disorder (ADD).

There is a lot of misinformation circulating on the Internet, in the media, and in books about ADD/ADHD. Please remember, in spite of all the negative media sensationalism, bad news sells. For example, thousands of jet aircraft take off and land safely every day around the world. It is much safer to fly than it is to drive a car. Nevertheless, when one US Air jet aircraft lands on the Hudson River near New York City, we hear about it nonstop on all of the news channels for the next week or two. Was it pilot error? Was it a flock of birds that got sucked into the engines? Was it mechanical failure? The cameras keep on rolling, reporters keep on asking questions, and the majority of the people keep on soaking it up. What we don't hear about or see on the TV news on a daily basis are scenarios such as this: "Here we are at Gate B-5 witnessing another successful passenger jet landing! Wait just one moment, I think I hear the passengers walking up the ramp. Yes! Here they are! More families reunited again and again!" The bottom line is, in spite of the negative media sensationalism, ADD/ADHD really does exist. For every negative story you can tell me about Ritalin or other psychostimulant medication, I can tell you a thousand positive stories about how the medication has helped individuals and families. Research studies show that the best way to treat this disorder is with a combination of medication and behavior modification working together, not one without the other. It's a good thing you are learning about the FAMILY Rules parenting system.

There has been a lot of hype about the over-diagnosing of ADD/ADHD in America. Granted, there probably have been individuals diagnosed with ADD/ADHD that do not have it. Likewise, others were not diagnosed with ADD/ADHD when they really did have the disorder. The most common way to diagnose ADD/ADHD in America is through a medical doctor. Unfortunately, although they are trained as physicians, their evaluation methods are very subjective at best. In other words, they ask a lot of questions or gather information on paper from teachers and parents. This method of gathering data is influenced greatly by the physician's bias, parental bias, and teacher bias. This means that the odds go up significantly of obtaining a false positive or a false negative diagnosis.

I am not minimizing the importance of obtaining subjective data; rather, I am pointing out the importance of obtaining objective testing data as a supplement. Objective testing options exist to identify the possible diagnosis of ADD/ADHD, but many physicians and psychologists are unaware of this fact. While conducting an assessment for ADD/ADHD, I administer an intelligence test; Connors' Rating Scales for Parents and Teachers; the Test of Variables of Attention - Visual and Auditory (TOVA); and the Wisconsin Card Sorting Test (WCST). I also utilize the subjective information I glean from the initial one-hour diagnostic interview. The TOVA test and the WCST are administered via a computer and the objective testing data is combined with the subjective data to reach a final diagnosis of whether or not the child, adolescent, or adult actually has ADD/ADHD. A thorough evaluation will use the best of both worlds – subjective and objective data.

Please be cautious while seeking evaluations for ADD/ADHD from physicians, psychiatrists, psychologists, or other mental health professionals who only utilize subjective data to formulate a diagnosis. Relying solely on subjective data that can be greatly influenced by the biases of a parent, teacher, or professional is not the best approach. Ask them about what objective tests they utilize in their diagnostic procedures to supplement their subjective data. Unfortunately, some of these professionals won't even know what you are talking about when you ask this question. Most of the hype out there in the media about misdiagnosis of ADD/ADHD is due to the lack of objective testing to supplement subjective information gathered by a professional.

A while ago, I had a young adolescent male, Paul, referred to me by a private school principal and his parents for an evaluation for ADD/ADHD. They were certain that he had this disorder. After giving him the tests that I previously described, it turns out that he was not even close to having ADD/ADHD. However, the objective testing data indicated the possible presence of depression, mild mental retardation, and the possibility of neuropsychological impairment. After additional testing, I was able to conclude that Paul was mildly mentally retarded and was experiencing a major depressive disorder. We were able to treat his depression, with the appropriate medication and counseling, and I referred him on to the public school system for special resource services. Although Paul was referred for ADD/ADHD, it turned out that his problem was altogether different. I believe that the subjective data combined with the objective testing data helped me to clearly differentiate between what Paul's parents and principal thought he was struggling with versus what he was really struggling with.

Finally, some school districts do a poor job of assessing and referring children and adolescents for evaluations for ADD/ADHD. I have lived in a community where the school district policy position concerning ADD/ADHD referrals was: "Don't ask - Don't tell." In this community, teachers often came up to me during my seminars and explained that they have been told, by the school district, not to tell a parent directly that their child needs to be evaluated for ADD/ADHD. Due to their interpretation of federal law, school district personnel believed it would be financially obligated to pay for the evaluation if the referral was made by a teacher.

When I attempted to talk about this with the school district superintendent and board members, I was told that teachers are not diagnosticians. They are not qualified to make such referrals. I chuckled and said, "So, if a child falls off of the playground equipment and breaks his arm, your teachers or school nurse won't make a referral to the emergency room to have the broken arm tended to because they are not professional diagnosticians?" The position of not making referrals for evaluations was a silly one, based on their fear of having to pay for the evaluation. My frustration with the school district heightened because I was dealing with the kids who were falling through the cracks. Children and adolescents with undiagnosed and untreated ADD/ADHD end up having academic struggles and disliking school. Their self-esteem starts to dive and they manage to hang out with other adolescents in a similar state of existence. With their mutual dislike for school and the authority figures that constantly put them down for their academic failures, they decide to spend more of their time experimenting with alcohol and drugs. I end up having to treat these kids when they are in their late adolescent years. After conducting my initial one hour diagnostic interview, I see "red flags" all over the place for possible ADD/ADHD. I end up evaluating the child for the disorder and confirming the reality that they have it when they should have been evaluated years ago. Now the parents and I have to work over time to get the child's feet and self-esteem planted back on the ground. We end up putting Humpty Dumpty back together again while the school district has saved itself some money.

It is very important that you explore your local school district policy concerning referrals for ADD/ADHD evaluations. Some school districts will identify and refer for evaluations while other school districts adopt a "Don't ask - Don't tell" policy. Don't assume your child is in safe hands and that your school district will tell you when they think there is a problem. To be fair to some school districts, we do live in a litigious society and they do have some legitimate concerns of fearing they would have to pay for making a referral for such an evaluation. You can work with your local school board members and school district administration in creating a policy of assurance where referrals can be made without threat of payment. Create a grass-roots effort and get the ball rolling. We started a grass roots movement and succeeded in opening up the doors to permit teachers the freedom to talk openly with parents. The best books to read about ADD/ADHD are ***Driven to Distraction*** and ***Answers to Distraction*** both by Hallowell and Ratey. Learn about the real facts and toss Grandpa Stewart's and Aunt Betty's opinions into the garbage can. Although your extended family members love you and Little Billy to pieces, often, they don't know diddily squat about ADD/ADHD.

4. Depression.

As time passes, we are learning more about the disorder of depression. Depression can definitely interfere with a child's ability to comply with adult authority at home or at school. Depression can affect one's self-esteem, energy level, and motivation, as well as the ability to pay attention and think clearly. Depression can be situational, such as being brought on by the death of a loved one. Depression can be caused by one's geographical local, such as the northern climates in Alaska, Canada, Europe, and Asia. Seasonal affective disorder is brought on by the lack of sunlight hitting the retina. As a result, a message is sent to the hypothalamus, which relays a message down to the pineal gland stating, "Hey, it's winter up here! It's time to hibernate!" People end up becoming grouchy, hungry, depressed, and they want to hibernate. Finally, depression can be caused by a biochemical imbalance in the brain. It is a well-documented fact that depression can be found in families due to a genetic predisposition. In other words, if you have one or both parents that have a history of depression, more than likely one or both of their parents had a history of depression. You or your child might end up experiencing a depressive disorder, too.

The best way to treat situational depression is through emotional support and time. The best way to treat a seasonal affective disorder is with a combination of an antidepressant and light-box therapy. Finally, the best way to treat a chemically imbalanced depression in the brain is with an antidepressant and therapy. It is best not to diagnose your children or yourself, rather, it is best to see a physician or a mental health professional for an evaluation.

5. Generalized Anxiety.

Anxiety is a real disorder and can be difficult to live with. It may cause children to disobey parental authority because they are trying to avoid facing their own fears and anxiety. They may not want to tell you about their anxiety or they may not even be consciously aware of their own anxiety and fears. Fortunately there is help for anxiety disorders. The best way to treat anxiety is with a combination of therapy and anti-anxiety medication. I believe the best therapeutic approach for treating anxiety is with a therapist who utilizes a cognitive-behavioral approach. In many cases, I believe, irrational and unhealthy thinking leads to problems with anxiety. When I help an adolescent or adult change their irrational thoughts to rational thoughts, more often than not, the anxiety eventually subsides. Eventually, they can go off their anti-anxiety medication and remain stable over time. Once again, don't diagnose your children or yourself, rather, see a physician or a mental health counselor for an evaluation.

6. Alcohol and Drug Abuse and Dependency.

More often than not, children with attitude problems toward authority figures at home and at school have experimented with alcohol and illicit drugs on at least one occasion. I stopped being surprised years ago when a child would eventually confess to using alcohol, marijuana, or other illicit chemicals. Seldom will an adolescent confess to their parents or therapist about their use of alcohol and other drugs. If and when they do, they often under-report their usage.

Two good personality profile tests that I utilize as a psychologist to evaluate the adolescent clients that I work with are the Minnesota Multiphasic Personality Inventory for Adolescents (MMPI-A) and the Millon Adolescent Clinical Inventory (MACI). Not only are these the two most commonly administered personality profile tests for adolescents used in the United States of America, but they are probably the two most commonly administered personality profile tests used for adolescents in the Milky Way Galaxy. However, I have not talked to any extraterrestrials to confirm this fact. Nevertheless, these tests are adequate psychometric assessment tools used to compare your adolescent child's responses with other adolescent children.

These tests help determine whether or not your child is experiencing depression, anxiety, eating disorders, low self esteem, family discord, peer insecurity, and body discomfort. They also help ascertain whether or not your adolescent child is experimenting with alcohol and drugs, or at least have the personality makeup of those who might be experimenting with alcohol and drugs. If I were you, and I thought my adolescent child was messing around with alcohol and other drugs, I would take my child to a psychologist and have these two tests administered. I would also take my child to get a urinalysis to see whether or not the urine is "clean."

Finally, you should know that the best approach to treating alcohol and drug abuse as well as dependency is in a group setting. Individual therapy with an alcohol and drug abuser is not as successful as group therapy in an outpatient or inpatient treatment setting. It is much tougher for the alcohol and drug abuser to pull one over on a group of people than it is to pull one over on an individual therapist.

As a side note, it is unfortunate that some parents won't take their adolescent child to a mental health professional if their child doesn't want to go. Taking your child to a mental health professional is no different than taking your child to a dentist for an abscessed tooth or taking your child to a physician for a broken arm. Your child may not want to go to the dentist or to the physician, but you take him or her anyway because that abscessed tooth or broken arm needs to be dealt with immediately. Likewise, when your child has emotional and psychological needs, those needs should be dealt with immediately.

In situations where your child is resistant to visiting with a mental health professional, you merely play the role of a Borg in a Star Trek episode and state the following to your child, "Resistance is futile! You will be assimilated!" In other words, you are the parent and your child is going to do what you want them to do. In some cases, I encourage parents to dangle a major consequence if their child does not comply, along with dangling a big reward if they do comply.

7. *Neuropsychological Impairment.*

Unfortunately, due to the alignment of the planets, the luck of the draw, the Leprechauns and Gremlins, the effects of general sin on mankind when Adam and Eve fell in the Garden of Eden, or the abuse of alcohol and drugs by a pregnant mother, some children are born with neuropsychological impairment. It seems like every book I read has a computer analogy to explain an author's point of view, so I might as well give it a shot, too.

Someone having a chemical imbalance in their brain that causes depression is equivalent to a computer with a software problem. Software problems can be corrected by reconfiguring the data, by simply deleting the software from the hard drive and getting a new disc, or by reinstalling the desired software again. The bottom line is, software problems can be corrected. However, hard drive problems cannot be reconfigured. If your motherboard goes belly up, it is history. It is time to get a new motherboard. When parts of our brain go belly up, they can't be replaced. Therefore, neuropsychological impairment tends to be a lifelong problem.

However, I have a very good psychologist friend who would adamantly argue against the above statement. He told me that he "fried" his brain on numerous illicit drugs when he was younger and that God healed him. Who am I to argue against his life experiences? He's certainly one of the smartest guys I know. If his brain was "fried" in the past, it has definitely been healed based on how he conducts himself today. Sometimes, existing neurons can develop new neuropathways in the brain to make up for deficiencies. The brain is a marvelously created organ. Today, he's teaching at a University on the east coast.

If you abused alcohol or other drugs while you were pregnant with your child, you may want to have your child evaluated by a pediatrician, neurologist, or neuropsychologist. Certainly a child with neuropsychological impairment will have difficulty complying with the rules at home and at school. You might have to adjust your expectations to match your child's ability to comply in this unique situation. On the other hand, it's possible that the FAMILY Rules system may be inappropriate for your child's developmental needs. By all means, if you suspect that your child may have some form of neuropsychological impairment, please have an evaluation done immediately by a neurologist or neuropsychologist.

8. Emotionally Disturbed.

Let's face it, we have some pretty sick puppies living in our society today. Unfortunately, there are many broken homes as the result of many extremely dysfunctional adults. Some children have been raked over the coals of emotional abuse during their short years on this planet. As a result of the emotional abuse, their trust level with anyone on this planet is zilch. These children fend for themselves, attempting to meet their own needs because they haven't perceived anyone else meeting their needs. They will do whatever it takes to meet their own perceived emotional needs, even if it means defying adult authority at home and at school. More often than not, these children are found in foster homes, group homes, and in families where multiple divorces have occurred. In these situations, your best bet is to put the FAMILY Rules system on hold and get your child the therapy needed to get his or her emotional feet on the ground. Only implement FAMILY Rules when the child is more emotionally stable.

9. Conduct Disorder.

I am seeing an increase in the number of conduct disordered children entering my office for help. Conduct disordered children have a real strong tendency to violate social norms, rules, and laws in their homes, schools, churches, synagogues, and communities. Conduct disordered children will lie, cheat, steal, use force to get what they want, and ultimately defy any perceived authority. As a matter of fact, they will tell most authority figures in their life to take a long walk on a short pier. When conduct disordered adolescents enter therapy, the odds of them turning their behaviors around without order and structure is next to nothing. Fortunately, FAMILY Rules has been used to turn many such children around.

To be honest, it is the teeth that can be found in the FAMILY Rules parenting system that helps some of these children turn their lives around in a positive direction. The teeth that I am referring to is the threat of being sent away to long term residential treatment if they continue to choose to disobey rules at home, school, church, synagogue, and in the community. With a conduct disordered child, you may have to be willing to work through your own guilt in order to get your child the help needed. Please don't forget that reverent fear of authority is good. The potential consequences the authority figure can impose upon a disobedient child can be a very productive motivational tool as long as it's legal, moral, and ethical.

Years ago, among some adolescents in Fairbanks, Alaska, I was known as the psychologist who sends kids away. I am now slowly developing this same reputation among adolescents in Grants Pass, Oregon. One evening, while standing in line at a video store in Fairbanks, a group of adolescent boys were whispering to one another and looking over their shoulders at me and whispering again. They left the store quickly. The young man behind the counter stated, "What is this 'Dr. J.' stuff? Why are they talking about you sending kids away?" I responded to the young man by saying, "I don't send kids away. Kids make the decision to send themselves away by disobeying their parents and school authorities. Besides, no kid is ever sent away without parental consent."

Recently, I had a parent call me up and ask, "Are you the psychologist who sends kids away? I want you to help me send my kid to long-term residential treatment right now." I responded by saying, "Hold on. Let's get together to talk about why you think your child needs to be sent away. Sending a child away to long-term residential treatment is a last resort option. I want to make sure we have tried everything else first. My goal is to turn your child around so that he or she can remain in your home." The moral of the story is this: don't be so quick to want to send your child away. Besides, residential treatment costs a lot more money than your local outpatient counselor does.

10. Undisclosed Abuse(s).

While providing therapy, it saddens me to discover that a child or adolescent has been physically or sexually abused by a family member, baby sitter, extended family member, or stranger. Obviously, a child that has been sexually abused and chooses to consciously or unconsciously suppress the memory finds it difficult to trust an authority figure.

There is a lot of controversy out there among mental health professionals concerning repressed memories. I really hesitate to go digging for repressed memories. The bottom line for now is research studies are showing that the retrieval of repressed memories via hypnosis is unreliable. Memory reconstruction can occur and events can be recalled that don't fit with reality. My belief is that memories will surface if the person is psychologically prepared to deal with them. I greatly discourage the use of hypnotherapy to retrieve memories because of it's unreliability. There are many variables involved such as how questions are asked, what someone wants to believe happened, or what someone doesn't want to believe happened. Hypnotherapy is useful for other forms of psychotherapeutic treatment, such as for the suppression of nicotine cravings or to help an athlete focus better during competition; however, as previously mentioned, hypnotherapy has not proven itself completely reliable concerning memory retrieval.

When I began my course work at Rutgers University in New Jersey to obtain my Master of Social Work degree, I was told that the best way to be a good therapist was to go through therapy myself. It was important as a clinician to know what it was like to be in the client's chair. Fortunately, Rutgers University provided free counseling for graduate students. I knew I had to deal with a lot of anger, grief, and loss issues in therapy. Therefore, I was more than happy to take advantage of the free counseling. I spent a year in therapy with a wonderful psychologist, who helped me to deal with many of my unresolved family issues from childhood.

During my year of individual therapy, I did not inform my psychologist about something that began years before. Since the age of nine, I had been having the same dream over and over again. The dream always started with me being a young boy sitting on the couch in my parents' home. I was home alone. It was dark outside and only the living room lights were on. Then as usual, in my dream, I would hear a noise upstairs in the large attic bedroom. The door at the bottom of the stairs would open up with a creaking sound. In my dream, as that young boy, I would be sitting on the couch shaking with fear as I watched the door open up to the living room. It was at that point in my dream that I would always wake up still shaking with fear.

For the first time in eighteen years, while primarily addressing my anger toward my parents as well as some grief and loss issues concerning a past relationship in my life, my dream began to progress beyond just sitting scared on the couch. There I was, a little boy, all alone, sitting on the couch again. Something was banging around upstairs and making noise in the large attic bedroom. The door at the bottom of the stairs creaked as it opened up. This time, I got up off the couch and nervously walked over to the door and opened it up. Then I woke up from my dream with overwhelming fear and trembling. In the next dream, on a different night, I made it to the bottom of the stairs and tried to turn on the light, only to be left standing in darkness. I woke up with fear and trembling again. In the next phase of the dream, I made it to the top of the stairs in the dark and tried to turn on the light without success. I woke up again with fear and trembling. In the next phase of the dream on a different night, I made my way up the stairs and down to the end of the attic bedroom in the pitch dark and tried to turn on the light without success. I woke up again with overwhelming fear and trembling. As an adult male, I found it hard to deal with feeling like a helpless little child. I couldn't talk with my psychologist or my wife about my dreams. I was too embarrassed. Hurray for the macho male ego!

Finally, toward the end of my year of individual therapy at Rutgers University, my dream progressed to a climax. During the last time I ever had that dream, I was an adult sitting on the couch in my parents' house, home alone. I was no longer the scared little boy. I heard the noise upstairs and began to breathe heavily with rage. Seriously, I probably sounded like a woman in labor breathing fast and hard while experiencing contractions. I ran over to the door at the bottom of the stairs, jerked it open, and did not bother to turn on the light switch. I ran up to the top of the stairs, into the dark attic bedroom, more enraged than ever. I made my way to the other end of the dark attic bedroom. I was flailing my arms in the dark trying to find whatever it was that had been making that noise all those years in my dreams. When I found it in the dark, I was going to kill it with every ounce of rage that my body and soul could muster.

While I was experiencing this climatic dream, my wife awoke because of my heavy breathing. She knew something was wrong because normally I am a very quiet sleeper. I seldom ever snore. She decided to wake me up from my obvious nightmare. She grabbed my wrist and began shaking it in order to wake me up.

Meanwhile, back to my climatic dream. I had reached the last spot in that large pitch black attic bedroom and whatever I was looking for grabbed my wrist. It's Murphy's Law to find what you're looking for in the last place you look. In my dream, I grabbed whatever it was, took it's hand off my wrist, clenched my other hand into a fist, and pulled my arm back to give this tormentor of mine the most powerful and deadly blow I could deliver. The heavy weight champion boxer of the world could not withstand my wrathful blow.

Meanwhile, back in the waking world, my wife began to scream my name, "Matt! Matt!" She was legitimately concerned that I was about to hit her. While sleeping, I had grabbed her wrist with my left hand, pulled her hand off my wrist and had cocked my right arm. Fortunately for her, she screamed out my name and woke me up before I hit whatever it was in my dream - and her. I immediately experienced a flashback memory.

For a brief moment, I saw something like a movie on a motion picture screen. The spot in the upstairs attic in my dream, where the thing grabbed my wrist in the dark, was the exact spot where an older adolescent male sexually abused me when I was nine years old. He was about six years older than me. I looked up to him. I trusted him. All the pain and anger came flowing out of me right there in my bed. My repressed memories were freed when I was emotionally and psychologically prepared to deal with them. I did not need hypnotherapy to accomplish this end result.

At my last therapy session, I informed my psychologist about the dream and it's progression during my year of therapy. She believed that my addressing the dysfunctional family issues I grew up with on a conscious level, freed me up to face issues of sexual abuse in my dreams at an unconscious level. For eighteen years I had stuffed the pain and anger of the betrayal I had experienced at the hand of my older adolescent male friend, whom I admired and trusted.

I can personally testify to the fact that my angry distrust toward authority figures pretty much diminished because my own issues surfaced when I was emotionally and psychologically prepared to deal with them. Never underestimate the power of the mind, especially the unconscious mind, and how it impacts the choices made by a child or an adult. If you suspect that your child has experienced undisclosed abuses, once again, please seek the assistance of a licensed mental health professional. Insist that the therapist doesn't try to force the issue to surface before your child is actually ready to face it. Your child's mind will allow him or her to process their issues when they are prepared to do so. In other words, you might have to wait until your child becomes an adult.

Part 2

The Mechanics of The FAMILY System

~Chapter Eight~

The FAMILY Rules Parenting System

This is the second longest but the most important chapter of the book. However, before you read this chapter, you really need to read and understand the first seven chapters. Have you read the first seven chapters yet? Yes, you! I'm writing to you! You know who you are! That's right! The individual who likes to skip ahead rather than take the time to read a book in its proper order. Well, aren't you special! The nuts and bolts of FAMILY Rules will not make absolute sense to you unless you first read chapters one through seven. So stop reading this chapter and start at the beginning of the book just like everyone else does. Hey! I said stop! A thorough understanding of the philosophical underpinnings of FAMILY Rules is essential to making complete and absolute sense out of the nuts and bolts of the FAMILY Rules parenting system. Okay, I'll catch up with you later after you enlighten yourself. I know. Life is difficult when you are sequentially impaired. You'll survive! Trust me! Go back to chapter one right this second. I'll see you back here in chapter eight in a little while. Bye!

For those of you who have actually read the first seven chapters, I wish to explain the ultimate goal of FAMILY Rules. The ultimate goal of FAMILY Rules is not to create perfect parents and children. Rather, the ultimate goal of FAMILY Rules is to improve communication in the home through clarification of the rules, consequences, and rewards. This process will eventually lead to less tension and conflict among family members and ultimately lead to more compliant and respectful behaviors from everyone toward everyone.

It is my most humble opinion that all families in America should be federally mandated to implement FAMILY Rules in their homes. What's funny is that you think I'm actually joking. However, I'm not joking. I'm being totally serious. Most problems in our society can be traced to the home and the lack of organized and structured discipline parents are providing for their children. As much as they might rebel and protest, children and adolescents want their parents to provide structure and guidance. They want to know that their parents are committed to keeping them safe and on the right path in life. Yet most parents don't have a game plan for parenting. They're flying by the seat of their pants while they parent with mood and energy level.

Although children have free will and can, therefore, make unhealthy choices, the provision of organized structure and clarified communication will help to significantly reduce the likelihood that they will make inappropriate choices. This is the ultimate goal of FAMILY Rules: To assist families via improved communication, learning to make appropriate choices, and taking responsibility for their actions. If you make a mistake while implementing FAMILY Rules in your home, admit it, get back up on the horse and keep riding. Don't quit because you are struggling with being consistent. Work on becoming more consistent. FAMILY Rules works if you work it! (Please see Chapter 12 and Appendix B for FAMILY Rules testimonials).

Before you implement the FAMILY Rules parenting system in your home, you will need the following materials:

1. Paper and pen or a computer and printer. You will be recording your parental expectations on paper. Hint: The age of computers is upon us and using one makes it a whole lot easier to add to the list, delete from the list, or modify the existing list of family rules. Get over your fears and learn how to use your computer.

2. A minimum of 55 (3 x 5) index cards which will be used for your Good Habit cards, Wild Cards, and Grace Cards.

3. A whole bunch of different colored poker chips or other similar items to be used as Daily Tokens and Random Acts of Kindness (RAK) chips.

4. If you don't want to take the time to go to the store and purchase all the separate items in order to put your parenting program together, you can always go on line and purchase a parenting kit (www.Family-Functions.com). You can order a parenting kit for two, three, four, five, or even up to six children.

5. A very serious commitment to the "correct and consistent" implementation of FAMILY Rules in your home (i.e., "the two 'C' words"). For the sake of beating a dead horse, "correct" means implementing the system the way I teach it to you in this book – no deviations. Please remember, I've taught this to several thousand families. I have taught FAMILY Rules to licensed mental health professionals. They have given me truckloads of feedback. We've already been there, done that, and got the T-shirt. What you're reading is what has been proven to work the best. So don't try and create a hybrid of FAMILY Rules. You may think your family is uniquely different, but it's not. We are all a lot more alike than most of us would care to admit. The kinks of FAMILY Rules have been worked out. This is an airtight parenting program. "Consistent" means keep your parenting roles properly prioritized and "keep on keeping on." This means implementing FAMILY Rules in spite of your changing moods or energy levels. Finally, keep on consistently implementing FAMILY Rules in your home especially when behaviors are going smoothly. Don't forget to take FAMILY Rules until it's all gone – until your last child is eighteen, graduated from high school, and has moved out of the home. Then you can go back to being an unstructured and unorganized slob if you so desire.

Please remember, "Every home needs a FAMILY." Now, without further adieu, it is a pleasure for me to introduce FAMILY Rules to you!

Fashion a List of Family Rules

1. Nothing goes on the list of family rules unless both parents are in agreement (i.e., both parents have equal veto power). I encourage cooperation and not a power struggle. If you can't work together on

something this simple, then you definitely need marital counseling before you implement FAMILY Rules. If you are a single parent, you can attempt to consult with your ex-spouse, in order to implement FAMILY Rules in both homes. If your former spouse is deceased, out of contact with the family, or uncooperative, then seek input from an adult friend. By the way, many divorced couples use this with their children in their two homes.

2. The list of rules are to govern behaviors for all family members at home, school, work, malls, church, synagogue, 35,000 feet up in the air in a jet, 2,000 feet below the surface of the ocean in a submarine, and everywhere else in between.

3. The rules are to be "Do as we say and as we do" rules. Parents are expected to practice what they preach. If you don't want your kids to swear, then you don't swear. If you want your kids to make their bed in the morning then you make your bed in the morning. The only exceptions to "do as we say and as we do" are issues of legal age (e.g., driving, drinking, smoking, movies, curfew, etc.) and the hierarchy model (e.g., parents tell kids what to do such as bedtime, phone time, etc.).

4. Parents may seek input from their child(ren) concerning what rules to put on the list but parents always have the final say (i.e., Authority flows downward). Remember, you are a benevolent dictator. If your child(ren) think(s) they are in control of the family, they may engage you in a power struggle in an attempt to maintain their perceived control. More often than not, it is best not to consult with your children, especially if they have an oppositional defiant disorder or have a conduct disorder.

5. Rules can be added to, deleted from, or modified on the list at any time as long as the parents talk with each other first and are both in agreement. Remember, this is a flexible, living, and breathing document. It is never chiseled in stone - FAMILY Rules is not rigid. FAMILY Rules can change with the needs of the moment and the developmental changes in your children.

6. If the rule is not on the list, then it is not a rule and your child(ren) did not break it. It would not be right if a State Trooper attempted to arrest you because he or she did not like the glasses you were wearing or the color of your hair. There is no state law telling us what kind of glasses we can and cannot wear nor is there a state law telling us what color of hair we can and cannot have. Therefore, you better thoroughly think through what rules you want to put on the family list and whether or not you are prepared to enforce them both "correctly and consistently." (Please see Appendix C for a sample of the most commonly used family rules).

7. You cannot create a new rule and retroactively go back and nail your child(ren) for breaking it. Your children must be informed first about any additions or modifications to the house rules list before they can be held accountable for breaking the rule(s).

8. On the average, most parents come up with approximately thirty-five rules. I have seen as few as five rules and as many as fifty rules. Please number the family rules for easy reference at a later time. Professionals who recommend a limited number of rules in a home are from another planet and have obviously never parented your children before. In the real world, we live by more than ten total rules and we all manage to cope just fine without feeling overwhelmed or having our self-esteem shattered.

9. I will not tell you what rules you should use to raise your children. FAMILY Rules is the skeletal framework of order and structure and you get to slap the meat on the bones and the skin around the meat in a manner that reflects your values and morals and how you want to train up your child in the way you think they should go. All parents need to work through what values and morals they want to teach their children. Every home is different; however, it is not uncommon for parents to want feedback from other parents or professionals to see if they are being too lenient or too rigid with their list of family rules (please see Appendix C for some ideas of rules or consult with an adult friend whose parenting abilities you respect). If you so desire, I am available for paid phone consultation

at 1-541-956-8585. You may also look at my website, to see if there is a counselor who uses FAMILY Rules in your community (www. Family-Rules.com). Ultimately, you have to make the final decision on what rules you need to have to raise your children.

Fashion a List of Family Rules

Add Good Habit Cards

1. Take forty-five 3x5 index cards and write various "Good Habits" on them that require approximately thirty minutes to complete the task. They can be shorter than a half-hour but never longer than a half-hour. These "Good Habit Cards" consist of chore-like activities as well as fun activities (e.g., sweep and mop the kitchen floor, clean the toilet and bathtub, clean out the inside of mom's car, bake a cake, write a letter to grandma, fifty jumping jacks/fifty sit-ups, read a book to your younger sibling, shoot baskets outside, etc.). You may create separate stacks of cards for older and younger children. (Please see Appendix D).

2. The good habit cards are to consist of tasks above and beyond your child(ren)'s daily and weekly chores (i.e., daily and weekly chores do not go on the good habit cards).

3. You may wish to designate some cards as seasonal cards (i.e., five yellow cards for outdoor summer tasks and five blue cards for outdoor winter tasks), or you may wish to divide one card with a diagonal slash and write "shovel drive way in winter/sweep drive way in summer."

4. Take five 3x5 index cards and simply write "Wild Card" on them. This means that your child(ren) has to do whatever you want them to do for approximately thirty minutes. Also, when you pull a "Wild Card," you have to do whatever your children want you to do for approximately thirty minutes. This teaches family members the principle of "what goes around comes around" or "do unto others as you would have them do unto you." In other words, my family

members usually pick interactive tasks such as playing catch or board games or going for a bike ride. You now have a total of fifty cards (i.e., you have forty-five "Good Habit Cards" along with five "Wild Cards", for a total of fifty cards).

5. Take an additional five 3x5 index cards and write "Grace" on them. If your child draws this card, they are off the hook for this particular card. They get some "amazing grace, how sweet the sound that saved a wretch like" them. You now have a total of 55 cards.

6. Assign good habit card values within the parentheses in the left margin of the page next to the numbered list of family rules (please see Appendix C). Start low and work your way up from there (i.e., one to three cards); however, start with a high number of "Good Habit Cards" for the most important rules. Most parents put all fifty cards next to "Obey all local, state, federal, and military laws."

Fashion a List of Family Rules

Add Good Habit Cards

Mix in Responsibility via Household Chores

1. Develop a list of daily chores. Daily chores need to have inspection times (i.e., feed and water the dog before dinner; brush your teeth before school and before bed, etc.). (Please see Appendix E).

2. Develop a list of weekly chores. Weekly chores need to have an inspection day and time (e.g., clean and vacuum your bedroom by 12:00 P.M. on Saturday). Note: Do not set an inspection time at a time when you cannot inspect it. If you don't get home until 5:30 P.M., don't set the inspection time at 4:30 P.M. Instead, set it at 6:00 P.M.

3. Parents, you don't need to nag your child(ren) any more about completing their chores. You just simply check them out at the inspection time and render a verdict. If the child didn't complete

the chore(s) on time, they will receive one "Good Habit Card" per unfinished chore and they will still need to complete their chore(s) immediately.

4. Parents, don't forget to make up your own list of daily and weekly chores. Yes! I know you already do plenty around the house. Writing down the daily and weekly tasks you do around the house allows your children to notice all that you do. Don't assume that they are completely aware of your contributions to the household. Also, wives, FAMILY Rules provides you with the wonderful opportunity to create a daily and weekly "Honey Do" list for your hubby. He will appreciate it. Spread your work load out and stop being a domestic martyr! Finally, I don't want to hear, "But no one does it as good or neat as I do." If your kids are slobs, then teach them to do it right. Otherwise, you are enabling them to be slobs.

This is How "F.A.M." Work Together

1. When FAMILY Rules is officially implemented, parents will no longer be in charge of whether or not their children are grounded nor will they be in charge of how long their children are grounded. Instead, their children will be in charge of whether or not they are grounded and for how long they are grounded. They will learn to take responsibility for their own choices.

2. If children break a rule or do not do their daily or weekly chores on time, then they are choosing to ground themselves. Parents never ask children to break rules — children choose to break rules.

3. When children choose to break a rule, they will need to randomly select the assigned number of "Good Habit Cards" from the front of the deck without looking at what they are drawing. The number of "Good Habit Cards" will have been previously designated by parents and placed in parenthesis next to each rule on their family rules list. The more significant the rule, the more "Good Habit Cards" they will receive for breaking it (please see Appendix C).

4. The child(ren) must accept their "Good Habit Cards" politely or they will be doubled each time they are inappropriate, so that 2 cards become 4; 4 cards double to 8 cards; 8 cards double to 16 cards; 16 cards double to 32 cards; and 32 cards max out at 50. Children feel like they are in a hole they can't climb out of if given more than 50 cards. Give your child a "ten minute cooling down period" in between doubling the cards for impoliteness. This will give both the child and you an opportunity to calm down and hopefully contribute toward de-escalating the situation. If you find yourself losing control of your temper, calm down first and then discipline. You will be much more effective in the long run.

5. After a child draws a card (or cards), he or she has two choices:

A. Do the Good Habit Card(s) immediately, or

B. Go to his or her room and do the Good Habit Card(s) later. With this option, the child is merely choosing to lengthen their grounding. The choice belongs to the child and not to the parents.

6. After a child completes the tasks on the "Good Habit Cards," he or she is required to have their parent(s) inspect the job to see if it was done correctly. If not done correctly, errors are politely pointed out and the child is asked to finish the job. Parents might have to show a younger child what is expected by helping with the chore. Once the "Good Habit Card" is completed correctly, it is returned to the discard pile and parents do not mention the offense again. After a child has "done the time for the crime," parents should cast their child's sins "as far as the east is from the west and remember them no more." However, if the chore is inspected for a second time and it's obvious that no effort was put into completing the chore correctly, even after giving specific instructions, then the child selects another "Good Habit Card." Have him or her complete the present task before moving on to the next one.

7. If the child chooses to go to his or her room instead of doing their "Good Habit Cards" right away, he or she may only do the following four things while in their room:

A. They can lay on the bed (this includes taking a nap);
B. Do their homework;
C. Engage in parent approved reading (boring subject matter that would gag your kid); or
D Clean their room.

The child cannot do anything else in their room. No TV, no stereo, no computer, no phone, no toys, no puzzles, no video games, etc. Nothing but the four above mentioned activities (which usually is perceived as absolute and total boredom). Bummer! If the child doesn't cooperate, see how to respond under "Y" in a few pages.

8.   If the child chooses to go to his or her room, there are only eight reasons for leaving their room:

A. To go to the bathroom for a brief period of time;
B. To eat a family meal (breakfast, lunch, or dinner – absolutely no snacking unless there's a physician's mandate for the child to eat a particular snack because of a physical disorder);
C. To go to school or participate in a school activity (drama, band, sports, etc.);
D. To go to work if he or she has a job;
E. To complete a Daily or Weekly Chore;
F. To go to church/synagogue (regular worship service and Sunday school only);
G. To go to a 12-step meeting or a scheduled appointment; or
H. To complete the good habit card(s) if it is not past their bedtime. If it is past his or her bedtime, then the card(s) carry over to the next day.

Note: Most children who choose to go to their room only stay there for ten to sixty minutes. They just want some space and time to calm down. Leave them alone unless they are destroying their room. If they are destroying their room, remind them about "Strikes" and "Pop Flies" (read about these under "Y").

9. If parents break a rule, they will need to do the assigned good habit card(s) immediately. The best parenting technique on planet earth is consistent role modeling (i.e., practice what you preach and walk the talk). "Do as we say - not as we do" is unacceptable. We all make mistakes from time to time; however, to knowingly practice hypocrisy is a major parenting mistake. If you make a mistake, admit it, do your cards, and keep on parenting. You cannot expect your children to change if you're not willing to change.

10. If a parent should ever refuse to do his or her card(s), children have the right to bring this issue to the attention of the other parent or mutually accepted adult mediator. The parents will have a private discussion. If the errant parent emerges from the bedroom with an attitude of humility and does the Good Habit Card(s), then the dilemma is considered resolved; however, if the errant parent does not change their position, then address this issue in therapy with a counselor who uses FAMILY Rules or give my office a call and set up an appointment for a paid phone consultation. We will get this issue resolved.

We are all hypocrites. No one is perfect. We all break the rules from time to time and/or occasionally violate our personal/spiritual morals, values and ethics. Hopefully, this doesn't happen very often. FAMILY Rules does not expect parents to be perfect; however, FAMILY Rules does expect parents to try and be the best role models they can be for their children. We need to strive to better our character and conduct on a daily basis. If you make a mistake, admit it and do your Good Habit Cards immediately, and keep on parenting. It's one thing to make mistakes or to occasionally and unintentionally break the rules. However, it's another thing to intentionally break the rules on a continuous basis without remorse or repentance. Knowingly and intentionally practicing ongoing parental hypocrisy is unacceptable and outright lousy parenting. Matter of fact, it's reprehensible and impeachable! Go to bed every night knowing you are a better parent than you were the day before. Always strive to be better. Strive for excellence even if you make mistakes along the journey of parenting. Don't settle for mediocrity. Your children are watching you. Monkey see - monkey do. The acorn doesn't fall far from the tree. They're a chip off the old block. Please don't make me come hunt you down.

Fashion a List of Family Rules

Add Good Habit Cards

Mix in Responsibility via Household Chores

Institute a List of Rewards

1. Sit down with your child(ren) and develop a "List of Rewards" that meet with your approval and fit within your financial realities. I have seen a variety of rewards offered by parents: ice cream cones, DVD rentals, video games, slumber parties, movies with a friend (popcorn and soda provided), shoes, CD's, clothes, fishing trips, concerts, shopping sprees, and many more items. Please number the rewards list for easy reference in the future (please see Appendix F).

2. Once you have developed the "List of Rewards" and numbered them, assign a Daily Token value for each reward. Rule of thumb: The bigger and better the reward, the more tokens it will cost your child(ren). (Please see appendix F).

3. Most parents place a minimum value of $ 1.00 per Daily Token. Sometimes, parents will choose to lower the number of Daily Tokens required to obtain a bigger and better reward to give their child(ren) extra incentive to obtain the desired reward (e.g., a $ 100.00 pair of designer tennis shoes could be offered for seventy Daily Tokens rather than one-hundred Daily Tokens).

4. Your children earn Daily Tokens as follows: Every night, at bedtime, you consistently and correctly recall the day to determine how your child(ren) behaved. If they didn't break a rule and they got all of their chores done on time, then they receive one Daily Token

at the end of the day. If they broke a rule and/or didn't get their chore(s) done on time, then they don't receive a Daily Token at the end of the day. Sorry parents, you don't get Daily Tokens ever. Peace and quiet via improved communication and increased compliance with the rules of your home is reward enough for most parents.

5.   Each child has his or her own color coded Daily Tokens (poker chips) to discourage stealing. Yes, your kids would actually rip each other off, so plan ahead and prevent it from happening.

6.   If your children receive all seven Daily Tokens for the week (Sunday through Saturday), they will receive three bonus Daily Tokens. Therefore, they will receive a total of ten Daily Tokens for a perfect week. Use a calendar to help you keep track of this.

7.   If your children receive Daily Tokens from the first day of the month through the last day of the month, they will not only receive ten Daily Tokens times four weeks (equaling a total of forty Daily Tokens), they will also receive ten bonus tokens for a perfect month (equaling a total of fifty Daily Tokens for their perfect month). Don't forget to use a calendar to help you keep track of the tokens.

A Side Note Concerning Allowance for Children

Some child psychologists believe that children should receive an allowance no matter how good or bad they have behaved (i.e., allowance should not be tied in with their behaviors). Instead, the allowance should be used as a teaching tool to help children learn how to manage their money. Most parents give their children a set amount of allowance on a weekly basis and then teach them to save twenty percent, give ten percent away to a local charity, soup kitchen, Red Cross, church or synagogue (i.e., teaching them to give back to their community), and do whatever they want with the remaining seventy percent. The amount you choose to give your children for their weekly allowance depends upon your financial realities. If you attempt to tie in their allowance with behaviors, then it interferes with your ability to teach them how to manage their money appropriately. Their behaviors will be dealt with sufficiently via the "Good Habit Cards" and Daily Tokens. Don't forget to "correctly and consistently" implement FAMILY in your home ("the two 'C' words").

Fashion a List of Family Rules

Add Good Habit Cards

Mix in Responsibility via Household Chores

Institute a List of Rewards

Love and Encourage Your Child(ren) Daily

1.   You can never overstate the fact to your child(ren) that you love them. Compliment and praise your children daily. Give them hugs and kisses. Tell them that they look nice. Let them know that you love them unconditionally. Brag about them to your friends. Don't worry if they think it's uncool. Deep down inside, they appreciate the positive attention. They really do! Really!

2.   If you catch your child(ren) engaged in Random Acts of Kindness, give them a RAK Chip. This RAK Chip obviously needs to be a different color than all of the other Daily Tokens. Three RAK chips equal one regular Daily Token. This way there is still incentive for your child(ren) to behave appropriately during the course of a day, even if they have already broken a rule and/or failed to complete their chore(s). They can exchange RAK Chips in order to acquire Daily Tokens and, therefore, still have a chance to obtain a perfect week and/or month (RAK Chips are like extra credit at school in order to help keep the grades up).

3.   Even though there is an opportunity for your child(ren) to earn rewards, this should not stop you from occasionally spoiling them rotten just for the fun of it. You can still take them out to dinner or buy them a gift just because they are special and have been behaving

well. They don't have to turn in Daily Tokens for everything. Just make sure you complement them while you're spoiling them so they can connect it together.

4.   Provide your child(ren) with opportunities to tell you how they think and feel about what is going on in the home. They must be respectful. Spend one on one time with them. In the midst of my very busy schedule, I try the best I can to take my kids out on a date more often than not. This provides them with a consistent opportunity to talk about anything they want to or need to with dad.

5.   Schedule a weekly family meeting. Place a family journal in a central location so that everyone in the family has an opportunity to write down what they want to discuss at the next family meeting. If it is not written down at least one-hour prior to the meeting, then it will not be discussed. It will have to wait until next week. Everyone needs to know what will be discussed so there are no surprises. Discuss old business first and then new business. Positive things may be discussed. This is not meant to just be a gripe session. The meeting length will vary from week to week.

Fashion a List of Family Rules

Add Good Habit Cards

Mix in Responsibility via Household Chores

Institute a List of Rewards

Love and Encourage Your Child(ren) Daily

Youth Residential Treatment if Needed or any other Creative Form of Teeth

1.   Rules without teeth are not worth the paper they're written on. There must be immediate "correct and consistent" consequences for inappropriate behaviors and attitudes. Otherwise, your children

will run your home and chaos will prevail (i.e., "He who spares the rod of discipline hates his child").

2.   If your children should ever reach the point where they totally and wholeheartedly defy your authority, in a "willful and prolonged manner" exceeding a twenty-four hour period of time, they will have committed "Strike-One" and they will be automatically grounded to their room for one week. They will miss weekend and extracurricular activities at school. They will also not be allowed to work at their job. If they end up being kicked off the team for missing practices and games or being fired from their job for not showing up to work, then tough luck! They shouldn't have defied your authority. It's the price they pay for outright disobedience. Upon completion of the one week of grounding to their room, they will have all fifty Good Habit Cards to do.

3.   If your children should ever reach the point where they totally and wholeheartedly defy your authority for a second time in a "willful and prolonged manner" exceeding a twenty-four hour period of time, they will have committed "Strike-Two" and they will be automatically grounded to their room for two weeks. Upon completion of the two weeks, they will have all fifty Good Habit Cards to do.

4.   If your children should ever reach the point where they totally and wholeheartedly defy your authority for a third time in a willful and prolonged manner" exceeding a twenty-four hour period of time, they will have committed "Strike-Three" and it will be time for you to pull out the nukes: long-term residential treatment. If you have a child that is that out of control, long-term residential treatment is your best option to help modify his or her behaviors and attitudes (please see appendix G). Don't forget to search the Internet, family magazines, or inquire at your church or synagogue. Your best bet is to contact an educational consultant (please see appendix H). Please see my website for more information (www. Family-Rules.com).

5.   Please don't forget that there is a difference between a "Strike" and a "Bad-Hair Day." A "Strike" is total and wholehearted defiance toward your authority in a "willful and prolonged manner" exceeding a twenty-four hour period of time. Defiance can be seen in a child's eyes and body language. Most importantly, you can see the total and wholehearted defiance in a child's actions (for example, dropping out of school, continuing to drink and do drugs, involvement in criminal activities, blowing out of therapy, having sex, etc.). On the other hand, a "Bad-Hair Day" will involve some defiance and willfulness but ultimately, your child submits to your authority, takes his or her cards and does them. Absolutely do not give a "Strike" to your child because they are having a "Bad-Hair Day." Consult with an objective third party before handing out a "Strike."

6.   In addition to "Strikes," there is such a thing as a "Pop-Fly." If your child earns a "Pop-Fly," the child automatically goes to long-term residential treatment. Don't even bother with "Strikes" when your child earns a "Pop-Fly." Just send him or her to treatment immediately. A "Pop-Fly" is defined as when a child goes above and beyond the call of duty with harm to self, harm to others, and/ or destruction of property. Sherry received a "Pop-Fly" when she did over ten thousand dollars worth of damage to her home. A "Pop-Fly" consists of behaviors that are way out of bounds such as running away for several days or weeks, major alcohol and drug use activities, assault, major destruction of property, and criminal activity.

7.   Sending your child(ren) to long-term residential treatment does not mean that you, your counselor, or FAMILY Rules has failed. This is the next logical option within the structure of FAMILY Rules to effectively deal with out of control children. If your child had a heart problem and the physicians in your local community could not treat it, you would not hesitate to send your child to a medical facility in another community. Likewise, concerning behavioral problems and attitudinal problems, if your child has failed outpatient therapy and is out of control at home, school, and in your community, then it

is time to send your child to the appropriate treatment setting. This is wise parenting regardless of the guilt trips you may put yourself through.

Please remember, your child has a free-will and makes his or her own decisions. Sending the child to live with a divorced spouse or distant relative is the next best option; however, the new household doesn't provide a therapeutic treatment setting with behavior modification. In most cases, the child's behavior worsens when sent to live with a divorced spouse or relative; however, if you can't or won't pay for residential treatment, then let your child terrorize your ex-spouse for a while. Maybe he or she will then be willing to help you out with the expenses of long term residential treatment (see appendix I for funding options). If you search the Internet thoroughly or inquire at your local church or synagogue, you'll eventually find a low cost facility (see appendix J for finding low cost options). Maybe your state Medicaid office will assist your child. Nevertheless, don't roll over and play dead in your own house. Do something about it!

Creative teeth simply means putting the "reverent fear" of authority within the heart of your child by threatening to send them to a place they don't want to go to. It doesn't have to be a group home or residential treatment facility. Years ago, I worked with parents who threatened to send their sixteen-year old son to live with his uncle. You're wondering what the big deal is? Well, the uncle lived in a cabin on the Yukon River in the middle of nowhere Alaska with the moose and grizzly bear. The kid would have been stranded there with his uncle for two years until he completed a home-based high school diploma program and he wasn't coming back home until he did. The sixteen-year old kid got off of the alcohol and drugs and graduated from a public high school in Anchorage, Alaska. Why? Because the fear of being sent away kept him from being sent away. Now that was some serious "Creative Teeth" that got their son's attention.

8.   The bottom line is your children are going to learn how to obey authority. The question is where do they want to learn to obey? Do

they want to learn how to obey authority at home or do they want to learn how to obey authority a few hundred miles away or a few thousand miles away in a long-term residential treatment facility? Most children decide to learn how to obey authority at home. Some children need to go bye-bye to learn how to obey authority. Ultimately, the choice to stay at home or go away is up to how your child chooses to comply with your authority in your home. They don't get to blame you and you don't get to blame yourself.

9.   Finally, the money you spend to send your child to a high quality long-term residential treatment facility is a worthwhile investment. The odds are very good that he or she will return home a changed individual with the learned ability to make more positive choices for themselves. If treatment will help your child stay off drugs, out of prison, or keep him or her alive, then no cost is too much. There are no guarantees, however, and your child has free will and may continue to make poor choices but at least you know you have done everything possible to help your child. That peace of mind is worth taking out an educational loan, spending their college money, selling an extra car, taking out a second mortgage on the house, selling your kidney, or all of the above. Well, okay, maybe you shouldn't sell your kidney (see appendix K for possible tax deductions).

But wait a minute, look beyond the fact that you are investing only in your child's future. In reality, if you are helping your child to be a better human-being, then ultimately, you are investing in your grandchildren's future as well. Can you imagine what kind of parent your out of control child will make someday if you don't deal with their destructive behaviors and attitudes here and now? Invest in your child's life and in the lives of your descendants. This is your parental responsibility and an awesome one at that. Go to your grave knowing you did absolutely everything you could for your children and your descendants. You can't take your money with you when you die. Invest your time and money wisely in the things that matter the most - your family. Meet your Maker with a clear conscience. Rest in peace! (Please see appendix L to find professionals who help transport children to therapeutic treatment settings).

~Chapter Nine~

Introducing FAMILY Rules In Your Home

How you present FAMILY Rules to your children and adolescents is very important. The ideal way to explain FAMILY Rules to your children is with the assistance of a therapist who is thoroughly immersed in FAMILY Rules training (i.e., they have attended one of my seminars around the USA or Canada). A counselor who uses FAMILY Rules will be able to offer objectivity to the implementation process. This counselor can also be the "bad guy", if necessary, to take the heat off of you. He or she can be available for ongoing monitoring of "correct and consistent" implementation of FAMILY Rules in your home if and when needed (i.e., "the two 'C' words"). To see whether or not you have a counselor who uses FAMILY Rules in your community, please go to my website located at: www. Family-Rules.com. There are counselors who use FAMILY Rules posted on my website and have a certificate in their office to verify their training (please see appendix A).

If you do not have a counselor in your area that uses FAMILY Rules, you may want to encourage your local therapist to contact my office so he or she can make arrangements to be trained to use FAMILY Rules. Have them call the FAMILY Rules office phone number: 1-541-956-8585. They can also learn more about how to become a counselor who uses FAMILY Rules by checking out my website: www.Family-Rules.com. Remember, your therapist must understand and be fully immersed in the FAMILY Rules parenting system or the odds might significantly increase that he or she may undermine your parental authority and turn your child into a monster. The democratic model of parenting (i.e., King Arthur's round table) inappropriately empowers children and undermines your parental authority.

The second best way to implement FAMILY Rules in your home is by having your entire family attend a FAMILY Rules seminar in your community. Attending a FAMILY Rules seminar is beneficial for your children because they get to see other families involved in the same endeavor. Many parents lack a reference point for parenting and they often learn just how "normal" they are when they attend a FAMILY Rules seminar. Parents hear other parents expressing concerns about whether or not they are being too strict or too lenient. Parents also get to hear other parents' children asking the presenter the same cute or defiant questions their own children ask at home. A FAMILY Rules seminar provides a place of connection, learning, and encouragement for all family members. To find out more information about how to sponsor a FAMILY Rules seminar at your school, business, civic organization, church, synagogue, or community, please call the FAMILY Rules, Inc. office number: 1-541-956-8585. You may also find out more information about how to sponsor a FAMILY Rules seminar by going to my website located at: www.Family-Rules.com (please see Appendix M).

The third option is to purchase my FAMILY Rules seminar on DVD and watch it together as a family. It has an excellent menu system which makes it easy to enter and exit any time you wish to do so. In other words, you don't have to watch the entire seminar in one sitting. I'm wild and crazy and will keep everyone's attention. You save money on line via my website if you buy the book and seminar on DVD together.

The fourth option, and soon to be the most commonly used method, is implementation of FAMILY Rules in the home by parents such as you. Although this approach lacks an objective third party, if everything has been screened concerning unresolved parent issues and children's issues (i.e., please read Chapters Four through Seven), it is very doable (see appendix N).

I have heard many stories through the grapevine regarding how parents and teachers have learned about FAMILY Rules. One evening, several years ago, while entertaining friends in our home for dinner, we heard one of the stories: The week before sharing an evening with us, our friends had dinner with a family who had recently learned FAMILY Rules. They were pleasantly shocked by the behaviors of this family's children. The kids were sitting well behaved at the table, eating with good manners, and they were not interrupting conversations. If that wasn't surprising enough, this family's children were not bouncing off the walls before and after dinner nor were they arguing or fighting. They were simply playing games and getting along. Can you imagine that? What is this world coming to?!!

I sat at our dining room table with a puzzled look on my face and asked our dinner guests, "What's the point?" They informed me that this family was neither a private practice client of mine nor did they ever attend one of my FAMILY Rules seminars. Instead, those parents knew another family that attended one of my FAMILY Rules seminars who shared the concepts of FAMILY Rules with them. As a result, chaos was eliminated from their home and everyone was getting along much better. They were able to do this without the assistance of a professional or by attending a FAMILY Rules seminar. Instead, they got their grubby little hands on my copyrighted materials and used the content for the benefit of their family without paying me a dime. I'm just joking!

I was genuinely pleased to hear about the positive results of FAMILY Rules and how it has helped to improve the home of one more family on this planet. My goal is to work myself out of a job. I seriously don't mind if I get occasional help along the way, but only as long as the FAMILY Rules fairies don't violate copyright laws in the process. Hint! Hint! The slogan of FAMILY Rules is "Every home needs a FAMILY." My very modest goal is to see FAMILY Rules implemented in every home on this planet. Please help spread the word. Let's restore proper love and respect for God, others, and ourselves in our homes, schools, churches, synagogues, and communities.

If you choose to implement FAMILY Rules in your home without the assistance of a counselor who uses FAMILY Rules or without attending one of my FAMILY Rules seminars, then you should proceed as follows (Remember: "correct and consistent" implementation is key – "the two 'C' words"):

1.   To the best of your ability, make sure that all adults are involved with the development of the list of FAMILY Rules (i.e., single parent, married parents, divorced parents who have remarried someone else, etc.). Agreement between all of the adults involved in your child's life helps to promote consistency in your child's world, especially when your child lives in two homes because of a divorce. I have had plenty of ex-spouses work together to develop a list of rules that would apply equally in both homes. Stability was provided for the children and manipulation of the parents was nipped in the bud.

2.   Make sure that FAMILY Rules has been edited by all adults involved in the process. Be careful concerning how you word your rules. Your children and adolescents are good little attorneys. They will spot a loophole anywhere and make you pay for it. Remember, your children may be consulted if you so desire, but you have the final say concerning how your home will be run. Authority flows downward. It's best to consult your children about the rules during a family meeting which would occur after you implement FAMILY Rules. Be very careful not to send your children and adolescents a message that they have an equal say in the decision making process in your home. No democratic parenting allowed! King Arthur is fictional and the knights of the round table never happened. Why would you allow a fictional story to shape your approach to parenting?

3.   Screen all children, adolescents, and adults for possible issues that might interfere with the successful implementation of FAMILY Rules in your home (i.e., psychological testing, medication management needs, counseling needs, etc.). For example, if you have a flaming ADHD child, have him or her tested and treated first before beginning FAMILY Rules. If you have a power struggle going

on in your marriage, first get marital counseling and resolve issues that might prevent FAMILY Rules from being successful in your home.

4. Find a safe and neutral environment to meet with the children in order to explain FAMILY Rules to them. Make sure that all adults are present during the explanation process.

5. Identify an adult to be the primary facilitator. This adult should be the most rational and emotionally controlled adult—one who won't be manipulated by a defiant strong-willed brat. Conduct business and don't lose your cool. You are a Wal-Mart cashier.

6. Begin with a very relaxed, laid back demeanor. Try to occasionally interject humor when it's appropriate. This approach helps to set a positive tone; however, if you meet outright resistance from one or more of the children, then you become an Alaskan Eagle. Instantly swoop down from the sky with a silent and swift grace, grab the little salmon from the river with your talons, and eat it for lunch. Symbolically, of course. No physical abuse or cannibalism allowed. In other words, calmly and swiftly cut to the chase and inform your children about the fact that FAMILY Rules has razor sharp teeth. If they should ever totally defy your authority, then the teeth will be swiftly implemented via a "Strike" or "Pop Fly. " The message is, "Don't push it with the parents or else you will go bye-bye!"

7. Ask your kids questions about why rules exist. Explain how rules are a part of everyday life no matter where they go on planet Earth. Discuss how they already live by rules at home, school, work, church, synagogue, on the road, on airplanes, etc. Ask your children and adolescents how they would feel if there were no more state or federal governments, no more police, no military, no laws, and all the inmates were let out of all the jails and prisons. If you have a smart-mouth child who responds by saying, "No laws. Cool!" Say something like the following back to your smart-mouth child: "Oh, I see. It would be cool if Joe Schmoe from down the street came into our home, ripped us off, killed your mom and me in front of all

the kids, raped you, then tied you and your siblings up, and burned you alive because he decided to set the house on fire? That would be cool?" The smart-mouth child usually understands the need for rules when you help him or her visualize being violated by another human-being. Discuss how rules keep us safe from others and from ourselves. Rules also help us be on the same page or sheet of music so we can all get along (i.e., I stop on red while you go on green and then you stop on red while I go on green).

8. Once your children and adolescents acknowledge the existence and need for rules, explain FAMILY in the correct order: F-A-M; how "F.A.M." work together; and finally, I-L-Y. In other words, follow the format of Chapter Eight. Read Chapter Eight out loud if necessary. Take time to answer questions along the way. Plan to take one to two hours for this initial explanation process. It's a good idea to read your family rules, out loud, once a week, during your weekly family meeting.

9. When you get to "Y," let your children know the difference between "Strikes" and simply having a "Bad Hair Day." "Bad Hair Days" are not Strikes. Also, let your children know that the razor sharp teeth clause is a last resort option and that most families never have to send a child to long-term residential treatment. Explain to them that most kids understand FAMILY Rules and will agree to comply because they don't want to be sent away for one or two years. However, assure them that you will not hesitate to use the teeth FAMILY Rules provides if and when necessary. You will not be a pushover. You have a backbone of steel.

10. Give your children a practice week consisting of seven days to transition into FAMILY Rules before giving out Good Habit Cards; however, start giving out Daily Tokens and RAK chips immediately. Give each child their own copy of the rules, chores, and rewards lists. Post your list of rules on the refrigerator. Inform your children that their friends will be subject to the rules. If their friends break the rules, they do the Good Habit Cards just like anyone else in your home. If they refuse to do their Good Habit Cards, send them home.

Let them know that they will not be invited back to your home unless they are willing to do their Good Habit Cards for breaking your rules in your home. Talk to their parents before subjecting your child's friends to your family rules. Most other parents will be pleased that you're taking an active role in community parenting.

11. Don't forget your weekly family meetings. You can use part of this time to tweak, tune, adjust and modify FAMILY Rules in your home if and when necessary. Remember, consultation with children is good, but adults have the final say. Parenting is not a democracy. Rather, parenting is a benevolent dictatorship.

12. Walk the talk. Practice what you preach. Do your Good Habit Cards immediately, even if your children didn't see you break the law by driving over the speed limit. You won't believe the powerful, positive effect of parental role-modeling when your children see you consistently tattle on yourself and immediately do your cards without their prodding. Your actions speak louder than your words.

13. If all else fails, buy my seminar on DVD and watch it with your spouse and kids. It has an excellent menu system which makes it easy for you to start and stop at your own pace. I'm very funny and I'll keep the attention of the adults and children in the room.

14. Finally, if you feel like you just don't have the time or "know-how" to get all the materials together to get FAMILY Rules up and running in your home, just go to my website and order the "Parenting Kit". It has everything you need to help you implement the parenting program in your home (see appendix N).

Please remember, when you are explaining FAMILY Rules to your children, you are conducting business. The Wal-Mart cashier never yells at the customer on the other side of the counter no matter how rude he or she becomes. Don't undermine your own parental authority by lowering yourself to the position of sibling. If you become emotional, they will have you right where they want you.

Don't fall prey to manipulation. Relax and have fun. FAMILY Rules works if you implement it "correctly and consistently." Please don't forget to let your friends, neighbors, and coworkers know that "Every home needs a FAMILY."

~Chapter Ten~

Rats And Cockroaches

No book about parenting discipline systems is complete without discussing rats and cockroaches. After helping to transport Carl to the residential treatment facility in the Western Samoa, I had time to kill on the island before I returned home to Alaska. The next plane wasn't going to leave the island for five days. What a beautiful place to kill time. I met with the staff and took a tour of the long-term residential treatment facility. I spoke with Carl's mother on the phone to inform her about our trip and the transitional time I spent with Carl before dropping him off at the facility.

While killing time on the South Pacific island, I decided to hike up a mountain to see Robert Lewis Stevenson's tomb. He was a famous author in the 1800s. When I reached the top of the mountain, soaking wet from the heat and humidity, I was greeted by a couple who hailed from southern California. They were on their honeymoon. We became acquainted via the usual process of exchanging names, professions, height and shoe size (I'm six feet, nine inches tall and I have size sixteen shoes. Almost everyone I meet asks me how tall I am and what size shoes I wear). I learned that they were attorneys. They learned that I was a psychologist. I agreed not to "shrink" them and they agreed not to "sue" me.

Anyway, our conversation quickly turned to the common denominator found in both of our professions - adolescents. We agreed that the 1960s and 1970s (the anti-establishment era) contributed to the decline of the traditional family and the values and morals espoused within the traditional setting. Respect for authority was replaced by questioning authority. Self restraint was replaced by "try everything at least once." Stamina and loyalty during trials and tribulations were replaced by "If the going gets tough, just quit. Try something different." Right and wrong were replaced with

"To each his own as long as no one gets hurt" and "Does it work for you or doesn't it work for you?" Well, you get the point.

While sitting on Robert Louis Stevenson's tomb, our conversation progressed. We were amazed by the fact that we were all gainfully employed in our respective professions as the result of the anti-establishment era. Families are breaking apart. Today's adolescents are facing many social pressures and they are a generation without a purpose or cause. These adolescents' parents and peer support groups have failed to pass on the traditional Judeo-Christian values and morals of our society. These traditional morals and values provided social skills and tools to successfully interact with others and to cope with life's many challenges.

As a result of the anti-establishment era, one of us picks up Humpty Dumpty's broken pieces due to his falling off the wall, another prosecutes Humpty Dumpty for falling off the wall, and another defends Humpty Dumpty's right to fall off the wall and to break into little pieces. We all agreed that we would rather have healthy families in our society and be forced to work in different professions; however, this probably won't happen in our lifetime. Unfortunately, I have job security.

Then our conversation took a turn for the worse. The prosecuting attorney talked about "the rats breeding behind the walls." With a puzzled look on my face, I asked for clarification, "What do you mean by rats breeding behind the walls?" Having lived in Alaska in the past, I had difficulty visualizing anything but ice behind the walls. He proceeded to discuss his fears about the problems our society will be facing in one or two more decades when this present generation produces the next generation of adolescents. In other words, the rats are breeding behind the walls. We concluded that there is a growing chasm in our society between those children who are being raised with respect and love for God, country, others, and self, versus those children who are being raised with a self-centered, victimized, sociopathic, defiant, godless existence. Unless things change quickly, we had better start building the walls around New

York City and Los Angeles because the "Escape From" movies will soon become a reality. Just watch the DVD's, "Escape from New York City" or "Escape from Los Angeles" and you'll get the picture. Please don't let your kids watch these movies!

The rats are breeding behind the walls and the only thing we can do about it is to help one family at a time. This is where you come into play. Yes, you! The reader of this book. You have the responsibility of analyzing where you are individually, as a spouse, if married, and as a parent. Are you honestly and seriously facing your issues? Are you receiving therapeutic, medical, and/or spiritual help as needed? How are you raising your children? Are you stressed out, tired, rolling over and playing dead while your children run the home and aimlessly run the streets? Do you have support and encouragement from a parents' group, 12-Step group, synagogue, or local church? Are you fulfilling the responsibility of proactively raising your children or are you hoping they'll grow up quickly and leave the home sooner than later? You can help nip tomorrow's problems in the bud by proactively raising your children today. I hope and pray you are not contributing to the breeding of the rats behind the walls.

Now let us contemplate cockroaches in the kitchen, which is another matter I have difficulty visualizing, having lived in Alaska in the past. A black bear in the kitchen? Yes. Cockroaches in the kitchen? No. Thank the Lord it is too cold in Alaska for cockroaches to thrive. Give me a grizzly bear or moose any day! We don't have cockroaches in our home in Grants Pass, Oregon either. Whew!

When you implement FAMILY Rules in your home, it will be like turning on the kitchen light at midnight in a Florida home. The cockroaches in the kitchen will scurry. They'll run for cover. They don't want to be seen. Likewise, FAMILY Rules will shed the true light on every member of the home and what role they play in the familial dysfunction. Is dad or mom over controlling and unwilling to share power? Are the adults parenting the children or are the children parenting the adults? Who tends to make up excuses and not take responsibility for their choices? Do one or both adults in the home walk the talk by practicing what they preach? Just how genuinely compliant or defiant are your children to your authority?

Rick and Delores attended a FAMILY seminar with their son, Frank. Afterwards, they contacted me to set up counseling sessions for their family. Rick and Delores were experiencing difficulty with the successful implementation of FAMILY Rules because Frank was being a good little attorney. He was finding loopholes and splitting hairs. In other words, he was being passive-aggressive toward his parents and the spirit of the law. Truth and genuine compliance were not at the forefront of Frank's mind.

As we upped the ante in therapy via FAMILY Rules consequences, Frank's absolute defiance became more and more clear to Rick and Delores. This was difficult for them to see and accept. Rick and Delores became nosy and found out that Frank had downloaded pornography from the Internet. He had also obtained information on how to make bombs. He had obtained a private mailbox in order to receive inappropriate letters. Finally, Frank obtained an internet account and paid for it with the money he made while working at a fast food restaurant. Rick and Delores had no idea that Frank was doing all this stuff behind their backs. After all, they had canceled their local internet account. Isn't it amazing what services our children can obtain without parental permission? The businesses didn't even try to contact Rick and Delores to see if it was okay with them. Talk about civil-suit possibilities!

In Rick and Delores' situation, FAMILY Rules clearly shed the light on where Frank's frame of mind was. As a result, Rick and Delores chose to send Frank to a long-term residential treatment facility in Montana. Frank is slowly making progress on his issues. He's learning to take responsibility for his inappropriate choices. Frank is beginning to face life in an honest manner. Obviously, Rick and Delores are ecstatic about Frank's progress and can't wait to have him come back home.

Another situation where the impact of FAMILY Rules clearly sheds light on a family's dysfunctional situation is in the case of Ken and Darlene. They brought their daughter, Sharon, in for therapy. She had a lifelong history of problems with anxiety and adjustment to new situations. She was finding their move to Grants Pass, Oregon to be a very difficult experience. Consequently, she was beginning to fall behind in school and was acting out her anger at home. Sharon repeatedly told and even yelled at her parents that she wanted to return to their home in the warmer southwestern part of our nation. Her parents were seriously considering putting in a request to the father's employer so they could return from whence they came. I informed them that such a move would be a major mistake and merely reinforce their daughter's irrational thinking and inappropriate behaviors.

Ken and Darlene agreed to attend a FAMILY Rules seminar with their four children. When they implemented FAMILY Rules in their home, Sharon became genuinely compliant and worked through her issues in therapy rather quickly. Once she realized that her manipulation tactics weren't going to work and that she was marooned in Grants Pass until high school graduation, she settled in and became more emotionally stable. I might add that medication helped her too.

The surprise for Ken, Darlene, and myself was the response of their younger child, Greg. His true colors came out because FAMILY Rules provided more structure in the home and shed the light on his manipulation tactics with mom. He was getting away with subtle defiant behaviors because Sharon's antics provided a diversion for him. FAMILY Rules shed the light on the cockroaches in Ken and Darlene's family kitchen and Greg's cockroach antennae were caught in the cookie jar. Darlene was confronted, by me, concerning her enabling and rescuing behaviors of her children. She decided to take a stand with Ken to confront Greg.

As a result of Ken and Darlene's united parental stand, Greg became superficially compliant for a few months. His parents were pleased and their family appeared to become more stabilized; however, they were merely in the eye of Hurricane Greg. A short time later, the torrential winds and rains of Hurricane Greg pounded down relentlessly on Ken and Darlene's shoreline. Greg was acting out with a vengeance. He made it clear that he was unwilling to submit himself to his parents' authority. School took a turn for the worse and he was getting into fights without remorse. He enjoyed it.

The straw that broke the camel's back for Ken and Darlene was when Greg had the audacity to file false complaints of physical abuse to school authorities. It was a desperate act on Greg's part to try and keep the upper hand with his parents. Unfortunately, this happens sometimes in families and the Child Protective Services agency treats the parents as if they are guilty until proven innocent. These state agencies are a necessary evil. They do help kids who are actually abused. Greg stated he hated his parents and siblings and did not care about what negative consequences his false allegation had on his parents' reputations or their careers. The matter was eventually cleared up and the truth prevailed. Greg also won an all expense paid trip to long-term residential treatment because of the "Pop-Fly" he earned due to his false reporting. He was out of control in a major way. Ken, Darlene, and Sharon continued therapy and attended self-exploration seminars. Their new-found awareness of their own personal issues assisted them in becoming better human-beings as well as better parents. Greg successfully completed his treatment in the Eastern Caribbean and the entire family is doing much better. No more cockroaches in the family kitchen.

FAMILY Rules really works, just not always in the way that some parents would like it to; however, pest control is necessary to prevent the rats from breeding behind the walls. We don't need another generation of troubled adolescents. Finally, it's better to know what's going on at night in a bright kitchen than it is to step on the little buggers in the dark with your bare feet. Denial is yucky! Parenting is a challenge, but, if you're proactive, everyone wins in the end. You win, your children win, your school wins, your church or synagogue wins, your community wins, and our society wins. There's no place like home (click, click, click) to begin making the positive and healthy changes made possible by implementing FAMILY Rules in your home. Goodbye rats and cockroaches! Hello FAMILY Rules! It's time to turn your family right side up with the mother of all parenting discipline systems.   Please don't forget, "Every home needs a FAMILY."

~Chapter Eleven~

Community Parenting

Y ou are to be commended for your obvious love and concern for your family and it's present and future well-being. You wouldn't be reading this book right now if this wasn't the case. We need many more proactive parents like you in our communities, involving themselves in the lives of their children. We need more parents who are constantly seeking to improve their family environment, staying on top of their children's behaviors, attitudes, their whereabouts, and who their friends are. This is truly positive parenting. However, your responsibility does not end with your own family. You belong to a much larger family called a community. In spite of our society's technological progress and our subsequent tendency to become isolated and self-sufficient, we are responsible for our neighbor's children, too. We truly are our brother's keeper.

Don't panic! I'm not talking about our social services system and government agencies raising our children. I'm a supporter of limited government intervention in the lives of families. Child Protective Services Agencies exist for a reason. Some children really do get abused and neglected by irresponsible parents. Those parents deserve to have their children taken away. Abused and neglected children really do need our help and an advocate. Okay, Child Protective Services Agencies sometimes make mistakes and inappropriately intervene. Often this is due to false allegations made by a lying child who is battling for control with his or her parents. Unfortunately, the agency sometimes treats parents as if they are guilty until proven innocent. This is very troubling for all involved parties. However, Child Protective Services Agencies are a necessary evil. If they didn't exist, who would take care of our community's abused and neglected children? Who would intervene on their behalf?

Nevertheless, the kind of community parenting I'm talking about is the kind that used to be common place in most of our villages, towns, and cities since the birth of our nation. Now it can only be found in smaller suburbs and rural communities, such as where we live in Grants Pass, Oregon. This is very sad. Community parenting went belly up in many larger communities due to increased population, technological and economic isolation, and because of the lack of involvement of parents who refuse to discipline their children (i.e., "Boys will be boys! Ha! Ha! He will grow out of it. Besides, it's none of your business!"). Many parents gave up on reporting inappropriate behaviors of some children to their uninvolved apathetic parents because the parents wouldn't do anything about it.

In spite of this sad scenario, you can still do your small part in reviving this very valuable tradition of community interdependence. Children and adolescents need to know that if they misbehave in public, their parents will find out later because another concerned community parent will make sure they do. Our nation's courts and state legislatures are finally starting to crack down on these uninvolved apathetic parents—the ones who have no interest in knowing whether or not their children are drinking, using illicit drugs, stealing, building pipe bombs in the garage, or purchasing guns and hiding them in their bedrooms so they can shoot up the school later on. If you see a child or adolescent misbehaving, do something about it. Communicate with the child's parents and include an expectation that they do something about it. If the parents respond in an uninvolved apathetic manner, inform them that you will contact the police, make a report to the Child Protective Services agency, or confront them in civil court. Your proactive involvement in community parenting will inspire others, whether or not they want to be inspired, into holding up their end of the stick. We all need to be involved in our children's lives.

My first involvement in community parenting was when I was approximately four years old. I was spending a couple of days at my grandparents' home in Portland, Oregon. Fortunately, my parents left my tricycle for me to ride. I clearly remember my grandma telling me where I could ride my tricycle and where I couldn't ride it (i.e., down the steep hill half a block away from my grandparents' home). When grandma went inside her house, I rode my tricycle down the sidewalk to the top of the steep hill, double checked to make sure she wasn't looking, and went for the ride of my life. After going about one-hundred feet down the steep hill, I realized I had no brakes. The stop sign and busy intersection were quickly approaching. I turned into someone's driveway and smacked right into a concrete wall. I woke up a few minutes later with blood all over me. An adult male was carrying me and my tricycle back up the hill, trying to find out who was responsible for me. My grandma came running out of her house in a panic. Boy! Did he let my grandma have it! She never let me out of her sight after that. If that's not community parenting, I don't know what is.

Another experience in community parenting involved my looking out the front window of my house and seeing an eleven year old boy start to beat up an eight year old boy. I opened up my front door and told him to stop. He ignored me and continued to hit the younger and smaller boy. I went out to the street and told him to stop. He said it was none of my business. As I was restraining him from beating up the younger child, I told him that it was my neighborhood and my driveway, therefore it was my business. I asked him where he lived and he wouldn't tell me. I told him if he didn't tell me, I was going to call the police. He told me where he lived. I walked this kid down the street back to his home. I rang the door bell and his mother opened it up. She was half drunk and looked surprised by my asking her to stay on top of her child's behaviors. She started to tell me that it was none of my business, but stopped when I told her I would call the police if she didn't change her tune. She complied and took her boy inside the house. He never fought in my neighborhood again. The younger boy played in peace and security because he knew a community parent cared enough to watch out for him.

Just prior to moving from Alaska to Oregon, I had an experience involving community parenting while I was driving approximately three hundred and sixty miles from Fairbanks to Anchorage along the Parks Highway. This is one of the most beautiful drives in Alaska and goes through the middle of the pristine wilderness, including incredible breathtaking views of Mt. McKinley and Denali National Park. It was early spring and still very cold. The sun was starting to go down. Well, smack dab in the middle of the three hundred and sixty mile stretch of highway, I came across a broken down vehicle with five adolescents. They were heading north toward Fairbanks. They informed me that they ran out of oil and that their engine seized up. They asked me if I had any oil and I told them that I didn't. The next stop was about twenty miles south down the highway. I drove south and was given oil by a very nice maintenance man at the Denali Princess Lodge. I was willing to pay for the oil but he refused to take the money after hearing why I needed it. He wasn't willing to charge a Good Samaritan who was trying to help out some desperate teens. I found out that there was a tow truck about fifteen miles south of the lodge.

I drove 20 miles north back to deliver the oil to the stranded teens. It was nearly dark. They informed me that they obtained motor oil from a passing motorist and learned that their engine was no longer operating. One of the teens hopped in the passing motorist's car and headed north to a gas station seventy-five miles away. He did not know that there was a towing company thirty-five miles to the south. When you are stuck out in the middle of the wilderness in Alaska, every mile counts because towing a disabled vehicle is very expensive. Three teens climbed into my truck and one of them refused to get in. He thought he should stay with the car. I reminded him that it was almost dark and very cold. I told him that he had no heat because his car was disabled and that Honolulu, Hawaii was going to freeze over first before I left him behind. I sternly told him to get in my truck so we could catch his friend before they traveled too far north. He complied and climbed into my truck.

While driving north to catch the passing motorist and their friend, the four teens in my truck caught me up to speed on how they ended up in their situation. Apparently, they were out and about having fun in Fairbanks and ended up violating their curfew. Instead of going home late and paying the piper, they impulsively decided to drive three hundred and sixty miles south to Anchorage. They made it to Anchorage and spent the night in a hotel room. Keep in mind, they never called their parents. Not one of them. I'll tell you what, I'd be freaking out if one of them was my child. On their way back from Anchorage to Fairbanks, their car engine seized because they ran out of motor oil. Does this sound like a bunch of impulsively out of control adolescents or what?

After driving about thirty miles north, we caught up with the passing motorist and extracted the fifth adolescent from the car. I informed him that there was a towing company thirty-five miles south of their stranded car and that he would save a great deal of money by having them tow his car. He got in my truck and we drove thirty miles south back to their car. We stopped so they could get all of their personal possessions out. Then we drove twenty miles south to the Denali Princess Lodge where I could make a phone call to one of the teen's parents. I could only imagine how that parent felt when a stranger called, introducing himself as Dr. Johnson, and telling him about his teen's dilemma. I assured him that I would take care of his child and the other four teens. They weren't going to be left alone in the dark of night and the freezing Alaska outdoor temperatures.

We drove fifteen more miles to the south. During our drive, I informed the teens that they had better eat crow and humble pie when their parents arrived the next morning. One of the teens said, "Why should we. We didn't do anything wrong!" Two other teens spoke up and said, "Oh, yes we did. We broke curfew, left Fairbanks and drove to Anchorage without our parents' permission, and got ourselves stuck in the middle of nowhere. We're lucky "Dr. J." stopped to help us out or we'd be freezing to death! We did plenty wrong!" We found the towing company. Fortunately, the Texaco gas station in Trapper's Creek had a restaurant so the kids could go inside to eat a late dinner and stay warm.

The kids didn't have any money so I gave the cashier my credit card and told her to write down the appropriate information. I informed her that the adolescents' parents would be picking them up tomorrow morning and that they would pay for the dinner and breakfast when they arrived. If they didn't pay her, she could put the kid's meals on my credit card. It was about 11:00 P.M. and it was too late and too far for the parents to drive from Fairbanks. So the cashier fed the kids and helped me find a local bed and breakfast in Trapper's Creek to put them up for the night.

I spoke to the tow truck driver and informed him of the stranded car's location approximately thirty-five miles to the north. I gave him my credit card information and informed him that the teens' parents would pay for the tow tomorrow morning. If they didn't pay for the towing, I told him to put it on my credit card. One of the boys hopped into the tow truck and drove north to retrieve his disabled vehicle.

When we arrived at the bed and breakfast, we were greeted by a very friendly older lady. I explained the situation to her and asked that she put the boys and girls in two separate rooms. She understood and told me that her room is located between their rooms. She assured me that there would be no inappropriate behaviors going on while she was on duty. I gave her my credit card information and informed her that the parents would pay for the rooms tomorrow morning when they arrived. I told her that if she was not paid, to charge the two rooms to my credit card. Fortunately, she was very willing to be flexible and help out the teens.

When I was saying my goodbyes to the teens at the bed and breakfast, they thanked me a thousand times. One of the girls stated, "You're Jesus Christ in the flesh, so loving and kind." Before I ducked out the door, I told her, "There's only one Jesus and I'm not him. However, I am a Christian and I believe in doing unto others as you would have others do unto you. If any of you were my kids, I would want someone to help you out in a time of need." They nodded their heads in agreement. Finally, I stated, "Please promise that you will

do one favor for me." They responded, "What? We'll do anything!"
I responded, "Please give your parents a big hug and apologize to
them for what you did. Treat them with respect and don't mouth off
to them in spite of the consequences you will receive and deserve."
They gave me their word that they would remain humble in spirit.
I arrived at my destination in Anchorage a few hours later than
planned. However, I slept well knowing that the teens were safe and
I was practicing what I preached.

Three cheers to all of the individuals who participated in the above
examples. If this isn't community parenting, I don't know what is.
These five teens were impulsively getting themselves into deeper
and deeper trouble as time passed. If it wasn't for the assistance of a
flexible maintenance man, a passing motorist, a cashier, a tow truck
driver, a bed and breakfast owner, and a traveling psychologist, these
kids could have died from hypothermia before they knew what was
happening. Please, dads and moms, practice community parenting.
We all need one another. You might have to help one of my kids
someday. If one of my kids are messing up, I want you to tell me.
Let's work together to love and protect our children. Community
parenting works!

Part 3

*Anecdotal and
Research Information*

~Chapter 12~

The Successes of FAMILY Rules with Parents and Professionals

Would you like me to let you in on a secret? The reason why FAMILY Rules is working so well all around the USA, Canada, Europe, Africa, India, the Middle East, Central and South America, Australia, and Asia isn't because I'm a brilliant guy. Nope! Actually, I'm just an average, laid back and funny guy who's done something brilliant. I've simply managed to take "common sense" and mix it in with "good old fashioned" parenting values. I've added a dash of "order and structure" along with a bit of "discipline and friendship." I tossed in "a whole lot of love" and cemented it all together with a pinch of "reverent fear of authority". These ingredients for successful parenting have been used by parents throughout the world for as long as man has walked the Earth. Not only that, but these ingredients for successful parenting are going to continue to work for parents for thousands of years to come. Seriously, I'm not a brilliant guy. Nope! I'm just a simple-minded guy who saw something that needed fixing and stepped up to the plate to "getter-done!" It's amazing how many lives can change for the better when chaos and dysfunction are eliminated through the implementation of a simple FAMILY Rules positive parenting plan in the home.

I've been teaching FAMILY Rules to parents and professionals since 1986. They demanded that I write this book. Since the first printing of my book in 2001, I've constantly been deluged with e-mails and phone calls from thankful individuals who want to share with me how FAMILY Rules has helped to change their lives for the better. There is no possible way that I can share all of their stories with you. There are just way too many stories to tell. However, I have selected a few stories (i.e., anecdotal information) as well as research information (i.e., data gathered through scientific means) to share with you. I want to give you hope that FAMILY Rules will work with your children too. You are not alone. The good news is that you actually bought this book, you're almost done reading it, and if you choose to implement it "correctly and consistently" in your home, you'll experience the same success that you're going to read about in this chapter. Don't just trust my word because, truthfully, I'm just a tad bit biased about the effectiveness of my parenting program. Instead, listen to others and learn from their experiences too. Rather than have me synthesize their stories and research information for you, I have chosen to let these parents and professionals tell you what they think you should know about FAMILY Rules in their own words via their own voice and pen. Please enjoy.

Children in California Love FAMILY Rules

We have been doing FAMILY Rules for five years. When our mom and dad are consistent with it, our home is calm, relaxed and not all tense. Without rules, our home is chaotic.

Our list of rules, and daily and weekly chores charts tell us exactly what we need to do every day so that our parents don't have to nag us. It's like a list that adults make, so they know what to do each day. It's our reminder. Our charts help us keep things in order and it is a constant progression. As soon as we get a responsibility down, it's taken off the chart and new responsibilities are added. It helps us see that we are maturing. I like when our family comes together and talks about things at our weekly family meeting. We can get input from each other and know what we need to work on, and how we are succeeding. Sometimes our family meetings are funny when our parents do role playing to show us right from wrong because they make it goofy.

It's nice that all the rules are written down so we know what they are and we don't have to guess and learn by getting in trouble. We like how our parents get Good Habit Cards too. When they receive a Wild Card, we have them play a game with us, wrestle, or pick up our room. We have learned how to take care of the house by doing cards so that when we grow up and move out, we will be able to take care of ourselves; it won't be scary.

The Daily Tokens and RAK chips are our favorite thing because it is a reward for a good day's work and for not breaking the rules. We are able to go with our parents and do fun things with the Daily Tokens and RAK chips that we earn. We like that we can control how many chips we earn in a week and it's up to us. If we decide that we don't want to follow the rules, then we don't receive as many chips. Finally, we like the Grace Cards because God forgives us for things that we do. It's like life, there are consequences but God loves us and wants us to learn and do well. We learn with this program every day. We love it!

N.W. and K.W.
California

I Would Never Be Like That

I told Dr. Johnson that I would be glad to write a testimonial about FAMILY Rules, so here it is: When I found out I was pregnant with my first child, I swore that I would raise my children and react differently than my parents did with me. I can always remember when I was a child with my brother in the back seat of the car. It would start off with my brother breathing on me. In response, I would poke him and then he would start to whine. Sometime during the duration of this conflict my mother, who was driving, would keep one hand on the wheel of the car and with the other hand reach back and flail it wherever, hoping to hit someone in the process. I especially noticed the veins on her neck popping out. I told myself, I would NEVER be like that.

Thirty years later, I found myself doing the exact same thing. Despite reading numerous parenting books and taking a number of parenting seminars, I found myself with bulging veins and having to repeat everything I said ten times because my kids seemed to be hearing impaired. I felt unappreciated and whatever happened would snowball emotionally until I blew up and got very angry with my children. I also found that my husband had a different set of rules with punishment. It seemed that he would become unglued over little things that the kids did that were due to childhood stupidity but the big things, like willful disobedience, did not merit severe consequences.

I honestly felt like I was a maid cleaning up after everyone's messes. No one seemed to respect the work I did in the house. Then there was the lack of respect of each child toward their siblings. I knew there had to be a way to teach children responsibility, both in the house and in terms of their behaviors. Then we went to a FAMILY Rules seminar. Boy, did our lives change!

First of all, I am not going to tell you that it is easy. It takes commitment to the "correct and consistent" implementation of the program in the home - especially because the parents have to work as a team. However, I feel that I can say I am a fair and objective parent. Any "consequences" my children have been given has been at their own hands. I have been able to sit back, point to the house rules, and put the responsibility of their woes on them. My house has never been cleaner and I feel that my children, both boys and girls, are learning lifetime skills that they will need when they live on their own (e.g., cooking, cleaning, washing dishes, etc.). They are learning to interact as well as not to react to their siblings. Our house has been so much more peaceful, my husband and I are more united, and our children have grown because of the implementation of FAMILY Rules in our home. The veins in my neck don't bulge and I feel I am a much better parent than I was one year ago.

The final point that I would like to make is that my children know that there are consequences for their chosen behavior. They are assuming responsibility for their actions and not blaming anyone else. This, to me, is the basis of character. FAMILY Rules has brought us closer together and is helping me to raise men and women - not boys and girls.

S.P.
Alaska

Helping an Out of Control Nephew

Security, structure, and peace have been introduced into my home with the Family Rules program. It didn't start out that way. A little history is called for here.

Once upon a time, just before leaving to go on a Christmas vacation, I received a call from my sister who has not talked to me for over three years. My sister said over the phone, "You want your nephew?!! He's yours!! He is out of control and I'm going to send him to live with his father!" My sister had reached the end of her rope. Knowing that my nephew has never seen or known his father, I immediately agreed to take him. Just after New Year's Day, our family grew to five. Prior to picking up my nephew, I set up an appointment with our family counselor. She told me that Family Rules was close to what I was doing, but with all the bugs and kinks worked out. I told my counselor, "I'm in!" My husband and I also decided to tell my nephew that he would be included as one of our own children. We didn't know if and when his mother would change her mind about him living with us. So we decided that we were going to raise him as if he were staying here until he graduated from high school.

Interesting enough, my other two boys have special needs. The FAMILY Rules program has been so helpful because of the added structure and constant positive reinforcement that they need. My nephew is learning to trusts us more and more. His guard is lowering and severe emotional wounds are being exposed. His emotional struggles are a formula for constant conflict and chaos. My nephew stated that he needs Family Rules to help him feel secure. As the younger ones grow up, they see what their cousin is going through. They see the rewards and consequences he receives because of his own choices. My nephew is a living example to my younger children concerning how decisions can impact their lives. We talk openly about decisions made by any member of the family and the power of choices. Family Rules gives us the skeleton, and we give it the muscle of morals, beliefs, and lots of personality. FAMILY Rules helps my family to engage in the process of teamwork and it's nice. I would recommend this program for any family, especially those dealing with children who have special needs and severe emotional wounds.

C. L.
Texas

Preventing a Train Wreck in the Home for a Single Mom

I started seeking parenting resources when my children were toddlers. I attended many parenting classes, counseling sessions, and family therapy. It was mostly useful and beneficial, but nothing really seemed to ever help me and the kids turn the corner completely toward family wellness. Nothing brought a lasting change to discipline, communication, and routine responsibilities.

By the time my children were adolescents things were out of control at home. There were short periods of calm and then the storms. My youngest daughter was the quiet one; being swallowed up by all the chaos and turmoil. My middle child, my son, was an angry, angry child. A day didn't go by without him kicking things, punching things, breaking things, or hitting others and himself. My oldest daughter could storm through the house as well, and began to threaten suicide. The police were called to our home on a couple of occasions.

I really didn't understand what was going so wrong. For crying out loud, I'd had tons of therapy, and so had the children. Things would improve from time to time, but never truly change; until one day, I walked into my psychologist's office and she said to me, "Lori, somebody wrote the parenting book I've been meaning to write; only he wrote it better than I would have." She gave me the book, "Positive Parenting with a Plan (Grades K-12): FAMILY Rules." She told me to read it and get going on the plan.

I wasn't completely sold on the plan. The psychologist was patient with me. She continued to meet with me for a year while I danced around the edges, sort of working the plan, but not really. Then one day she told me to get serious about FAMILY Rules or get out of her office. She told me, "I'm no longer willing to stand by and watch the train wreck unfold."

Long story short, I got serious about FAMILY Rules and fully implemented it at home. Within a month or two, things had drastically improved in our home. My kids were no longer throwing temper tantrums. They were choosing their behaviors wisely. I was parenting with a sound plan. I couldn't believe I had fought it for so long.

No other parenting program had ever worked for me as a mom. Believe me, I have tried a lot of parenting programs! I now consistently use the mechanics of FAMILY Rules. I am also a member of the free parent list serve "Dr. J." offers via his website. It is a tremendous tool of support and for promoting lasting change. I am very grateful to "Dr. J." and my own psychologist who had the guts to believe in me, and to believe in the philosophical underpinnings of the FAMILY Rules parenting system. I wish you could have been there to see it all unfold. It truly is beautiful and powerful. We are a calm and rational family today.

Lastly, when "Dr. J." says a family has to take all the medicine until it is all gone – I strongly believe he's right. I go back and re-read the book, different chapters at times, on various occasions, even after four years with the program because it brings me back to the philosophical base and the parenting mechanics that keep our family on the track to wellness.

L.G.
Wisconsin

Blended Families Experiencing Bliss

After marrying and blending our family in 2001, it became evident we were not exactly a happy family. After fumbling around for a couple of years, trying everything available to us; counseling, support groups, friends, pastors, and parenting mentors, we were left on our own to continue in our CHAOS (i.e., Can't Have Anyone Over Syndrome). In 2003 our son's youth pastor invited us to a seminar he was conducting at our church and that is where he told us about FAMILY Rules. We immediately saw hope in "Dr J's" parenting system and rushed home to implement FAMILY Rules with our children. We did not see instant success! Our kids went wild and would throw their cards on the ground and said they were not going to do them! They were acting out in a big way. Their behaviors got crazy for a bit, but we knew we had to be CONSISTENT. We stuck it out and the kids realized that we were not giving in. Something had changed in our approach to parenting and their tactics weren't working anymore. In the mean time we ordered the book so we could CORRECTLY adhere to the program and the new way of life for us. Our kids learned in a short amount of time that they needed to work within the FAMILY Rules parenting system or life wasn't going to be fun for them in our home. In the end, our children chose to comply with our authority.

The FAMILY Rules parenting system was something that brought us to another level of togetherness within our home. But there was something else missing. My husband, the stepfather, was not spiritually mature (i.e., one of the reasons FAMILY Rules can fail in the home). This was causing marital and parent/child relational issues in the home. My husband dealt with this part of his life and asked his stepchildren (i.e., my kids) for forgiveness. He never went back to his old ways. He walked the talk. My children instantly bonded with their stepfather and we went to yet another level together as a family. Our kids are all over eighteen now, but FAMILY Rules still remains a part of our home. Our children plan to use FAMILY Rules with our grandchildren someday.

TM & JM
California

Everything is Cherry in Idaho

I have been amazed by the positive changes I have seen in our students in large part due to "Positive Parenting with a Plan (Grades K-12): FAMILY Rules." For most boys and families, the outcomes have exceeded my already high expectations. The staff at Cherry Gulch loved the seminar presentation on DVD. FAMILY Rules is an outstanding system because it ensures that key principles of parenting are in place. I have had a number of students ask if they could use FAMILY Rules with their kids in the future. The boys do not enjoy having to pull "Good Habit Cards." However, there is no question that they want to avoid having to pull "Good Habit Cards" so they end up breaking their bad habits and learning some good habits instead. The parents I work with have greatly appreciated having a plan of action for parenting. FAMILY Rules has decreased their anxiety, increased their confidence as a parent, and ultimately turned a chaotic and conflictual home into a peaceful one while improving their children's behavior and attitude. The families that implement FAMILY RULES have a better relationship with their children. Also, their children are better behaved and more likely to reach their potential. So thank you Dr. J. for developing a great parenting program so I would not have to try and create one from scratch.

I wanted to share just one of the many positive testimonials we have received, since a positive comment about Cherry Gulch is also a positive comment about FAMILY Rules: "Dear Dr. Sapp, I am Michael's grandfather, and his mother is our daughter. I am grateful beyond measure for what you and the staff have done, not only with Mike but for our daughter. We watched and tried to be supportive throughout these difficult years. We saw and felt the terrible toll that has been paid. We watched and hoped for an outcome like what has occurred to dare and the results exceed what we could imagine. I have spent time with Mike since he was born and have enjoyed him enormously. The work that was done at Cherry Gulch produced results better than anything I have seen in 40 years as a child psychoanalyst and psychiatrist. Despair has been replaced by joy. Thank you."

Andrew D. Sapp, Ph.D.
Cherry Gulch Therapeutic Boarding School
Emmett, Idaho

Awesome in Arizona

I am the clinical director at Copper Canyon Academy (CCA), which is an all girl's therapeutic boarding school for girls ages thirteen to seventeen. We have been using FAMILY Rules as part of the parent workshops over the last two years. Many of our parents, when I asked them what their plan was when they graduated CCA and got home, most of them told me I really don't have one.

Years ago we used to have the girls draft a home living agreement, which was fundamentally flawed from the beginning and not many, if any, used it effectively or at all. Since using FAMILY Rules, it has empowered our parents, has given them a plan, and it has shown them how to implement the plan. The families that use it "correctly and consistently" have given me great feedback on how it has changed their family life. Of course there is resistance from the siblings and from the girls here at CCA, but if the families stick to the "Two C Words" ("correct and consistent"), we have had amazing results. The reason the girl's are successful in our program is that it is structured and consistent and that is what FAMILY Rules provides for our parents, is a model of structure and consistency in the home. FAMILY Rules has reduced the control/power struggles once found in the familial relationships, the parents have learned how to set structure and boundaries and then let the choice be up to their children.

Another aspect that is great is the "Random Acts of Kindness" (R.A.K.) chips. Our parents have literally been traumatized by their experience with their children prior to CCA. Therefore, it is imperative that they acknowledge in their kids what is going right or working well, and not just focus on waiting for something to go wrong. They need to stop seeing their children for who they were and start seeing them for who they have become. The R.A.K. chips allow the parents to focus on what is going right in their daughters behavior, even in the midst of a mistake. They can now recognize improvements by focusing on what is going right. I have seen that single piece of FAMILY Rules alone improve the trust and relationships and lower the fear and anxiety in the family upon their return home after they leave CCA. I have also seen it do wonders for the parents to get on the same page as they discuss what their family rules should be. Because nothing goes on the list unless they both agree, it has helped so much to stop the "divide and conquer" problem we see so many times in families. Other parents have told me that they love the flexibility of the program. Obliviously, FAMILY Rules is ordered and structured, but they can tailor it to their values and needs of their family.

I fully believe that one of our main roles as parents is to teach. If we teach correctly, we cannot do enough of it and FAMILY Rules parallels my belief that one of the mains roles of a parent is that of a teacher. It does not dish out punishment, but asks the question, "What can they learn from their choice?" This rings true with what I teach as a clinician and what CCA is trying to instill in the students and families here. FAMILY Rules has been a great marriage with CCA from a philosophical standpoint and we will be using it for years to come.

Personally in my own family we have been using FAMILY Rules for two years and the results have been amazing for us. It has been a great tool for teaching our kids who are ages: 10, 7, 5, and 2. They are learning that they have a choice and with every choice comes a result. This program makes it so easy to turn it back to them and have them own their choices. FAMILY Rules has taken away the power struggle we used to have with our children. Also, we love the part of the parenting program that focuses on what the children are doing that is good. We have seen this program help our children learn there are more people in this world than just themselves. As they receive R.A.K. chips for kindness shown to other people, they are learning that the world does not revolve around them. My oldest has also learned delayed gratification using his Daily Tokens to budget for his rewards. For example, my ten year old and seven year old saved for eight months to get a Wii game system. They went without many other rewards in that time period to save for their game system. It was great to see them work together to achieve a combined goal. We also love the flexibility of FAMILY Rules as we can consistently adjust it to our growing family and the different needs we see with each of our kids.

Mike Gurr M.S., M.A., L.P.C.
Clinical Director
Copper Canyon Academy
Rimrock, AZ

Adolescents and Their Families are Restored

We provide a supervised 24-hour in-patient residential treatment program, a partial hospitalization program, and an intensive out-patient program for adolescents ages 12-17 who have found themselves in crisis. The behavioral manifestations demonstrated can include, but are not limited to, drug abuse, eating problems, self-abusive behavior (cutting), academic problems, major depression, and violent behaviors.

Our mission is to facilitate healing in a holistic manner effecting mind, body, and spirit. It is understood that no lasting change can take place unless intervention is focused on an internal and external basis. Fundamental change must, therefore, affect what a person thinks, what a person does, and who a person believes in.
Through psychological intervention, we seek to increase our client's dignity and self-respect by encouraging them to understand that they have a purpose in life. And to educate each youth in crisis to the impact that they have on the outcomes in their lives based upon the choices they make.

We also seek to educate their moms and dads by providing them with an "ordered and structured" approach to parenting so they will maintain at home, the progress their child has made while going through our treatment. The approach we use is Dr. Matthew A. Johnson's "Positive Parenting with a Plan (Grades K-12): FAMILY Rules." Over the years, we have found this parenting approach to be simple to teach, easy for our parents to learn and implement in their homes, and the effectiveness of the outcomes second to none.

We believe it is a blessing to work with adolescents and their parents and I have a few experiences to share with you. I was teaching a group of parents the FAMILY Rules process for setting up consequences and one of the parents stated, "So does this mean I have to do more work and set up assignments added on to what I already have to monitor in my home? Am I supposed to find time to do all of this in my busy schedule? My response, "No, this means that you get to provide your child with lessons about consistency to help him for the rest of his life. This will help him in school with his teachers, when he goes to college with his professors, when he gets married with his wife, when a policeman pulls him over, and in every relationship he will have in the future." She kind of mumbled, "Wow, I had no idea it was this important. Do you have the book right here so I can buy it and start reading it now?"

I like the fact that FAMILY Rules provides parents with an approach to parenting other than "flying by the seat of their pants" or parenting with "mood and energy" level. Recently, one of our moms, who had Dr. Johnson's book, had implemented the strategies in her home. She shared with us that after there was considerable improvement in her adolescent son's behaviors and attitudes, she was asked by her younger four-year old son, "Is there some kind of "Plan Book" you can use with daddy so you can stop yelling at him too?" Isn't it amazing that young children can see and understand the importance and benefit of having a "plan" up and running in the home?

Finally, what I really love about FAMILY Rules is how it helps to restore the individual, the family, and the relationships within.   One father informed me that his son's behavior has improved so much since he started implementing the FAMILY Rules in their home. He indicated that this book brought out the best in his son. He said that prior to implementing the FAMILY Rules parenting plan, his son had become some other person. He then said to me, "I want to thank you for giving me my son back". We strongly recommend the FAMILY Rules parenting plan to all parents who want their child and family back.

Joilyn Lewis, Psy.D., LMFT
Licensed Marriage and Family Therapist
Abundant Life and Adolescent Growth, Inc.
Commerce, California

Race and Culture Don't Matter

My private practice, like others have rewarded me with a vast array of situations. I have used FAMILY Rules with parents and children that are together, and those that are divorced. It has helped the children. It has also helped the parents to become better parents. My guess is that is the goal of most parents.

Unfortunately, there are reasons that "Dr. J." has so simply stated in this book as to why FAMILY Rules might fail in the home. Even though the parents or parent may not be able to implement FAMILY Rules immediately, what I find is that they are still able to take moral ideas; philosophical underpinnings; and/or behavioral support techniques (i.e., consistency of consequences between parents, in all settings; immediacy and specificity of consequences, etc.) and implement at least some piece(s) into their home. So it really is a process of change and each family has its own unique start.

Race and culture don't matter with this parenting program. The internal changes that parents need to come to in helping themselves and their child is the point at hand. It is far better to do this constructive process rather than continue on the destructive practices they might be involved in. This book is a must read for all parents and professionals since it has something for everyone to learn.

Simon Azavedo, MSW, LCSW, CCBT, DAPA
Bergen County, New Jersey

No More Flying by the Seat of Their Pants

I have been using the FAMILY Rules model for about a year. I am a child therapist and I see children from ages two to eighteen years-old related to some sort of trauma in their life - mostly sexual abuse. Even though we know all parents should be consistent, they usually are not. However, the most important time for them to be consistent is when their child or the parent has been traumatized. I have been trained in many parenting programs and I choose to use FAMILY Rules consistently with the majority of the families who enter my office. I love the FAMILY Rules program. The parents I work with love it too because I am not teaching them anything that is unfamiliar and therefore it does not scare them away.

I educate parents about FAMILY Rules who have children that are just about to get the boot out of the house. Those parents that just needed to learn a parenting program to help put them on the right track. I would say I have used FAMILY Rules with about thirty-five families thus far. What I LOVE about it is the QUICK turnaround in their home. Almost all of my families that I work with had a new household in two weeks. The one family that did not turnaround was because mom chose not to follow the rules and did not make the child do the "Good Habit Cards." The child turned her in to me for not following the program correctly.

I have had many success stories. The one that sticks out to me is when I had a sixteen year old young man with severe depression, sexually assaulted within the past few months, and the week before he saw me he was in a psychiatric hospital due to anger outbursts at his parents, not going to school, no friends and suicide notes. His psychiatrist and his parents no longer knew what to do with him so they sent him to me. I received the intake and thought, "Why is he not in a residential treatment facility?" I always have hope for every child and family that I see, as most therapists do, so I agreed to see the family.

I met with the adolescent male two times. Then I had the parents come in for a special meeting. I had a gut feeling that this kid is not that bad so it must be someone else provoking him. I found out that his mom was so controlling that the young man couldn't breathe without her permission. I offered to teach them FAMILY Rules and the parents decided to do it. The next session they brought in his daily chores list that was a page long. It was detailed by half hour increments of what this young man will be doing during the entire day. I taught his mother over the next few sessions about why she needs to lighten up a little bit on the chores and surprisingly, she did.

Two weeks later, the adolescent male was stable, going to school, working a part time job, and finally enjoying some time with his family without constantly yelling at them. Once again FAMILY Rules has saved some parents and children from chaos and conflict. Being educated in the FAMILY Rules model not only prevents parents from flying by the seat of their pants, it also gives therapists a solid parenting program to teach to the parents we work with so we, as therapists, are not flying by the seat of our pants while we are providing therapy to families who need our help.

Valerie Meyers, MS, LPC
Child Therapist
Bismarck, ND

Kids Buy In To the FAMILY Rules Program

I have been working with families for over thirty years. I took "Dr. J's" FAMILY Rules seminar in 2004 for Continuing Education Units. At present, I have over thirty families on this parenting program. I have used many other behavioral modification programs over the past several decades without success. The FAMILY Rules parenting program works because it is for the entire family - not just the children. In my community, I provide three one hour workshops for the entire family over a period of four months. I usually have four to five families at one time. I insist that the children attend too. There is a certain "buy-in" when the children know other kids are doing the program too. I have a family with two boys who learned the program five years ago. They have found the parenting program to be so useful that they volunteer to come to the last meeting of each group to discuss problems. The boys tell the other children why they like the program.

Peggie Wiseman, L.C.S.W.
Licensed Clinical Social Worker
Truckee, California

One of My Favorite Specialties in My Private Practice

I am often referred families for parent consultation who are struggling with the issues discussed in Chapter Seven of this book. Both parents and children can struggle with a clinical issue. For instance, a child in the household may have an executive functioning weakness (cognitive inflexibility, ADD, language/auditory/ sensory processing issues, or even depression/anxiety) that is still problematic despite medication and thorough, effective, ongoing treatment. A parent may have alcoholism, cancer, depression, or a major life event, such as job loss, that is affecting functioning. There are some cases where I postpone teaching FAMILY Rules until further treatment is accomplished. However, in most cases, I still see value in teaching FAMILY Rules, having the parent(s) read the book, and designing a program for their household. I explain that implementation may not be the goal right away, but it is critical to prepare for when the time comes when the clinical issues are treated enough such that implementation is appropriate. This teaches a unified front philosophy, healthy development, and healthy role-modeling. A way to get the buy-in is to convince the parent(s) that the clinical issues are temporary and will improve with treatment, so in the meantime, parents need to prepare themselves for appropriate parenting and a positive family plan for when the clinical issues are treated and ready for it.

FAMILY Rules can also be a way to support and even provide treatment, when designed and managed by a therapist. Parents in this situation usually feel freshly empowered, rather than stuck in feelings of hopelessness. Most of the time, we are able to proceed with implementing FAMILY Rules. For parents who are initially resistant to take on the whole FAMILY Rules commitment, I often have them start by listing the values they want their children to learn and have with them when they leave the nest (i.e. honesty, work ethic, health, self-respect, etc.). Often parents have these values swarming in their heads and they subtly affect parenting decisions and behavior. When they are asked to think about it and put it to paper, with clear definitions, they feel the warmth, love, and significance of getting their parenting out of their heads and committed in writing. Parents are often triggered into having feelings of anxiety or resistance when they think about things like authority, discipline, and the "meltdowns" that can occur with strict rules and consequences. Having parents focus on something meaningful, but benign, like values, makes FAMILY Rules more approachable for some parents. It also teaches the importance of parents communicating with each other and reaching agreements on paper. I am also able to convince parents that it is these values that drive their rules and the "Good Habit Cards." For instance, parents who value "taking responsibility" can say to their kids, "We have the rule about cleaning your room because we have a value about taking responsibility for our spaces and belongings." This helps parents feel empowered to stand by their rules. Parents tend to feel like they have accomplished something with this exercise and are usually eager for me to assign another exercise. We wind up building their FAMILY Rules program in these steps, which feels more manageable to them.

I often get the kids to buy-in to the program by using school as an example (i.e., most of the kids I work with do not have significant school problems and generally comply well with school system). I explain that they walk around school and do stuff in class without really thinking of the rules and consequences. They usually do the right thing and stay out of trouble. I explain that this is because they learned the school system, the clear rules, predictable consequences, and expected behavior. Therefore, the kids run themselves on automatic pilot pretty well. I explain that once they learn the FAMILY Rules program for their household, and get past the initial discomfort, they will walk around the house and do stuff at home without really thinking of the rules and consequences. They will usually do the right thing, stay out of trouble, and run themselves on automatic pilot. I explain that school is designed that way to keep chaos low so kids can focus on the lessons they need to learn and so they can have fun. I explain that home is supposed to run the same way for the same reasons and that's where I come in. I explain that the purpose is also to make it easier on them when they get into society, so they run themselves well on automatic pilot and enjoy the rest of their lives.

The biggest obstacle I have found is getting the parents to take their "Good Habit Cards" for breaking rules. They often "forget" or feel they don't have to do the "Good Habit Cards" because they already did so many "chores" during the day to make up for breaking a rule. I explain the philosophy to the parents. I remind them that by dismissing their own "Good Habit Cards", they are teaching their kids to squirm out of or protest doing their own "Good Habit Cards." In the end, the parents are missing opportunities to role model "being accountable" and handling consequences with grace. Often they understand and agree with the philosophy, but they still slack on the "Good Habit Cards." So, one thing I started to do was have them accrue and do "Good Habit Cards" in my office (with their advanced permission). For instance, with one family, I smugly suggested that for every "Good Habit Card" they skipped doing during the week, they leave 5 minutes early from my session but still pay me for the whole session. In these tough financial times, no one likes to pay for my time when they are not in session. This helped as a motivator with this particular family. They'd rather do the 15-30 minutes of washing mirrors vs. pay me for session time that they had to miss. With another family, I asked kids to email me and "cc" the parents when they felt that the parents were not complying with doing their "Good Habit Cards." The parents felt embarrassed when I would reply, "Well, sorry mom, cancel fun plans until you get them done." This maintained the kids buy-in and increased the parents' compliance with doing their own "Good Habit Cards." Obviously, this would not work with every family and it requires particular informed consent from parents to serve in this role. But it's this creativity in the therapist that can help make FAMILY Rules successful for parents and children.

Another way to get families to buy-in and comply with doing their "Good Habit Cards" is to use the "digital craze." I ask kids and parents to take pictures with their cell phones or digital camera of infractions (i.e., when a child leaves their empty soda can in their room; When it's 5:15pm and the cat litter is still messy; When it's 11:00am on Saturday and someone's room is still a mess). I encourage them to take a picture of the infraction with a clock nearby to verify timing. Teens especially like catching their parents this way. However, I have also seen some particularly "lawyer-like" ten or eleven year-olds complying quickly when mom says, "You claim this room is clean and you therefore should not get "Good Habit Cards" but I disagree. Because this is a fair and just system, I will take a picture and email it to Dr. Hartman as evidence for her to help us decide." The child has often said, "Okay! Give me fifteen more minutes to tidy up, then let's decide." There's something about this level of digital accountability that can motivate people to comply.

Recently, I had to recommend implementing the "Pop-Fly" and "Strike" part of FAMILY Rules (i.e., The "Y" part of the FAMILY acronym). It became evident that an adolescent male client was not responding to FAMILY Rules. I met with the parents weekly and the family as a whole biweekly for several months. Over time, I could tell that something was fishy. I began to suspect that this teen was using marijuana regularly when he came to my office with his parents for our FAMILY Rules meeting. He smelled like incense. Another time, he came to my office but he barely spoke. This was different than usual. He appeared stoned. I suggested the parents get him drug tested. When the test results came back positive for marijuana, I referred the family to a substance use specialist. However, we maintained a commitment to FAMILY Rules to maintain structure and to measure his improvement in substance treatment. I had a release and often spoke with the drug counselor.

Additional rules were set-up involving regular urine-testing and compliance with outpatient substance treatment meetings. He continued to use marijuana and boycott FAMILY Rules. It became clear that he needed a more intensive level of treatment and care. At one point, he said, "I want to do the right thing, but I can't." I recommended a residential drug treatment program followed by a therapeutic boarding school. I referred them to an educational consultant who assisted them in finding the right match and within several weeks, his parents coordinated an escort to help transport him to treatment. The parents kept in touch with me and reported over time that he was doing significantly better. Also, they reported feeling good about the order of their decision-making process in eventually choosing to send him there (i.e. Using FAMILY Rules helped them feel they did all they reasonably could for their son before having to send him away for help). Teaching FAMILY Rules to parents is one of my favorite specialties in my private practice.

Julie Hartman, PhD
Licensed Psychologist
Corte Madera, California

FAMILY Rules Goes Global

I have been using FAMILY Rules for a few years now at our House of Hope-Fort Bend in Texas. One of the mom's that went through the program is now a coach and she is an excellent teacher of the FAMILY Rules parenting program. She will be my coordinator while I am gone and she will have the team to share the load. Recently, we moved to Abu Dhabi because of my husband's employment. We have taken FAMILY Rules with us in order to help "Dr J" take over the world one family at a time.

While we were living in Texas, we had one Vietnamese couple go through our parenting program. The dad had already sent the son off to an academy, but felt he and his wife needed help before the son came back. They went through our four-week program. Not only did they change their style of parenting, but we helped to heal their marriage.

We had a divorced couple come to our FAMILY Rules parenting program because their eighteen year old son was dragging them through the mud. This kid was a real class act and knew how to manipulate his parents. The dad was even suicidal when they all came to us. I told the dad that his son was eighteen, and according to Texas law, he was on his own now. The dad was not responsible any longer to clean up his son's messes. Talk about enablers! They took our four week FAMILY Rules class and dad was no longer suicidal. The dad made up rules for his home and told his son, "It's my way or the highway." Although the parents were divorced, they worked together and made up a plan so they could tag team this kid. It was totally amazing. They nipped their scheming son in the bud!

Finally, just before we moved to Abu Dhabi, a Hispanic lady called our office. She said, "We don't have any problems so far but I'm concerned that my twelve-year old son, my oldest boy, may get into problems in a couple more years." She found us on the internet. She wanted to nip any potential problem in the bud so she called us for parenting support. We require both parents to attend. In Texas, we sometimes experience the cultural issue with the Mexican machismo. Some Hispanic men tend to leave most of the discipline to the women. They just want to be the good guy. One reason why I love FAMILY Rules is because it makes this issue disappear. Regardless of culture, the parents must team up together to parent their children. While we are away in Abu Dhabi, we will have the team continue with their work in Texas. Leon and I will be a satellite team in Abu Dhabi. How's that for taking F.A.M.I.L.Y. Rules global?

Janeen Smith
Licensed Minister
Certified Marriage and Family Therapist
Abu Dhabi, United Arab Emirates

Children Want Order and Structure

I am the director for the community support division of our agency. I do carry a case or two from time to time. I think this is important to keep my saw sharp. I am currently working with two other families along side of other community support workers. At our agency, therapists are required to watch Dr. Johnson's seminar on DVD that I purchased via his website. They are working on implementing the Family Rules plan with the parents and children they serve in our community. Aside from the very compelling vignettes "Dr. J." shares in his seminars, I have a few testimonies of my own to share with the readers of this book.

One of the better examples is about a single mom and her two teenage boys. The mom is a recovering heroin addict. She has been clean for a few years and is in the process of completing her degree in criminal justice. She has a sixteen year old son, who at the time of working with the family, had just completed a two year commitment with the juvenile justice system for untold crimes. The identified client was a thirteen year old boy who had been expelled from school for drug use on school grounds, assault, and a list of other offenses.

During my first visit to the home to conduct my assessment, the mom explained to me that her boys did what they wanted, when they wanted. They did not follow her rules. The oldest was on probation and house arrest. He was not supposed to use any controlled substances. However, mom disclosed that he was using and that his probation officer was not enforcing that part of the probation as long as the sixteen year old stayed close to home. Later on, I was informed that he actually would take off at night and return early in the morning. The identified thirteen-year old client was following in his brothers footsteps. After all, who else did he have to be a role model for him? Ever since his older brother had gotten out the detention center, he started using marijuana with him. Both boys were extremely disrespectful of their mother and had no problem using profanity when referring to her in person. Mom on the other hand, while making strides to make a better life through her program and school, had not changed in some areas such as parenting. Her method of parenting and enforcing the rules came down to her yelling and screaming at her two sons. I had the privilege on more than one opportunity to witness this most ineffective method of parenting.

Upon completing the assessment, I was able to identify many needs which were addressed in therapy, some advocacy, and probably the most important piece in the home was the parenting piece. I asked the mom on my second visit if she would be interested in a parenting plan that would make her life easier. Her response to me, as is often the case, "I have tried all those parenting plans." I asked her why she was not following one at the present time. Her response to me was, "Oh, you know, they don't work." I listened to her tell me how none of those plans really work. When she was done I asked her, "If I could show you a plan that was different and really worked, would you be interested?" Her response was, "Yeah, if it really works." I began to explain the basics and she stated, "That is a lot of work." I pointed out, just like "Dr. J." does in his seminars, that she was already spending the excessive amount of time and energy via flying by the seat of her pants. I pointed out that what I was suggesting was channeling her energy in a more ordered and structured manner. After more conversation she agreed to try the plan.

We sat down and made the plan of implementation. I told her first off, that the yelling and screaming had to stop. She agreed. The next thing I directed her to do was not to tell her two sons that she was implementing anything new in their home. This visit had already taken up a considerable amount of time so we set our next appointment for a few days later. I gave her homework which was to come up with a list of rules and some "Good Habit Cards." I gave her a list of supplies she would need.

At our next appointment we reviewed the rules which she had nicely typed up. This was helpful for when she might add, delete, or amend any of them at a later date. She had come up with a nice stack of "Good Habit Cards" too. We reviewed her homework and in one or two cases, there were a few that we talked about that seemed to both of us to be a bit punitive. She obtained her Daily Tokens and RAK chips. After about a week we had everything in place. While this was happening, I had made a referral for therapy and had gotten the therapist on board with what we were doing.

The next appointment was the "Great Reveal." She was going to tell her two boys about the rules of the home. Did I mention that her sons were using marijuana and possibly other illicit drugs too? Also, the older boy is a self professed gang member and the younger boy is affiliated - not initiated. I showed up for the appointment and the mom told the boys to have a seat at the kitchen table. The younger one reluctantly sat down while huffing and puffing, and rolling his eyes. The older boy made some gestures and said, "F_ _ k that! I am not sitting down." Up to this point in time, this young man and I had not had a lot of interaction. I reached over and pulled a chair out and told him, "Have a seat." He looked me straight in the eyes. At this point, I didn't dare look away. I wanted him to know that I was not asking. After a moment, which seemed like an eternity, he made another gesture with his hands and arms and reluctantly sat down. At this point I was not sure how this whole thing was going to go down.

The mom began to explain that the present situation was not good and that there needed to be some change. She spoke about her past and the negative affects it has had on the family. She stated things were going to change. Previously, when mom would yell and scream, she would yell at the top of her voice, "This is my house! You WILL do as I say or get out!" On this day, instead, she calmly sat at the table and said, "This is my house. You WILL do as I say and as I do or you will get out. Is that clear?" What was different was that she did not yell and scream as she said it. I think she was as surprised as I was with the response of her two boys. They sat there and said nothing and gave her their full attention.

She began to tell them how the Family Rules program was going to work. Both of the boys gave her some lip service, but she reminded them these rules were not optional. She explained that the same rules applied to her, except for where age or the law made the difference. I said very little during this whole time. Mom had become a student of Family Rules and understood it pretty well. I left there that day and mom, along with her two boys, seemed to be in good spirits as evidenced by their demeanor and their interaction between one another. The older boy actually shook my hand before I left. I called mom the next day to check in and see how things were going, she reported that things were going well. She stated a few "Good Habit Cards" had been pulled. None the less, they were on task and things were peaceful around her home. I had the services in place which were identified to address the needs.

Over the next few weeks, I checked in with mom, and monitored the services I had made referrals for their family. When I visited the home, I noticed a completely different energy. It was peaceful. The tension I had previously experienced was not there. Both boys were respectful toward mom and just seemed like different boys altogether. It had the appearance of the same home, but felt completely different. I called a month later to see how things were going. The mom confessed to me that things got a little sideways because she was not following the Family Rules plan. What she noticed was that as soon as she quit, so did her boys.

This made her realize the power and safety that Family Rules provides for the parent and children. I followed up with mom a few times since and she reported that the plan continues to work well in their home. She has had some issues, but the Family Rules plan has stayed in place. Nothing ever changes except for a rule and maybe a "Good Habit Card" is thought of and added to the deck. I have to be honest, I was not sure how this hardened sixteen year old gang member was going to respond. It made me a total believer in FAMILY Rules when I saw him follow the rules and become a productive member of the family. I worked with another family where the only parent in the home was the dad. They lived on a two acre lot. Weeds grew exceptionally well on this lot. One of the "Good Habit Cards" that dad put in the deck was to cut weeds down on the lot. This was not so bad except dad had to be reminded that the task had to last for no longer than thirty minutes. His response was, "There is no way my kid can chop all those weeds down in thirty minutes." Dad did not get it. Later dad put a "Good Habit Card" in the deck that removed meals from the kids if they broke a rule. I found this out through the school counselor. This is unacceptable. A parent should never deprive a child of food at any time. The school called and made a report to child protective services because the child had disclosed this to them. It was reported to us directly that dad was physically abusing his children. Our agency made a report to child protective services. Dad stated that he felt violated by us. Excuse me! He was beating his kids and he felt violated by us? He declined services from our agency. I later found out that he moved his kids to another school. We can change our surroundings but the problems only follow. In this case, dad was the main problem. He did not get it. The kids were in therapy addressing their issues and I believe they were making progress. Dad did not get it.

I would have to say, out of all the families I serve, regardless of where a family falls within the socioeconomic strata, the number one missing element is "order and structure" in the home. Children are asking for order and structure in one way or another. I think the problem is that parents do not know how to provide it. I have never seen this parenting program not work with a family as long as they follow the plan to the letter of how it is laid out and not change a thing. One has to be aware of the underlying personal issues and see to it that they are addressed. As longs as the parents implement the program "correctly and consistently," it really does work.

My wife and I have also been treatment foster parents for seven years. As a part of maintaining our license, we are required to attend twenty-hours of training annually. I have been to a variety of parenting trainings. They intrigue me, believe it or not. I paid for the seminar "Dr. J." put on when it came to our town because I wanted to check it out. I have to say, I think FAMILY Rules is by far the best parenting program out there. It is the most practical and the most hands on. I am able to sit down with a family and help them put it in place step by step. It is simple and that is the nice thing about it. As long as you follow it just as it was intended, not much if anything can go wrong. Finally, I can also say, that in every case – without exception – where FAMILY Rules did not work, it had everything to do with the parents' refusal to participate fully as the role models this wonderful system expects them to be as parents. FAMILY Rules is great. I'm as excited to share it now as I was two-years ago when I was first introduced to it. It really works!!!

Bill Reinicke
Director of Hogares, Inc.
Albuquerque, New Mexico

Tickled in Texas

I went to "Dr J's" workshop in Austin, Texas a couple of years ago, and was so excited to introduce his parenting program to the families I see in my practice. His parenting method has worked with people when nothing else has! It is simple, precise, clear, concrete, and easy to implement. Here are just a couple of examples of families who have used this parenting model with success.

Susie was the youngest of three children and the only girl. At fourteen, her grades were poor; she did not work around the house, and she was sarcastic. At times, she even was abusive to her mother. Susie's mom was rather passive, and let her get away with this behavior, as her own mom had done with her sister when she was growing up. Susie's dad traveled a lot, but when he was around, she behaved better. When her dad would try to set limits, her mom would not be able to follow through when he was traveling. Susie's mom had read a couple of different parenting books, and even attended a short workshop, but gave up quickly in the face of Susie's rather formidable resistance to anything new.

As I worked with the couple to join together on a parenting plan they could both embrace, they found FAMILY Rules to be a really workable solution. They especially liked the first half of the book, saying it "opened their eyes" to mistakes their own parents had made with them when they were growing up. This book helped them understand how they might sabotage their own progress as parents. Susie's parents followed the steps precisely, and within two weeks of introducing the plan to their daughter, they could already tell a difference. Her behavior, especially her attitude and demeanor, improved immediately. Yes, Susie tried to sabotage her parents' new parenting plan. She tested them to see if they meant business; however, they held firm and she learned that her parents were in charge - not her. Life became easier for Susie when she chose to follow the fair and consistent rules. Today, at sixteen, she is an "A" student and is looking forward to going to college.

I would like to share one more story. Dana was a single parent with two boys, eight and ten years old. She was chronically stressed, and found herself yelling at her kids far too much. On her good days, she could be loving and nurturing, but found that her hardest times were when her boys came back from their father's house. At dad's house, there were no rules, no bedtimes, and they could do what they wanted when they wanted. When her two boys came back home, they would continue their rather chaotic, unruly behavior. Dana was afraid that if she was firm with the rules in her home, her boys would prefer to live with their father. This was a threat that the boy's dad had used many times to intimidate her.

As I introduced her to FAMILY Rules, I reassured her that the kids were crying out for order and structure. It would help them to settle down and feel safe in their home. Over time, she began to trust that setting rules and limits, delivered calmly and clearly, along with the nurturing relationship she already had established with her boys, was in everyone's best interest. After we introduced the rules to the kids in a family session, both children complained and questioned the process. However, it was easy to see that they were actually intrigued. Within a month, Dana noticed that her two boys were settling down much quicker after returning from their father's house. She also noticed that she wasn't yelling at them anymore. Two months later, during a family therapy session, the kids asked me to invite their dad in to teach him the FAMILY Rules parenting system too!

Truthfully, I could go on and on. Suffice it to say that I am committed to teaching every parent who comes in my office a better way to do things. The FAMILY Rules system is the best parenting program I have seen to turn things around quickly. I'm grateful that I can use a parenting program that helps families, not only in being more responsible citizens, but especially to be more loving and supportive toward one another.

Pamela J. Monday, Ph.D.
Licensed Professional Counselor
Licensed Marriage and Family Therapist
Austin, Texas

Adopted Children Love the FAMILY Rules Program

I am a social worker who has an international hosting program for orphans from Eastern Europe. Through our program, we bring between one-hundred to one-hundred fifty children each year to stay with host families around the USA. Afterwards, many of the families go ahead and adopt those children who they came to love during the four to five weeks of the programs. We have decided to implement FAMILY Rules as a concept for the hosting families to use while the children are here. With this up and running in their homes, it will help alleviate misunderstandings due to languages as to expectations of the children and of the host parents. We are so excited to be using this plan.

Also, we implemented FAMILY Rules in my home after I attended "Dr J's" seminar in Chattanooga, Tennessee. It took a few months for my husband to watch the seminar on DVD and read the book. He reads maybe two books a year, and they usually revolve around some Christian athlete. After he watched the DVD, we went to Latvia for the adoption of our eighth child, who is fourteen. While there, we stayed in an apartment at the orphanage for the required one week. Of course, there was nothing much we could do. So, he read the book and told me we were going to do this program. We created a list of rules, Good Habit Cards, and everything that is required. I had my laptop there, so I typed as he and I talked.

Our new daughter happens to speak a good bit of English and was very interested in our plan too. She actively helped with the program and proudly told all her friends about rewards for tokens and so forth. Three weeks after we returned home, everyone is on the same page. The transition with a new child was very easy and whenever someone breaks the rules, everyone is equal. This is especially important for a new child entering the family, who may feel that existing children have some advantage. Not to mention, we fired the twice a month housekeeper since there was nothing for her to do last Friday.

On a couple other notes, we have entertained an assistant director from one of the orphanages that we work with in St Petersburg, Russia. She has been intrigued with our FAMILY Rules program. She told me that she will go back to the orphanage and use FAMILY Rules there too. She can't wait for the book to be translated into Russian.

Our nanny took a few of the kids to an animal preserve last Friday for a daytrip during spring break. She is a very responsible young woman from Connecticut. She has read the book as well, and helped me beg my husband into watching the seminar on DVD. Well, she got caught for speeding and received a ticket. This was her first ticket ever. She has been doing fifty "Good Habit Cards" for the past two days for breaking a state law. The kids have developed so much respect for her now as they watch her do her cards that she doesn't normally do. It's been totally awesome.

Le Ann Dakake,
Director of Hosting Programs
New Horizons for Children, Inc.
Acworth, Georgia

Mandated by the Los Angeles Superior Family Court

I am a Licensed Marriage and Family Therapist in Sherman Oaks, California. I also provide services as a Child Custody Evaluator for the Los Angeles Superior Family Court. I attended Dr. Johnson's "Positive Parenting with a Plan (Grades K-12): FAMILY Rules" seminar in the early part of 2005. I have been including his book as a mandated source in my parenting plan recommendations to the family court. Dr. Johnson's book is now a part of the family court orders, believe it or not, when the divorce cases settle. The divorced parents must read it, implement the FAMILY Rules program in their separate homes, and then, six months later, report back to court about their progress. I just wanted to let the readers of this book know that Dr. Johnson is now famous amongst the Judges in the Los Angeles Superior Family Court system. So far, it's going really well. I strongly believe it would work equally well in other divorce courts across the USA.

Bruce Harshman, Ph.D.
Child Custody Evaluator
Sherman Oaks, California

Happy and Healthy HMO Clients

When given the opportunity, I had to write to express my sincere appreciation for the invaluable FAMILY Rules parenting program. I work as an out-patient therapist both in private practice and within a large Health Maintenance Organization (HMO). I met "Dr J" in 2006 at a continuing education workshop in San Diego, California. I already had a professional reputation as an effective therapist with a specialty in child and adolescent psychotherapy. My doctoral thesis was on the value of family recreation between parents and their middle school age children (6th, 7th and 8th grade). At the time that I took "Dr J's" seminar, I was already leading a group for parents and their middle school age children within the HMO setting. I would teach the families some valuable skills, like communication skills building, assertiveness training, and a discipline model where parents were taught how to assign consequences to whatever the child or adolescent did wrong. It made perfect sense to me; however, only the psychologically sophisticated parents were able to catch on to this cumbersome method. In retrospect, the absence of clearly written rules made this process too hard for most families.

During the FAMILY Rules workshop, I was impressed by this simple, yet air-tight parenting program. By that I mean that there is virtually no wiggle room for therapists or parents to modify the program. "Dr J" covered everything a family needs in order to move out of chaos and into peaceful order and structure. Needless to say, I stopped teaching families the consequence assigning method of discipline and started teaching FAMILY Rules.

For the past three years, this is how I have used the "Positive Parenting with a Plan" program within the HMO setting. While all therapists are assigned adult and adolescent cases, most therapists dislike working with this population. All too often, their sessions dissolve into power struggles. So I put the word out to the other therapists within the HMO: "Send me your difficult cases." I welcomed parents and their middle-school aged children (6th, 7th, and 8th grade) to attend an orientation. At the orientation, I introduced the FAMILY Rules parenting program. To participate in group, the families have to agree to attend seven sessions on a weekly basis, and if at all possible, I want all of the adults in the home to attend all seven sessions. I have them fill out a questionnaire about their approach to setting limits with their children and ask them to list some of the things they argue about. I am fortunate to have a co-therapist who works with me. We make time in every group, where I meet alone with the parents and my co-therapist meets alone with the kids. We come back together at the end of each session for a review, wrap up, and homework assignments for the parents.

In my private practice, I introduce the families that I work with to this program. This parenting program has worked miracles with some very difficult families that I have worked with. I receive referrals from four clinics and find the experience of working with these families to be joyful and rewarding. I recommend the "Positive Parenting with a Plan (Grades K-12): FAMILY Rules" program without reservation.

Frank Patti, Psy.D.
Marriage and Family Therapist
Santa Ana, California

Great for Teaching Graduate Students

In our counseling programs here at New Orleans Baptist Theological Seminary, we focus some on counseling theory in our classes, but also we like to teach our students skills that will empower them to help families learn how to resolve their problems. It is a thrill when the students go out to the clinical practice settings, and we receive reports about how well trained they are. "Positive Parenting with a Plan (Grades K-12): Family Rules" is one of the tools we teach them to prepare them to work with parents and children. It is one of the most practical, and least complicated (which means more likely to be used) programs I have seen to prepare parents to use behavioral techniques. Dr. Johnson's material is easy to understand and full of illustrations and examples to make it easy to apply to everyday life. The "Good Habit Cards" are a wonderful change for most families after months, sometimes years, of attempting to remove toys from children or privileges for teens. Their old approach wasn't working because they can't take away "all" the toys. Also, they would often over-react in the length of the restrictions. FAMILY Rules eliminates these futile and unproductive attempts and provides more positive and effective disciplinary interventions.

Not only is Dr. Johnson's Family Rules program fairly easy to teach parents to use, as well as successful when parents implement it "correctly and consistently", but it is also easy for the graduate students to learn how to use it. The free power point training slides Dr. Johnson has made available via his website are clear and entertaining! Our students always enjoy the training, and feel like they can walk away ready to use the material immediately. I would encourage all undergraduate and graduate programs that are seeking to prepare students to use behavioral training or token economy methods to teach this material to their counselors-in-training.

Dr. Kathy Steele, PhD, LPC, LMFT
Assistant Professor Psychology and Counseling Department
New Orleans Baptist Theological Seminary
New Orleans, Louisiana

Works Wonders with Juvenile Offenders

We have been using the "Positive Parenting with a Plan (Grades K-12): FAMILY Rules" program since 2003 and it has been very effective. We use the program with Level 5 & 6 adolescents which represent the highest level of acuity in our Juvenile Justice System. We work with adolescents and their families from the Departments of Juvenile Justice and Family and Children Services, as well as direct referrals from the Juvenile Courts. We work in twenty-two metropolitan Atlanta counties and use the program with both English and Spanish speaking families.

We have found FAMILY Rules to be the most effective parenting program for behavior management with adolescents who have a history of oppositional and defiant behaviors. Our research data shows that we have less than a 20% re-offending rate with those whom we have used the program, as opposed to those who didn't complete or were not involved in the program. Re-offending is defined as returned to court involvement, re-arrests and probation violations by this agency. All of our field clinicians are trained in the use of the FAMILY Rules parenting program at orientation. We are Nationally Recognized by the National Center for Mental Health and Juvenile Justice as a Best Practice organization.

David F. Anthony, Psy.D., ACS
Clinical Director
Family Intervention Specialists, Inc.
Atlanta, Georgia

Measuring Success Several Families at a Time

I have been using Dr. Matthew A. Johnson's "Positive Parenting with a Plan (Grades K-12) FAMILY Rules" program for several years. It is the most effective and valuable parenting plan I have ever taught. While serving as a Director and as a Child & Family Therapist for a non-profit agency, I put together several parenting groups teaching this method. Sometimes the group consisted of only five parents while other groups had as many as twelve parents.

The makeup of families was quite varied: foreign born, military, low income, high income, parents with mental health issues, and families of children with disabilities, such as Asperger's Syndrome. These groups were run by the generosity of grant providers. Because of their generosity, I felt it important to have a method of showing whether or not the groups they were funding actually helped parents to improve their parenting skills.

I developed a Pre-Test/Post-Test questionnaire. There are fifteen questions. During the first session of the group, the parents would complete the Pre-Test via the following options for their answers: 1-Fully Disagree, 2-Somewhat Disagree, 3-Agree, 4-Somewhat Agree, 5-Fully Agree. The survey asked questions such as: (1) I feel I know all I need to know about disciplining; or (5) I discipline my child without losing my temper; and (15) I am consistent in my discipline method. During the last session, the parents completed the Post-Test with the same fifteen questions and the same options for their answers (1-5 above). These questions are the same as in the Pre-test but are phrased like, "I have learned." Fifty-five parents were surveyed. Of the fifty-five parents, 78% fully agreed that they had poor parenting skills and their children acted out more than other children; 4% Somewhat Agreed; and 18% Agreed. Of the fifty-five parents surveyed with the Post-test, 96% agreed that their child's behaviors and their ability to discipline in a more positive manner improved significantly; 3% somewhat agreed; and 1% Agreed.

One family who came to the group consisted of a husband in the military. His wife was born and raised in Japan. They had a kindergartner and a two-year old. This couple initially came into therapy due to the wife's anger outbursts. She was raised by a very abusive father, while living in Japan. He continued to emotionally abuse her after the recent death of her mother. She was finding herself treating her son in the same manner as her father had and was still treating her. She was adamant that she did not want to perpetuate the same pattern with her own children. The couple agreed to come to the next FAMILY Rules group while we continued working individually on other issues. Fortunately the husband was not abusive and he was very supportive of his wife. Occasionally, there were some cultural differences that had to be taken into account. Although she spoke English well, translation was sometimes a challenge. Her husband spoke Japanese and was able to help her understand when needed.

This couple was able to quickly implement the FAMILY Rules plan in their home and stuck with it. For the mother, the parenting program took away her angry emotions connected to her previous parenting style and assumptions (i.e., "My son is acting up just to make me angry!"). Concerning her son, he thrived with the positive parenting plan and readily took his "Good Habit Cards" when need be. He would even go take a "Good Habit Card" when he did something wrong before his parents had a chance to tell him to take one. Eventually, their son was getting a card about once a month, if that. In addition, the father was able to stop being the mediator between the mother and son. Their two-year old daughter was learning by watching her kindergartner brother. Even at age two, mom and dad used the positive parenting plan with their daughter, without the "Good Habit Cards." Those were introduced later as needed when she reached kindergarten age. This family had a six-month, one-year, and eighteen month follow-up. They are still using the FAMILY Rules plan successfully and the mom's parenting style continues to be positive.

As I continue to work with families in private practice, I teach this method one-on-one. Parents love the simplicity and effectiveness of FAMILY Rules and learn quickly to become consistent.

Candis K. Sollars, MSW, LCSW
Astoria, Oregon

No Horsing Around in a Kentucky Treatment Facility

The Efficacy of using "Positive Parenting with a Plan: FAMILY Rules"
In a Crisis Stabilization Unit at a Residential Treatment Facility
Written in 2006 by Denise Greenhalgh,
Former Supervisor and Employee
at the Christian Care Communities at Woodlawn
in the State of Kentucky

The Research Question: *If the "Positive Parenting with a Plan (Grades K-12): FAMILY Rules" parenting program works well with families in various home settings across the USA, can it also work in therapeutic treatment settings with improving the attitudes, behaviors, and compliance of "At-Risk" children?*

Background Information:
The Sanders Crisis Unit accepts children who are in a behavioral, emotional, and/or family crisis. The "At-Risk" child needs an immediate placement and does not meet the criteria for hospitalization. The Sanders Crisis Unit has seen a significant shift in the severity and diagnoses of the "At-Risk" children referred for placement over the past few years, which in turn has created a need to change in the therapeutic milieu.

The Sanders Crisis Unit program is structured to be a seven to ten day placement for stabilization of the child's mood and behavior, or longer if treatment or placement goals are not met and further crisis stabilization is needed. The therapeutic milieu is designed to help the child or adolescent return to the parent or guardian, or to a less restrictive treatment environment. The behavior modification program used in the milieu is adapted from the "Positive Parenting with a Plan (Grades K-12): F.A.M.I.L.Y. Rules" parenting program, authored by Dr. Matthew A. Johnson (2001). This allows the therapeutic staff to work with the parent and foster parents to implement the original program in the "At-Risk" child's home environment while the child is stabilizing under the same basic behavioral modification program. Therefore, providing continuity for an "At-Risk" child who will eventually return home.

Traditionally, treatment milieus have used incentive systems similar to those in many homes or school based behavioral modification programs. These incentive systems are usually based on points and levels. During my many years of working in residential treatment settings, I've found several shortfalls in these programs. One such flaw in many programs is how to keep "At-Risk" children from getting into a "no win" situation for the day once they have had problems. Let's just say that a child had a rough night of sleep, woke up in a bad mood, and ended up breaking rules in the morning. In many incentive or point systems, the child may now have no incentive to work on improving their behavior the rest of the day. Further, let's say that this "At-Risk" child does end up pulling it together some time in the afternoon, but when their points are reviewed for the day, potentially ending up drawing them back into problems once they find out that they didn't get there points for that day. The "Positive Parenting with a Plan(Grades K-12): FAMILY Rules" program addresses this by allowing the child to correct their behavior with Good Habit Cards, and then get on with their day. The Random Acts of Kindness Chips (RAK Chips) further keeps the child from falling into this trap by encouraging them to work above and beyond their Good Habit Cards to make their day successful.

Other problems occur when residential treatment-staff develop the mindset that their job is to "control" or "fix" the behaviors of the "At-Risk" children. This inevitably leads to power struggles and frustrates the residential staff who cannot "make" the children behave. With the "Positive Parenting with a Plan (Grades K-12):

FAMILY Rules" program, the residential treatment staff continually put the responsibility back on the children for their behaviors. The residential-staff become more like facilitators rather than enforcers. Through directing the kids to take responsibility for their behavior, the staff see behavior problems as opportunities to work with them - not control them. The focus of redirection becomes choices of the child and how their choices result in either positive or negative consequences. If the focus is on the child's choices, there is no more power struggle. Instead of the residential treatment-staff coming at problems, attitudes, and behaviors with highly confrontational re-directions, staff can refer back to the rules and the number of Good Habit Cards the child will receive if they break that particular rule. Since the "Good Habit Cards" are predetermined and random, there is little room for staff to overreact or become punitive. In the Sanders Crisis Unit, "Wild Cards" were also developed and shuffled into the deck to further address and alleviate the potential for staff to overreaction.

The Sanders Crisis Unit faces several other challenges for implementing a therapeutic treatment milieu that may not be found in other residential facilities. One challenge we faced in implementing a behavioral modification system was finding one that would meet the behavioral and developmental needs of the age range of 6 to 18. Let's face it; time outs have no behavioral modification benefits for a sixteen-year old. Further, most seven-year olds cannot process their behavior in a three page written essay. The "Positive Parenting with a Plan (Grades K-12): FAMILY Rules" parenting program addresses this by allowing for multiple sets of "Good Habit Cards" that focus on the age, therapeutic, and developmental needs of the kids (i.e., It's a flexible, adaptable, adjustable system that can be tailored to meet the unique needs of every home environment and/ or therapeutic treatment environment). The set of "Good Habit Cards" are not necessarily assigned by age groups, but are instead assigned by colors (we used yellow, orange and green "3 x 5 cards") so that the child could be given "Good Habit Cards" at a lower level of difficulty if they struggle with emotional or cognitive deficits. The colors do not draw attention to the level of cards that are assigned. While it is important for the child to correct their behavior, it is also important for them to be able to successfully complete their "Good Habit Cards." Please see Sample Chart on the next page:

Sample Chart of Colored Good Habit Cards used by the Sanders Crisis Unit:

Cards allowed to still receive a Day Bead			
	Green	Orange	Yellow
Level 1	7	5	3
Level 2	5	3	1
Level 3	3	1	0

Another challenge that the Sanders Crisis Unit faced in implementing the "Positive Parenting with a Plan (Grades K-12): FAMILY Rules" parenting program was the nature of the acute crisis that the "At-Risk" child and or family was currently involved in. To expect a child in a crisis to follow every rule from the time of admission would be to potentially set them up for additional failures. This was addressed by using levels to phase in higher behavioral standards by ability and age, once again basing this on the card color of the child.

The goal is that as the child's behavior stabilizes, they receive fewer "Good Habit Cards." As they progress on the levels, they are experiencing success with the "Positive Parenting with a Plan(Grades K-12): FAMILY Rules" program, avoiding feeling the "I can't do this" mindset from settling in. They actually learn that they can succeed.

This success was realized by one twelve-year-old foster child with Fetal Alcohol Syndrome (FAS). The foster parents had tried practically every possible parenting system available in the USA over a 4-year period. The foster parents and the outpatient therapist could not find a parenting program that would work for their foster child. Trying to implement the last parenting program resulted in the need to place him in the crisis unit.   At first, he struggled with completing the "Good Habit Cards," and continued to engage in tantrums if he received cards for breaking rules. He continued to struggle with this until the day before his discharge. The foster parents had tried so many variations of parenting programs that they were uninterested in learning the "Positive Parenting with a Plan (Grades K-12): FAMILY Rules" parenting program. However, about three days after discharge from the Sanders Crisis Unit, the foster parents contacted the unit to ask about this new parenting system.   Apparently this 12 year old foster child told the foster parents that he thought that the "Good Habit Cards" could help him and that he wanted to try them in his foster home. Seriously, how many other behavioral modification systems are requested to be put in place by the kids?

A Summary of the One Year Research Study:
The Sanders Crisis Unit used a Pre-Test/Post-Test model to assess the degree of change in the symptoms the child is experiencing from intake through discharge. The Symptom Checklist/Behavior Assessment (ScuBA) were used in this process to self-report of symptoms.   A self-report behavior assessment was used for the child or adolescent to report their current symptoms. If a child or adolescent's discharge plan included placement in another agency program, an interagency referral was completed if the referral source has not already initiated that referral.

"At-Risk" children were placed in the Sanders Crisis Unit for many behavioral and emotional problems.   The diagnoses that these children had were grouped into four categories:

- Behavioral and Relational Problems (Oppositional-Defiant and Conduct Disorder, ADHD) - 60%

- Mood Disorders (Depression and Bipolar Disorder) - 14%

- Anxiety Disorders and Posttraumatic Stress Disorder - 18%

- Abuse or Neglect - 1%

- Other Disorders - 7%

The statistics continued to show an increase in the number of children reporting at least one form of abuse or neglect. This percentage increased to 88%, which is well above the percentage for the general population in the USA. This research study included 148 of the 168 children who were placed in the Sanders Crisis Unit. The number of children who reported witnessing or being involved in domestic violence in the past year continued to be at a high rate (41%). The significance of these statistics directed the Sanders Crisis Unit toward the continuing process of adjusting the treatment milieu to meet the changing needs of children in our care.

The Sanders Center Behavior Assessment (SCuBA) is a symptom checklist given to each "At-Risk" child upon their intake session to provide the treatment team with an indicator of the issues that the child may be experiencing. The symptoms are grouped into ten categories, which include: Coping Skills, Social Skills, Self-Esteem, Education, Depression, Anxiety, Posttraumatic Stress Disorder, Control of Circumstances, ADHD, and Oppositional – Defiance.

The SCuBA was also completed at discharge, and the two results were compared to measure the effectiveness of the Sanders Crisis Unit treatment program. If the "At-Risk" children's scores decreased, then child was reporting fewer symptoms, which indicated that they had made improvement during their treatment in the Sanders Crisis Unit. The overall results of the SCuBA scores demonstrated positive results for children placed in the Sanders Crisis Unit.

The Outcome Results of the One Year Research Study:

- The percentage of "At-Risk" children who showed improvement in at least one or more of the SCuBA scales was 97%

- Although the "Positive Parenting with a Plan: FAMILY Rules" parenting program helped to improve the attitudes, behaviors, and compliance among most of the children in the Sanders Crisis Unit (i.e., 97%), the SCuBA scales which indicated the greatest percentages of improvement include decreased Depression, improved Coping Skills, and improved Self-Esteem.

The Conclusion of Research Study at the CCC at Woodlawn:

It appears that the "Positive Parenting with a Plan (Grades K-12): FAMILY Rules" program is just as successful in the therapeutic treatment setting at the Sanders Crisis Unit as it is in the various homes across the USA. The parenting program helped the staff to behave as "facilitators" rather than "enforcers" by redirecting the "At-Risk" children to deal with the consequences of their own choices. The parenting program was easily tailored to the unique needs of the children in the unit. Acting out children still had an opportunity to pull themselves out of their "nose-dive" and still end up having a good day. Finally, although it helps "At-Risk" children with all sorts of issues (i.e., An impressive overall improvement of 97%), it especially helped children who were struggling with depression, coping skills, and low self-esteem. It is my hope that other therapeutic treatment facilities will conduct research in the future utilizing the "Positive Parenting with a Plan (Grades K-12): FAMILY Rules" parenting program. **NOTE:** Sunrise Children's Services acquired CCC in November of 2007.

"Where's the Beef?"

Wow! You made it through the plethora of anecdotal stories and research data. I'm very proud of you! Now, I'm going to share with you why I included this new and necessary lengthy chapter in my revised book. Prior to 2001, I had been using FAMILY Rules in various treatment settings that I worked in as well as with my private practice clients. Everyone I taught it to, and I do mean everyone, loved the FAMILY Rules parenting program. Occasionally, I would get speaking engagements here and there at schools, churches, and universities and they all loved the FAMILY Rules parenting program too. After fifteen years of prodding, I finally gave in to the pressures from parents and professionals to write this book. After the first printing in 2001, a door immediately opened up for me to speak for Cross Country Education around the USA and Canada.

Shortly thereafter, my speaking schedule grew by leaps and bounds. Occasionally, while on the road speaking, I became frustrated by a small percentage of professionals attending my seminars who wanted to know if I had any research to back up the effectiveness of my parenting program. They were like the real old lady in the Wendy's TV commercials back in the 1980's (i.e., She would scream loudly at the camera, "Where's the beef?!!"). In the minds of some of these professionals, they were not going to accept the fact that FAMILY Rules helps parents and children unless I had the research data to back up what I was teaching.

In response to their skepticism, I decided to begin my seminars by holding up a chair in the air while addressing the crowds. I would ask all of the professionals in the room, "How many of you read numerous research studies in the past month, reviewed the graphs and charts, and conducted statistical analysis studies before you chose to sit in your chair at my seminar this morning? Hmmmm? Please raise your hands." My audience would just sit there in silence looking at me like I was asking a very stupid question. I responded to their blank stares by saying, "That's right! None of you reviewed any research studies before you chose to sit in your chair this morning. Do you want to know why? I'll tell you why. It's because you have decades and decades of experiences sitting in all types of chairs in many different environments and your common sense told you that chairs work. That's why you didn't review any research studies before sitting in your chairs this morning. You didn't need any research studies to arrive at the factually accurate common sense conclusion, based on anecdotal information alone, that chairs really do work."

I would go on to say, "How many decades, like the very old lady in the Wendy's TV commercials, did the tobacco industry shout out, 'Where's the research?!!' as they denied the common sense anecdotal fact that tobacco was creating addictions and killing thousands upon thousands of people worldwide every year? Just ask the spouses and children of dying loved ones lying in the hospital beds. They'll tell you that their common sense doesn't lie. If you smoke cigarettes for decades, they're going to give you lung cancer and you will die a premature death. We didn't need any research studies to know that this was the truth. The truth is the truth regardless of whether or not you have any research studies to back it up."

Then I would share with the professionals in my audience, "My graduate statistics professor at George Fox University, Dr. Neal McBride, taught us that good research proves to be true that which everyone already knew to be true. In other words, good research confirms common sense. Do you want to know why? Well because good research springs forth from anecdotal information. People see others dying in hospital beds after smoking for several decades. Their common sense tells them that smoking is killing them. Someone does a research study. The research data proves to be true what everyone's common sense was already telling them is true: Smoking causes lung cancer. Duh!!! We didn't need any research to know that and you don't need any research to know that what I'm about to teach you is the truth. When you walk out those doors at the end of my seminar, you will know that I speak the truth. You will know in your heart of hearts that my FAMILY Rules parenting program, if implemented correctly and consistently, will help change the lives of the families you are working with."

Thank goodness I was right. It would have been pretty embarrassing if I was wrong. However, I assure you that I'm not going to dedicate my entire professional career to promoting something that doesn't work. I'm not going to travel all over the world speaking to parents and professionals if it doesn't make dramatic changes in the families who are using my parenting program. I'm very pragmatic and I don't like wasting my time or the time of others.

Fortunately, since the first printing of my book in 2001, I've received a never-ending onslaught of e-mails and phone calls from parents and professionals who are using FAMILY Rules with success. Much like the stories you have already read in this chapter. It works for everyone in spite of their ethnic, political, religious, financial, or geographical differences. By the way, successful parenting has absolutely nothing to do with these diverse variables. It has everything to do with the proper mechanics of parenting regardless of our diverse backgrounds.

The great news is that recently, I've been receiving information from others who have conducted their own research while using FAMILY Rules with their client populations. To be honest, I just don't have the time and resources to invest in doing the research. I already know the chair works. My common sense doesn't lie to me. I need to spend my time teaching others and let them do the research. I'll most certainly provide consultation if they would like my assistance as they conduct their research studies.

Guess what? The research data is starting to come in and is proving to be true that which everyone already knew to be true. If you take good old fashion parenting values and put them in a "new and improved" package, minus corporal punishment, it works! My thanks to all the parents and professionals who are spreading the good news and conducting the research to help others understand that parents and children can live happy and peaceful lives in their homes. Seriously, I really appreciate your assistance in helping me take over the world one family at a time. Muhahahahaha!!! I mean that in a good way of course.

In closing, I want you to pretty please consider doing the following two things for me: (1) I want you to get my parenting program up and running in a "correct and consistent" manner in your home. I want you to feel the bliss of peace and harmony at home. It may take a little time and effort to make it through the transitional phase but there's a big pot of gold waiting for you at the end of the rainbow. Hang in there and "getter done"; and (2) I want you to run up and down the streets of your neighborhood totally butt-naked and scream out to all of your neighbors: "If you're not using FAMILY Rules in your home, then you're a Silly Billy!!!" I'm just kidding. Please don't run up and down the streets of your neighborhood totally butt-naked. That could be really scary for a lot of innocent bystanders. Also, that just might get you thrown in jail and I don't want to have to pay your bail. My point is that I would really appreciate it, pretty please, if you would tell your neighbors, coworkers, parents at school, fellow worshippers, and extended family members to get their hands on my book, too. Please help me spread the love. I wish you and your family all of the best of God's blessings. Please don't forget, "Every home needs a FAMILY." Live long and prosper. Peace out.

Part 4

*Questions About
FAMILY Rules*

~Chapter 13~

Questions & Answers

Undoubtedly, you have nit-picky questions concerning the implementation of the FAMILY Rules parenting system in your home. Well, there's good news! I am going to try my best to anticipate every single question you can think of about FAMILY Rules and attempt to answer those questions here and now. I'm also going to admit I'm one hundred percent human and I'm going to forget to include a few questions and answers in this chapter. However, thanks to the modern miracles of technology, you will have the opportunity to go to my website and join the free parent listserv and ask other parents questions about my FAMILY Rules parenting program. Most of the moms and dads on the free parent listserv have been using FAMILY Rules for years and know the program like the back of their hand (www.Family-Rules.com). You may also go to my website, click on the online store, then click on the "Phone Consultation" picture, and pay for a "twenty-five minute" or "fifty-minute" phone consultation session with yours truly. Once your internet order has been placed online, and your payment has been received, my office will call you and set up a time for our phone consultation appointment. Now, on with the questions and answers.

A QUESTION CONCERNING A "FAMILY RULES" GUARANTEE:

1. IS THE *FAMILY RULES* SYSTEM GUARANTEED TO WORK WITH NO MORE PROBLEMS IN A SITUATION WHERE NO SYSTEM OF DISCIPLINE WAS IN PLACE - JUST CHAOS? No more problems? Wherever you find human parents and children, I guarantee you will always find problems. However, if you "correctly and consistently" implement FAMILY Rules in your home (i.e., "the two C-words"), you will find that the chaos will diminish to a relatively sane level of tolerance. Don't forget the stalled car analogy mentioned earlier in the book (i.e., there may be some stressful transition time but it will get easier).

QUESTIONS ABOUT CORPORAL PUNISHMENT:

1. SHOULD A PARENT PUT SPANKING ON THE LIST OF RULES, RESERVING THE RIGHT TO IMPLEMENT THIS? No! I made it pretty clear, earlier in the book, that FAMILY Rules is for children from Kindergarten through the 12th grade. These children are too old to spank! Time outs are appropriate for children from age two through preschool. You should try other interventions such as redirecting their attention elsewhere, turning off your TV and playing with them (i.e., sometimes kids act out because you're spending way too much time watching TV or playing on your computer). FAMILY Rules will help to correct their behaviors if you implement the system "correctly and consistently" (i.e., "the two 'C' words").

QUESTIONS ABOUT GOOD HABIT CARDS:

1. MY WIFE AND I WERE UNDER THE IMPRESSION THAT THE KIDS ONLY RECEIVED ONE CARD OR CARDS, DEPENDING ON WHAT WE SET, IF THEY DO NOT COMPLETE THEIR CHORES. Most families give one card per incomplete chore. Some families choose to give two cards per incomplete chore. However, my vote is for one Good Habit Card per incomplete chore.

2. ARE WE TO GIVE A CARD OR CARDS PER CHORE LEFT INCOMPLETE? Yes!!! Most families give only one card per incomplete chore (please read above question).

3. WHAT IF SOMEONE PULLS A CARD, THEN SOMEONE ELSE BREAKS A RULE AND PULLS THE SAME CARD? CAN WE PUT IT BACK? When a Good Habit Card has been pulled and completed, place it in the discard pile. No one else should be able to pull this card again until the rest of the cards have been completed and end up in the discard pile. When all the cards have been completed and are placed in the discard pile, reshuffle them and start all over again. **NOTE:** The discard pile is behind the divider in the Good Habit Card box.

4. WHAT IF SOMEONE HAS ALL 50 CARDS, AND THEN SOMEBODY ELSE BREAKS THE RULE? Give the second offender their good habit cards from the stack of 50 cards. Once they have been completed, put them back into the stack of 50 cards. The individual who has 50 cards to do will still have to do all 50 cards. So what if some of the cards were just done! The toilet, stove, or kitchen floor can't be cleaned too many times.

5. IF THE PARENT FEELS THAT ON ONE OCCASION TOO MANY GOOD HABIT CARDS WERE GIVEN, IS IT APPROPRIATE NEXT TIME TO DECREASE THE NUMBER OF GOOD HABIT CARDS GIVEN? One of the great things about the FAMILY Rules parenting system is it tends to limit the influence of emotions on parent's decision about discipline. Please take note that nowhere in the "Mechanics of FAMILY" section did you read where a parent's "feelings" play a role in determining how many cards a child receives or doesn't receive. Once again, the number of Good Habit Cards are predetermined and placed within the parenthesis next to the numbered rules (see Appendix C). When a child or adult breaks the rule, he or she receives the number of Good Habit Cards adjacent to the rule. No more and no less. Please implement FAMILY Rules the way you were taught and don't deviate from the program because of the way you feel. If you allow your feelings to dictate your decisions, then you will undermine your own authority. Also, if you give one child a break, the other children will want breaks too. If you don't give them the same break, then you will be accused of favoring one child over another. Just stick with the program and set your feelings aside. Remember, you are conducting business like a Wal-Mart cashier. In your case, the business of parenting.

6. IS IT OKAY TO START LOW, LIKE 1 OR 2 GOOD HABIT CARDS, AND GRADUALLY INCREASE THE NUMBER OF CARDS WITH EACH OFFENSE? Yes and no. As I stated in a previous answer, please start off low and work your way up from there. However, you should not increase the number of cards with each offense. You should give your children time to see if their behaviors settle down. If a certain rule continues to be broken then, after some time has lapsed, consult with your spouse and increase the number of cards. Remember, you both have to be in agreement before you raise the number of good habit cards. If you don't have a spouse or partner, then arrange to bounce your decisions off of someone you respect such as a friend, neighbor, counselor, clergy person, etc.

7. BECAUSE SOME CHORES NEED TO BE DONE MORE OFTEN THAN OTHERS, CAN THE PARENT SUBSTITUTE CHORES WHEN GOOD HABIT CARDS ARE DRAWN? Yes, but only when a "Wild Card" is drawn. Otherwise, stick to the Good Habit Cards drawn. Please remember to implement the FAMILY Rules parenting system "correctly and consistently." Don't deviate from the program for the sake of convenience. Remember, if you choose to have the rule, "Do what you're asked to do immediately without complaining," on your list, then you can simply ask them to do the chore. Also, don't forget to make up a list of daily and weekly chores.

8. IS IT OKAY TO HAVE MORE THAN 50 GOOD HABIT CARDS IN A STACK? Yes. You can have 500 Good Habit Cards in a stack. However, no child or adult can ever receive more than 50 cards total. I learned early on during the development of this parenting system that anymore than 50 cards is seen by children as too deep of a hole to dig themselves out. They went belly-up into a state of "learned helplessness" and gave up. Therefore, we capped it at 50 Good Habit Cards.

9. IF WE, AS PARENTS, HAVE A HECTIC SCHEDULE, CAN WE SET A TIME LIMIT WHEN WE NEED THE CARDS DONE? No. As I explained earlier in the book, the children are now in charge of whether or not they are grounded and for how long they are grounded. When they choose to break a rule or not get their chore done, they are choosing to ground themselves. When they are grounded, they have two choices: (1) Get their Good Habit Cards done right away, or (2) Stay in their room until they choose to leave their room and complete their Good Habit Cards. Please don't allow your hectic lifestyle to undermine your parenting priorities. Cut back on your schedule if it is interfering with your most important responsibility - your kids.

10. ARE CHILDREN ALLOWED TO DO THEIR GOOD HABIT CARDS WHEN IT IS BEDTIME? No. If they still have Good Habit Cards at bedtime, then the cards carry over to the next day. Don't allow your children to manipulate their bedtimes. This will motivate them to get their cards done before bedtime or immediately upon returning home from school.

11. WHAT IS THE DIFFERENCE BETWEEN BREAKING THE RULES AND PULLING GOOD HABIT CARDS AND NOT COMPLETING CHORES AND PULLING GOOD HABIT CARDS? When a child breaks a rule, they are to receive the predetermined number of Good Habit Cards found in the parenthesis adjacent to the numbered rule. When a child does not complete a chore, they normally receive one Good Habit Card per incomplete chore. A few families decide to give two good habit cards per incomplete chore. However, my vote is for one Good Habit Card per incomplete chore.

12. SHOULD WE HAVE A TOTAL OF 55 CARDS IN THE DECK, INCLUDING WILD AND GRACE CARDS? Yes. There are a total of 45 Good Habit Cards, 5 Wild Cards, and 5 Grace Cards. However, you can't do a Grace Card because it simply lets the child or adult off the hook for that particular card (i.e., They receive some amazing grace, how sweet the sound, that saved a wretch like them).

13. IF YOU HAVE LIMITED WAYS TO GET GOOD HABIT CARDS, CAN YOU CHANGE THE RULES TO ALLOW DAILY/ WEEKLY CHORES TO ACQUIRE GOOD HABIT CARDS? As previously explained in the book and in this question and answer chapter, most families give one Good Habit Card per incomplete chore. A few families choose to give two good habit cards per incomplete chore. My vote is to only give one Good Habit Card per incomplete chore.

14. IF YOU HAVE MULTIPLE CARDS, BUT YOU GET A GRACE CARD, SHOULD YOUR CARDS BE CANCELLED? No. If you receive five Good Habit Cards and one of those cards is a Grace Card, then you only get off the hook for that one Grace Card. You still have to do the other four Good Habit Cards.

15. WHAT IF THE CHILD WRITES OR SCRIBBLES ON A GOOD HABIT CARD? Messing with the FAMILY system in any way results in the child receiving all 50 cards. They are not to mess with the lists, cards, or chips! No! No! Please read the last rule on the list of sample rules (Appendix C).

16. WHAT IF WE HAVE A CHILD WITH A SERIOUS DEVELOPMENTAL DISABILITY, DO THEY DRAW FROM THE SAME DECK OF CARDS AS EVERYONE ELSE? This is the beauty of the FAMILY Rules parenting system (i.e., It's flexible, adaptable, adjustable, and can be tailored to meet the unique needs of every family). If you think your special needs child is capable of doing the same Good Habit Cards as everyone else in the family, then the answer to your question is "Yes." On the other hand, if you don't think your special needs child is capable of doing the same cards as everyone else in the family, then simply create a deck of Good Habit Cards that are tailored to meet their developmental needs.

QUESTIONS ABOUT RAK CHIPS AND REWARD TOKENS:

1. CAN WE PUT A LIMIT ON RAK CHIPS? Yes. However, lean in the direction of graciously rewarding your children for their kindness. All too often, parents naturally focus on their children's negative behaviors while taking their children's positive behaviors for granted. Let them know you appreciate their Random Acts of Kindness. Bless their buns!!!

2. HOW MANY REWARDS SHOULD BE ON THE LIST, AND CAN WE HAVE A SEPARATE REWARDS LIST FOR EACH CHILD? There is no minimum or maximum number of rewards required on the list. It's up to you. You're the parent. You need to determine how much time and financial resources you have available to provide the rewards. Yes, you may have separate reward lists for your children.

3. READING THROUGH THE BOOK, I NOTICED A FEW THINGS THAT WERE NOT MENTIONED. MY QUESTION FOR YOU IS WE HAVE NOT BEEN GIVING THE KIDS RAK CHIPS FOR DAILY CHORES. YOU NEVER MENTIONED IT (OR WE DON'T REMEMBER) SO I WANT TO KNOW IF WE SHOULD INITIATE THIS PRACTICE? Yes, if you want to do so. Please keep in mind that doing their daily and weekly chores and not breaking the rules is rewarded with a "Daily Token" at night time just before they go to bed. Try to focus on giving your children RAK chips for Random Acts of Kindness - not daily and weekly chore requirements (i.e., my daughter made the bed for her brother because he flew out of the house this morning. She did it out of the kindness of her heart without being asked. She gets a RAK chip. He gets cards when he gets home for not completing his chore). Nevertheless, you are not violating the gist of my parenting program if you should choose to give your children RAK Chips for completing their chores on time. I'm all for leaning in the direction of positive reinforcement via praise and rewards.

4. IF WE DO INITIATE THIS PRACTICE, DO WE GIVE THEM ANY REMINDERS (REFER TO QUESTION #1)? CAN WE SUBSTITUTE A REMINDER FOR A RAK CHIP OR VICE VERSA? No. Please remember to "correctly and consistently" implement the FAMILY Rules parenting system as previously explained. Deviations from the order and structure of FAMILY Rules cause the program to collapse.

5. SHOULD WE REWARD A CHILD WITH GOOD GRADES WITH A SECOND CHILD WHO HAS LEARNING DISABILITIES? Once again, FAMILY Rules is flexible - not rigid. You can write rules that apply to both of your children's unique learning abilities as you see fit. Just make sure that you are both in agreement before you write down the rule. We are not going to short-change a child because they have a learning disability.

QUESTIONS ABOUT STRIKES:

1. IF THE CHILD IS DEFIANT AND NOT WILLING TO COMPLY WITH THE RULE, AT WHAT POINT IN TIME DOES THAT BECOME A STRIKE? When a child continues to defy a parent's authority in a "willful and prolonged manner" exceeding a period of 24 hours, they are pushing their luck and may receive a "Strike." Please go back to "Y" in Chapter Eight and read the difference between a "Strike" and a "Bad Hair Day." Also, check out the information on "Pop-Flies." In a nutshell, if a child makes it clear via their body language, words, and actions that Honolulu, Hawaii will freeze over first before they will obey their mom and dad, then they will receive a "Strike." Consult with an objective third party before giving your child a "strike" (i.e., Your counselor who uses FAMILY Rules, members of the free parent listserv, etc.).

QUESTIONS ABOUT YOUNGER CHILDREN:

1. IS IT OKAY TO NEGOTIATE HAVING THE PARENT HELP THE CHILD WHEN THE JOB IS TOO DIFFICULT

FOR A YOUNGER CHILD TO DO? Yes. However, to avoid this problem, consider creating two separate decks of Good Habit Cards. One deck of cards can be used by the older children and adults. The other deck of cards can be used by the younger children. This second deck of Good Habit Cards can consist of easier activities to do for the younger children. Finally, it's okay to jump in the tub the first couple of times, with your kids, and teach them how to clean it. After the initial instruction and assistance, they will be on their own.

2. WITH SMALL CHILDREN, IS IT WISE TO START THE FIRST FEW DAYS WITH DAILY TOKENS AND REWARDS BEFORE USING GOOD HABIT CARDS? Yes! Let them taste the sweet before they taste the sour. The Daily Tokens, Rewards, and RAK Chips help the children to buy into the FAMILY Rules parenting system. You can do this for one week when you first start the program in your home. It's called a "practice week." Once "practice week" is over, then the Good Habit Cards need to be handed out when they break rules or don't get their chore(s) done on time.

3. WHEN CHOOSING THE NUMBER OF GOOD HABIT CARDS, SHOULD AGE OF THE CHILDREN BE A FACTOR? No. The number of Good Habit Cards should be predetermined by the parent(s) ahead of time and placed within the parenthesis, next to the numbered rules, on the family's list of household rules (please see Appendix C). Keep in mind that you want to start off low (i.e., 1 to 3 cards) and work your way up from there. However, start with a large number of cards for the most important rules (i.e., "Obey all local, state, federal, and military laws," etc.). Don't forget, you can have two separate decks of good habit cards: one deck of Good Habit Cards for the older children and the adults and a different deck of Good Habit Cards for the younger children.

4. WHAT DO YOU DO WITH A YOUNG CHILD WHO DELIBERATELY BREAKS THE RULES JUST TO GET ANOTHER CARD? Some young children have fun doing the

Good Habit Cards and like the attention they receive in the process. Don't worry, the novelty of FAMILY Rules will wear off. They will stop. A positive alternative is to inform them that they can do chores around the home without breaking the rules. Offer them RAK chips for doing chores. Remind them that they lose their Daily Token if they break the rules or do not complete their chores on time. Finally, as previously mentioned, if a child continues to break a certain rule on a continuous basis, then consult with your spouse or partner and increase the number of Good Habit Cards.

5. SHOULD THE PARENT GIVE A YOUNG CHILD ALL 50 CARDS TO DO WITHIN A WEEK IF HE CONTINUES TO BREAK THE SAME RULES REPETITIVELY? Don't allow yourself to be manipulated by guilt. If your young child earns all 50 cards, then give them all 50 cards. Let them experience the natural consequences of their choices. Don't bail them out. Otherwise, you are enabling them to become a defiant monster. Remind them about "Strikes" and "Pop-Flies."

6. CAN YOU ADJUST THE CARDS FOR THE YOUNGER KIDS AND ONE FOR THE OLDER KIDS? Yes. You can have a deck of cards for the older kids and adults, as well as a deck of cards for the younger kids. You can also have a separate deck of cards for a child with a developmental disability. FAMILY Rules is flexible.

7. IS CRYING OVER A PULLED CARD CONSIDERED IMPOLITE? No! Defiance and rudeness are impolite! Let the tears flow without consequences; however, absolutely do not allow your child to guilt trip you with their tears. Remember "the two C- words" - correct and consistent implementation.

8. WHEN I WAS A KID, THERE WERE SOME INSTANCES WHEN IT SEEMED LIKE I JUST COULDN'T HELP CRYING. Me too!! I was a big cry baby sometimes. I still am at times. Don't repress your child's tears.

9. WHEN CHILDREN ARE OVERLY TIRED, SHOULD THE PARENT SHOW GRACE WHEN THEY ACT OUT? I don't know about you, but I can be a grouch sometimes when I'm tired. However, being tired is no excuse for inappropriate behaviors. It's okay to use your parental wisdom and bestow grace upon your children once in a while. Please be careful! Make sure you don't bestow too much continual grace upon your children. You may end up teaching them that it's okay to misbehave if they are tired. They need to get a grip on their emotions, even when they are tired.

10. IS IT OKAY TO REMIND THE KIDS ABOUT THEIR CHORES OR SHOULD WE ZIP A LIP SO THEY PRACTICE RESPONSIBILITY? A little bit of grace at first wouldn't hurt, but only for the first week or two of implementation at the most. Then zip the lip so they learn responsibility.

QUESTIONS ABOUT OLDER CHILDREN/ADOLESCENTS:

1. IF YOU HAVE 18-YEAR-OLD, MATURE, COMPLIANT, AND OBEDIENT TEENAGER WHO IS DOING WELL BEFORE *FAMILY RULES* WAS IMPLEMENTED, SHOULD YOU MAKE HIM ADHERE TO THE FAMILY SYSTEM, ESPECIALLY WITH TWO YOUNGER CHILDREN IN THE HOME? Your 18-year-old is an adult just like you. You are much older and hopefully were mature and compliant before FAMILY Rules was implemented in your home. Nevertheless, you are adhering to the FAMILY Rules parenting system and so should your 18-year-old son. When your children turn 18, they change to the status of a tenant. If the tenant doesn't obey the landlord's rules, the tenant is evicted. After the 18-year-old graduates from high school, he doesn't receive Daily Tokens or RAK chips, but he does receive the Good Habit Cards just like you do. Finally, if your 18-year-old is truly mature, compliant, and obedient, he or she won't have any problems with adhering to the FAMILY Rules system just like you have to do. Otherwise, if there is a problem with adhering to the FAMILY Rules system, then I guess the teenager wasn't so mature, compliant, and obedient after all.

2. IS THERE DANGER IN PARENTS USING THEIR AUTHORITY TO CHALLENGE THE WISHES OF A BRIGHT, RESPECTFUL, AND OLDER ADOLESCENT, FORCING HIM OR HER TO OBEY THEM? You are joking, right? Please reverse the question. "Is there danger in allowing a bright, respectful, and older adolescent to disobey his or her parents?" If this child is truly respectful, then this shouldn't really be an issue. They will naturally obey.

3. AT WHAT AGE SHOULD YOU ALLOW CHILDREN TO PURSUE THEIR OWN INTERESTS? You should be helping your children pursue their own interests from the time they are knee high to a grasshopper. Allow them to explore new areas of interest throughout their years at home as long as it is legal, ethical, and moral. However, if their own interests are alcohol, drugs, sex, and gangs, you better put your foot down.

4. SHOULD YOU HAVE DIFFERENT RULES REGARDING TELEPHONE USE FOR DIFFERENT CHILDREN, DEPENDING ON THE CHILD BEING COMPLIANT, HAVING GOOD GRADES, ETC.? As explained earlier in the book, FAMILY Rules is a skeletal framework of organization and structure for parenting. You get to slap the meat on the bones and skin around the meat that reflect your unique morals and values. No two families are the same. FAMILY Rules is flexible - not rigid. If you want to craft a family rule with your spouse that covers the above issue, go for it! You can word a rule anyway you want to as long as both parents are in agreement.

5. SHOULD YOU STOP THE *FAMILY RULES PARENTING* SYSTEM AT THE AGE OF 18 EVEN THOUGH THE CHILD IS STILL IN HIGH SCHOOL AND LIVING AT HOME? Earlier in the book, I talked about taking the medication until it is all gone. Please remember, the medication is not all gone until the last child turns 18, graduates from high school, and moves out of your home. At age 18, high school graduate or not, he or she becomes a tenant and you are the landlord. If the child continually disobeys you, evict him or her from the premises! You can't permit the 18-year-old to set a bad example for the young ones or else you will pay the price as they get older.

6. WE HAD AN INCIDENT TODAY WHERE ONE OF THE KIDS LEFT TRASH IN THE OFFICE. WHEN I QUESTIONED EACH OF MY FAMILY MEMBERS, EACH ONE REPLIED THAT HE OR SHE DID NOT LEAVE THE TRASH. CONSIDERING THE LACK OF OFFICE USE, THAT WRAPPER COULD HAVE BEEN SITTING THERE FOR DAYS AND KNOWING MY FAMILY, SOMEBODY PROBABLY REALLY CAN'T REMEMBER. WHAT SHOULD I DO? GIVE EVERYBODY A CARD OR LET IT GO? Let it go. Exercise grace and wisdom in this matter. If it were ketchup all over the kitchen floor and counters, you might want to turn up the heat — but not for one wrapper left a couple of days ago. Pick and choose your battles wisely.

7. WHEN A CHILD IS NOT ACTING CORRECTLY, HAS BROKEN A RULE, AND WANTS TO TALK AND EXPLAIN OR ASK QUESTIONS, DO YOU ALLOW THE CHILD TO TALK OR MAKE HIM OR HER WAIT UNTIL THE WEEKLY FAMILY MEETING? This is another opportunity for your use of parental wisdom, grace, and discretion. If your child is a defiant little brat who is simply engaged in disrespectful back talk, then make the child wait until after completing the Good Habit Cards. If he or she doesn't take the cards politely, keep on doubling them until the child is polite, but don't forget to give them a 10-minute cooling period in between the doubling of the cards. On the other hand, if your child is fairly mature and responsible and wouldn't normally want to talk or explain his or her behavior, then you best give him or her your ear for a few minutes — not hours. You might possibly have made a mistake in judgment. Be fair, but don't be an enabler of parental disrespect.

QUESTIONS ABOUT PARENTAL CONSEQUENCES:

1. CAN A PARENT BE GROUNDED? Yes. If a parent breaks a family rule, then he or she is grounded until the Good Habit Cards are completed. The parent needs to be working on the cards or sitting in the bedroom until they are ready to complete their cards.

2. WHAT HAPPENS IF ONE PARENT REQUESTS A JOB TO BE DONE IMMEDIATELY THAT CAUSES EVERYONE ELSE TO BREAK ONE OR MORE RULES, SUCH AS BEING ON TIME?

If a parent pulls rank and places a demand on the family that causes them to break a rule, such as being on time, then they are off the hook. Otherwise, we have a pretty unfair and inconsistent parent at the helm who needs a reality check.

3. WOULD IT BE A MINOR INFRACTION TO ROLL THROUGH A STOP SIGN IF YOU WERE GOING SLOW? The law is the law.

A policeman would give you a ticket for this offense except in New Jersey. In New Jersey, motorists speed down the side street and through the stop sign just to get in front of you. They don't know what the word "stop" means in New Jersey. If your parents have a rule on the list about obeying all laws, then you will receive the number of Good Habit Cards found in the parenthesis adjacent to the numbered rule. Parents receive cards too if they roll through stop signs.

4. IF A PARENT IS GROUNDED, DOES HE OR SHE GET TO TAKE A LONG- DISTANCE PHONE CALL FROM MOM? No.

The grounded parent should complete any Good Habit Cards first or sit in the bedroom until he or she decides to complete the cards. No phone calls until the cards are done. If you get to deviate from the FAMILY Rules parenting system, then so do your kids. Think this one through. The whole system will collapse if you start doing this. Please implement the system "correctly and consistently" in your home (i.e., "The two C-words"). Don't make me hunt you down.

5. DO PARENTS HAVE TO GO TO LONG-TERM RESIDENTIAL TREATMENT? No. Long-term residential treatment is only for

children who disobey their parents over and over again. However, I have met many parents who wouldn't mind being sent to long-term residential treatment just to get away from everyone.

QUESTIONS ABOUT TWO HOMES DUE TO A DIVORCE:

1. WHAT SHOULD OR COULD WE DO TO MAKE THE TRANSITION SMOOTHER IF THE *FAMILY RULES* SYSTEM IS ALREADY BEING DONE IN MY EX-SPOUSE'S HOME FOR THE CHILD? Great question! Unfortunately, divorces stink for everyone, especially the children. They end up being shuffled between two homes and receive mixed messages galore. This becomes really complicated when the ex-spouses are at war with one another. The children end up in the crossfire. Fortunately, I have worked with several ex-spouses who were willing to remain cordial with one another for the sake of their children. I have had plenty of blended families in my private practice setting and at my seminars who worked together to create a list of rules equally applied in both homes. As a result, the children are provided with much more consistency between the two homes and their transition becomes smoother. If you can attend counseling and avoid a divorce, please do it. If not, please work together with your ex-spouse to develop a list of FAMILY Rules that will be implemented in both homes. By the way, the Los Angeles Superior Family Court mandates divorced couples to use this parenting program as a part of their divorce settlement (Please read Chapter 12).

2. IN A TWO-HOUSEHOLD SITUATION, IF MAYBE 30 OF THE CARDS ARE THE SAME, CAN YOU TAKE ALONG THOSE 30 CARDS TO THE OTHER HOUSEHOLD? Yes. Consistency between the two homes is a must for the sake of the children. If you can maintain a cordial relationship with your ex-spouse for the sake of your children, please do so. This way your children can't divide and conquer.

3. IN A DIVORCED (TWO-FAMILY) SITUATION, COULD A CHILD DRAW TWO CARDS AT ONE HOME, AND WIND UP GOING TO THE OTHER HOME AND DRAW 50 CARDS THERE, TOO? If both parents are working together to maintain consistency between the two homes, then the answer to this question is yes. You simply take your 50 cards to the other parent's home and work on them there or stay in your bedroom until you're willing to get them done. However, if both parents are using the FAMILY Rules parenting system but they aren't working together to maintain consistency between the two homes, then the answer to this question is no. Unfortunately, you will have 50 cards to do at both homes.

QUESTIONS ABOUT SINGLE PARENTS:

1. IS *FAMILY* **JUST FOR MARRIED COUPLES OR CAN SINGLE PARENTS IMPLEMENT IT IN THEIR HOME TOO?** Forgive me. I know I keep talking in terms of couples. Yes. Single parents can implement FAMILY Rules in their home just as successfully as a married couple. Please assume that anything I write about married couples applies to you, too. However, since you don't have a spouse to consult with, you might want to consider consulting with an adult who's judgment you trust (i.e., a neighbor, family member, coworker, pastor, rabbi, milkman, etc.).

A QUESTION ABOUT SCHEDULING FAMILY SEMINARS:

1. HOW DO I SCHEDULE A *FAMILY Rules* **SEMINAR IN MY COMMUNITY?** Contact me ("Dr. J.") via the following phone number: 1-541-956-8585. You may also contact me by my e-mail address (DrJ@Family-Rules.com). Finally, don't forget to check out the FAMILY Rules website (www.Family-Rules.com) to see if a FAMILY Rules seminar is already scheduled in your community. My seminars are normally posted on my website at least two to three months in advance.

A QUESTION ABOUT STARTING A FAMILY RULES SUPPORT GROUP:

1. HOW DO I START A *FAMILY RULES* **SUPPORT GROUP MEETING IN MY COMMUNITY?** Contact me at my private practice phone number, e-mail address, or website listed above. Check out the website because we might have an already established

FAMILY support group in your community. If you want to start a support group, we will list it on the FAMILY Rules website.

QUESTIONS ABOUT COUNSELORS WHO USE "FAMILY Rules":

1. WE WOULD LIKE OUR THERAPIST TO BECOME A COUNSELOR WHO USES "FAMILY-RULES." HOW CAN THIS HAPPEN? Have your counselor contact me at the FAMILY Rules, Inc. via my office number (1-541-956-8585), e-mail address (DrJ@Family-Rules.com), or have the counselor check out my website (www.Family-Rules.com).

2. WE ARE SEEING A COUNSELOR AND WOULD LIKE TO IMPLEMENT *FAMILY RULES* IN OUR HOME. WHAT IF OUR COUNSELOR ADVISES US NOT TO DO SO? Your counselor knows your family situation better than I do. Please review chapters 4 through 7 with your counselor. If you have unresolved issues in your life, marriage, or family, you had better wait to implement FAMILY Rules in your home. However, this is America and you do have freedom of choice. If your counselor leans in the direction of democratic parenting (i.e., King Arthur's round table), you can choose to see a new counselor that offers a different approach. This is your consumer right. Just go to my website (www.Family-Rules.com) and find a counselor who uses Family Rules in your community or near your community.

Part 5

Appendices

~Appendix A~

How to Become a Counselor who uses FAMILY Rules

If you are a lay counselor or a licensed clinician (i.e., LPC, LMFT, Licensed Clinical Social Worker, Psychologist, Psychiatrist, etc.) and/or an ordained clergyperson, and you want to become a "Counselor who uses FAMILY Rules," please contact Dr. Matthew A. Johnson via the following options:

Office: 1-(541)-956-8585
Fax: 1-(541)-955-7165
E-mail: DrJ@Family-Rules.com

What are the benefits of becoming a "Counselor who uses FAMILY Rules?" Well, to begin with, you get to receive very practical training that will help you teach the order and structure that most families need. Second, as a "Counselor who uses FAMILY Rules," you get to have your name placed on the FAMILY Rules website referral page for free. Readers of the book, "Positive Parenting with a Plan (Grades K-12): FAMILY Rules" will be able to access the website and find your name and office location. You will be allowed to have a link from the FAMILY Rules website to your website provided your website is ethical and is done in good taste. Finally, you will be able to get families in and out of your office quicker (2-6 months) which will please the managed care companies. Prolonged therapy sessions will become a thing of the past. Yes, this will eat into your business profits initially; however, the increased number of referrals you will receive as a result usually makes up the difference.

Training consists of you're attending a six-hour seminar. Dr. Matthew A. Johnson is willing to travel to your community and train multiple clinicians and/or clergy or you can contact him and travel with a group of clinicians and/or clergy to Grants Pass,

Oregon. This may help you write off a part of your southern Oregon vacation. There's great fishing and hiking in Oregon! Lots to see and do. Talk with your Certified Public Accountant (CPA) about the tax laws because they are constantly changing. Finally, you can simply go to www.Family-Rules.com and click on "Future Seminars" to find out where and when "Dr. J." will be speaking in a city near you. His speaking engagements are normally posted on the website at least two to three months in advance.

Note: If you're a parent who would like to find a counselor who uses FAMILY Rules, simply go to my website (www.Family-Rules.com) and click on "Locate Counselors Who Use FAMILY Rules". If you already have a counselor and you would like them to consider using FAMILY Rules as a part of their practice, simply direct them to my website or have them read this book.

~Appendix B-1~

An Adolescent's Perspective about Residential Treatment

Before I went to long-term residential treatment in the South Pacific, I would explode with anger at almost anything. This I attributed to drugs, which I did every day during the last summer before I left home for Paradise Cove. I stole money from home. I smoked weed and drank a lot. My parents did not know about this. I was also smoking cigarettes for about six years. I didn't care about anything. Whenever something didn't go my way, I got mad and yelled and hit things or I ran away. My older brother and I got in a lot of fights. When he told on me for smoking, I ran downstairs and got a baseball bat and hit him three times. Mom had the police called, and we fought until the police showed up. I went to jail overnight, since formal charges were made against me. I got kicked out of school because of drugs. That was all my life revolved around.

When my parents first sent me to long-term residential treatment, I was so mad at them that I just wanted them to die or something. I couldn't see the things that I was doing when I yelled at them. It just made me hate them more. As I was being escorted out the front door of my parent's home to catch my plane, I yelled at them that I hated them and that they would never see me again.

While I was in residential treatment, I learned a lot about the pain that I caused my parents and the pain that I didn't deal with myself. This also opened me up to see and change what I was doing to make my life better. It helped me to see that I didn't have to be a failure and a messed up person. I could live happy and deal with things that bother me in a different way.

Since I got home three months ago, things have been great and I am building more and more trust every day. I am really happy for once.

I am building my relationships stronger every day and we all get along. I am having fun with my family.

Well, now I thank my parents for sending me there and loving me enough to do that. I know that it was as hard for them to send me there as it was for me to be there. All in all, I love them for doing it. Going to long-term residential treatment did save my life. I was in the fast lane and heading for a ditch a couple of times. I did almost die. I almost died from alcohol and driving high; also just smoking cigarettes (which I quit).

I think that if your child is out of control in your eyes then it would be good, for both the child and the parents, for the child to be treated. I know that there are also things that you can't or don't want to see your child doing. There is probably a lot you don't see and know about. You could save your child's life and improve your life. You can help your child.

~Appendix B-2~

An Adolescent's Perspective About Being Escorted to Residential Treatment

Dear Dr. J.

I hate you! You screwed up my life and me.

Ever get a letter like that from someone you escorted to a program? I'll be honest, I wanted to write a letter like that, but I guess I never got to it. I'm glad that I didn't though. This program has helped me out a lot and I don't regret having to come here anymore.

Anyway, I met the latest **VICTIM** you brought here. Guess what? He's in my family. I remember him from home, also. We didn't get along too well, but since I've changed we seem to get along fine now.

So how are things with you? I'm doing well here. Still level 3. I keep choosing out of the Accountability Seminar, but will have another chance soon, and this time I should do well. I was Assistant Family Leader for awhile which helped me out a lot, but no longer do I have the position, which is fine with me.

Well that's it I guess. I just wrote to say "hi." Adios! Have a happy Thanksgiving!

Your Friend,
(Name withheld to protect confidentiality.)

~Appendix C~

A Sample List of FAMILY Rules

The _____ FAMILY Rules

**Good Habit
Cards**

(50)   1. Obey all local, state, federal, and military laws.

(1)   2. Do what you are asked to do immediately without complaining.

(1)   3. "No!" means "No!" Don't ask again.

(1)   4. Don't interrupt others. Wait your turn to talk.

(10)   5. Treat people and animals with respect (e.g., no verbal or physical abuse of others).

(3)   6. Obey all authority at home, school, church, synagogue, and in the community.

(2)   7. When you are angry, talk with an adult. Don't act out your anger inappropriately.

(1)   8. No inappropriate facial expressions or body gestures.

(5)   9. No stealing (i.e., borrowing without permission from the owner is stealing).

(10)   10. You must receive parental permission before you go anywhere at any time.

(10)   11. You must stay where you receive permission to go. If plans change, call and ask parents.

(50)   12. Never run away from anywhere unless you have been abducted and/or are in danger.

(3)   13. No swearing or talking about inappropriate subject matter.

(10)   14. Parents' room is off limits. Knock and ask for parental permission before entering.

(2)   15. No eavesdropping on private parental conversations.

(20)   16. No lying, sneaking, or cheating (i.e., dishonest behaviors will not be tolerated).

(50) 17. No destruction of property regardless of who it belongs to.

(5) 18. No getting up at night to eat, watch TV, or to use the telephone or computer or play video games.

(3) 19. No eating certain foods when it has been explained to you that you are not to eat it.

(30) 20. No playing with matches or lighters (Use of such items with parental permission only).

(2) 21. Do not overuse your bathroom time or lock the door to keep others out. Be considerate.

(5) 22. Participate appropriately in family devotions and meetings (e.g., no joking, no mocking).

(10) 23. No use of telephone, cell phone, video games, or computer without parental permission and parental supervision.

(2) 24. Do not keep others waiting when it is time to leave to go somewhere. Be on time.

(20) 25. No use of make up and/or jewelry without parental permission.

(1) 26. Always sleep with sheet on bed. Don't sleep in your regular street clothes.

(1) 27. No dishes, food, or trash left in the living room or your bedroom.

(1) 28. Eat with good manners.

(50) 29. No sexual activities with another person unless you are married to them.

(10) 30. Follow all school rules, obey all school personnel, and be on time to school and all classes.

(5) 31. No listening to inappropriate music or watching inappropriate videos or movies or inappropriate texting.

(5) 32. No faking sick or insisting on staying home from school.

(10) 33. Bring homework home from school. Don't forget!

(10) 34. Do all homework on time and turn it in on time.

(2) 35. Don't leave clothes, shoes, lunch utensils, or other personal belongings at school.

(10) 36. Obey all bus rules.

(5) 37. Behave appropriately at church/synagogue and follow parental directions. Sit with parents in church/synagogue.

(2) 38. Behave appropriately in the car. Don't play inside or on top of the car.

(1) 39. Complete all daily and weekly chores on time.

(3) 40. Attend all scheduled appointments on time and without complaining.

(10) 41. Take all medication as prescribed.

(→) 42. You shall receive the following rewards and consequences for grades: A+ = \$8; A = \$7; A- = \$6 B+ = \$5; B = \$4; B- = \$3; C+ = \$2; C = \$1; C- = 0; D+ = 4 cards; D= 8 cards; D- = 12 cards; F= 20 cards.

(→) 43. School year curfews are: 9:00 P.M. (Sun - Thurs nights) and 11:00 P.M. (Fri & Sat nights). Summer curfews are: 10:00 P.M. (Sun - Thurs nights) and 12 midnight (Fri & Sat nights). You will receive 5 cards for the first 15 minutes being late. After the first 15 minutes, you will receive 1 card for every minute you are late. The satellite that sets the cell phone clock is the official timekeeper.

(10) 44. No hitting, kicking, scratching, pushing, shoving, fighting, etc. If you are caught arguing and/or fighting, everyone involved will receive cards. Parents will not be detectives.

(50) 45. Any attempt to tamper with the family rules, good habit cards, daily and weekly chores lists, and/or the rewards list will result in receiving all 50 cards.

~Appendix D~

A Sample List of Good Habit Cards

1.   Scrub tub and tile in downstairs bathroom.
2.   Scrub tub and tile in upstairs bathroom.
3.   Clean toilet in downstairs bathroom.
4.   Clean toilet in upstairs bathroom.
5.   Clean floor and wall in downstairs bathroom.
6.   Clean floor and wall in upstairs bathroom.
7.   Clean washer and dryer.
8.   Clean refrigerator.
9.   Dust and polish all furniture in the living room.
10. Dust and polish all furniture in the dining room.
11. Clean windows in the living room.
12. Clean windows in the dining room.
13. Clean windows in the bedrooms.
14. Clean freezer.
15. Vacuum the living room.
16. Vacuum the bedrooms.
17. Sweep and mop the kitchen floor.
18. Clean out the inside of mom's car.
19. Clean out the inside of dad's car.
20. Wash mom's car.
21. Wash dad's car.
22. Shovel/rake/sweep parking area.
23. Twenty-five pushups and twenty-five sit ups.
24. Fifty jumping jacks.
25. Remove all DVDs from the cabinet. Clean and dust them and put them back in alphabetical order.
26. Shovel/rake/sweep next door neighbor's parking area.
27. Dust and clean fireplace area.
28. Clean up all the dog poop in the yard and throw away in a garbage bag.
29. Wash, dry, and put away dishes.

30. Clean microwave oven (inside and outside).
31. Clean all mirrors in the house.
32. Clear snow and ice from the walkway.
33. Dust all pictures.
34. Dust all books.
35. Write, "I will not break the rules" (100 times).
36. Do a daily chore for a sibling.
37. Clean and polish silver.
38. Clean all sinks in the house.
39. Write a one-page essay on why you shouldn't have broken the rule you just broke.
40. Remove sheets and blankets from your bed. Wash and dry them. Put them back on your bed.
41. Remove sheets and blankets from your parents' bed. Wash, dry, and put back on their bed.
42. Vacuum hallway and stairs.
43. Clean laundry room floor.
44. Clean garage.
45. Write an e-mail to an extended family member (e.g., grandma, grandpa, aunt, uncle, cousin, etc.).
46. Bake a cake or a batch of cookies.
47. Walk the dog.
48. Give the dog a bath.
49. Dust baseboard heaters.
50. Straighten out coat/boot closet(s).
51. Play a board game with one or more family members.
52. Bake a batch of cookies for the family.
53. Shoot baskets in the drive way.
54. Kick the soccer ball around in the yard.
55. Play catch with a football, baseball, softball, or frisbee.
56. Ride your bike around the neighborhood.
57. Read a book to a younger sibling.
58. Ask the neighbor if you can help them do something for a half-hour.
59. Read a passage a scripture selected by a parent and write a one page essay on how it applies to life.
60. Give everyone in the family a genuine hug.

61. Say one nice thing to everyone in the family.
62. Write down three things you like about yourself and three things you want to change about yourself.
63. Play a video game with a parent.
64. Talk with a parent or neighbor about what they do for a living and how they ended up doing it.
65. Write a one page essay on what you want to be when you grow up and how you plan to get there.
66. Listen to classical music.
67. Listen to spiritual music.
68. Listen to a self-affirmation tape or CD.
69. Write ten self-affirmations and read them out loud.
70. Memorize and verse selected by a parent and repeat it out loud.
71. Memorize a hymn and sing it out loud.
72. Play a musical instrument.
73. Study foreign language self-help book.
74. Color, draw, paint, or sketch.
75. Work with play-dough or clay.
76. Knit or crochet.
77. Go outside in the yard, look up at the sky, and think about why you're here.
78. Talk with an adult about why they think we are here.
79. Plan a family vacation.
80. Plan a day trip or weekend trip.

NOTE: When a parent or child breaks a rule or doesn't get a daily or weekly chore done on time, we consider that a bad habit. Therefore, we are going to give them an opportunity to learn one or more good habits to replace the bad habit with. This is not called "Punishment Parenting with a Plan." It's actually called "Positive Parenting with a Plan." Discipline comes from the root word - "Disciple." We need to teach, guide, direct, correct, and instruct. Punishment lasts for a moment. However, replacing bad habits with good habits will change a child for a lifetime. With this program, we are exchanging good habits for bad habits. We are not punishing them. Create a balance between the chore-like cards and the fun ones.

~Appendix E~

A Sample List of Chores

Daily Chores

1. Eat breakfast before you go to school or before you go out with friends on the weekend.
2. Make your bed in the morning before you leave for school or leave the house on the weekend.
3. Brush teeth and comb your hair in the morning before leaving for school.
4. Take a shower nightly before bedtime and use lotion on skin to keep from drying out.
5. Feed and water the dog/cat by 5:00 P.M.
6. Clean dishes immediately after dinner.

Weekly Chores

1. Clean and vacuum your bedroom by 12:00 P.M. on Saturday.
2. Take garbage cans out to the street on Thursday evening before bed time (garbage is picked up on Friday morning).
3. Cook and have dinner ready by 5:30 P.M. on Tuesday evening.
4. Split and stack wood immediately after school on Monday. Must be done before dinner.

~Appendix F~

A Sample List of Rewards

Tokens

(2)	1.	Ice-cream cone at the ice-cream parlor of your choice.
(3)	2.	DVD Rental.
(25)	3.	Pizza party with five friends.
(15)	4.	Slumber party.
(70)	5.	Tennis Shoes of Your Choice.
(12)	6.	Music CD (must be approved by parent).
(7)	7.	Roller skating.
(10)	8.	Hat.
(40)	9.	Concert with a friend.
(15)	10.	Baseball game with a friend.
(15)	11.	Hockey game with a friend.
(25)	12.	Dinner at your favorite restaurant.
(100)	13.	Bike.
(→)	14.	Toy (8 tokens for every $10 increase in price per toy).
(200)	15.	Solo trip to a relatives' home.
(30)	16.	Fishing trip.
(600)	17.	Snow machine.
(200)	18.	Your own bedroom.
(10)	19.	A two-hour extension on your curfew, providing the extension is within the law.
($$)	20.	Money for tokens to be determined by the parent(s).

NOTE: Although you are the benevolent dictators in the home and determine what the rules, chores, and "Good Habit Cards" are going to be, if you're wise, you'll seek input from your children concerning what they would like to see go on the Rewards List. You may think you know what motivates your child but you might be surprised at what they would like to have you put on the list. Even though you're seeking their input, you still have final say as to what actually goes on the Rewards List. By the way, most families across the USA assign a one-dollar value per Daily Token. Therefore, a two-dollar ice cream cone will require two Daily Tokens. A fifteen-dollar music CD will require fifteen Daily Tokens. Finally, with the big-ticket items, most parents decide to cut some slack on how many tokens they will require. In other words, although a pair of real nice tennis shoes may actually cost one-hundred dollars, the parents may only require seventy Daily Tokens instead of one-hundred Daily Tokens. This gives the child more incentive to work harder to save up for the big-ticket items. That means they're behaving and getting their chores done on time. That means you're happy. That means it's worth doing it.

~Appendix G~

"P3" Preferred Therapeutic Treatment Programs

"P3" Preferred Programs: The five programs listed in this appendix are preferred by Dr. Matthew A. Johnson because they use "Positive Parenting with a Plan" ("P3") either as (1) their core treatment model, and/or as (2) a part of their parenting training model, and/or as (3) a part of their aftercare model.

Note: If you believe your therapeutic treatment setting qualifies for "P3" preferred status, please contact Dr. Johnson.

Cherry Gulch Therapeutic Boarding School ("P3" Preferred)

Cherry Gulch is an award winning ranch-style, therapeutic boarding school designed specifically for 10-14 year old boys. Cherry Gulch's supportive, encouraging and respect-based approach is designed to build students up—rather than tear them down. Cherry Gulch is passionate about providing early intervention and prevention to help boys reach their full potential and become well-rounded, pro-social young men. We are dedicated to providing outstanding therapeutic and academic services to students and their families. This is accomplished in the context of a safe environment working toward **"Building Brighter Tomorrows for the Boys of Today."**

P.O. Box 678
Emmett, Idaho 83617

Office: 1-208-365-3437, Ext. 502
Fax: 1-208-365-7235
E-Mail: info@cherrygulch.org
Website: www.CherryGulch.org

Copper Canyon Academy
("P3" Preferred)

Parents looking for help outside the home often feel uncertain, scared, and many times doubtful about the future. The decision to place a child outside the home is one of stress, tension, and turmoil. Copper Canyon Academy girls boarding school is truly a trailhead to success. We understand your concerns and together we can face the difficult challenge of turning these teens around. The staff at Copper Canyon Academy is comprised of seasoned and well trained professionals experienced at working with adolescents. Copper Canyon Academy boarding schools for girls assists families and gives them the reassurance that there is a wonderful future ahead for their child and family. Copper Canyon Academy is a boarding school for girls with behavioral problems, emotional problems or learning problems. Nestled in a scenic Central Arizona valley Copper Canyon Academy allows junior high and high school young women the opportunity to progress to their fullest potential. We believe that by combining a warm, caring, structured environment, students will develop self-esteem, self-awareness, self-reliance and self management.

P.O. Box 230
Rimrock, Arizona 86335

Office: 1-928-567-1322
Fax: 1-928-567-1323
E-Mail: admissions@coppercanyonacademy.com
Website: www.CopperCanyonAcademy.com

Abundant Life and Adolescent Growth, Inc.
("P3" Preferred)

Our programs are licensed by the State of California. We provide a 24-hour supervised treatment in residence program and a partial day/intensive outpatient treatment program designed for adolescents (ages 12-17) who have found themselves in crisis. The behavioral manifestations demonstrated can include, but are not limited to, drug abuse, eating problems, self-abusive behavior (cutting), academic problems, acute depression, and violent behaviors. The purpose of the program is to therapeutically challenge inappropriate cognitive and behavioral responses. We teach our clients socially fitting problem solving skills through participation in daily psychotherapy. As we grow up, we acquire various beliefs and self-statements that are faulty and distort the truth. These beliefs and assumptions contribute to the feelings of fear, sadness, and anger which produce a behavioral response of addiction, self-abuse, and anti-social behaviors. At Abundant Life, our goal is to examine and replace faulty beliefs, thereby producing emotions of hopefulness, thus making a link back to the truth.

6055 East Washington Boulevard, Suite 240
Commerce, California 90040

Office: 1-323-722-8950
Fax: 1-323-722-8952
E-Mail: information@adolescentgrowth.com
Website: www.AdolescentGrowth.com

National House of Hope-Orlando
("P3" Preferred)

The National House of Hope-Orlando is a non-denominational, not-for-profit organization established to serve as a catalyst to the development of a network of Houses of Hope around the USA, a Christian residential program for troubled boys and girls ages 14-17, across the country. This work is based upon Biblical principles, proven to provide both workable and successful solutions in restoring troubled teens and their families, resulting in these teens becoming solid citizens and effective, contributing members of society. Dr. Johnson serves on their Advisory Board.

PO Box 560484
Orlando, Florida 32856
Office: 1-407-843-8686

Fax: 1-407-422-3816
E-Mail: houseofhopebren@aol.com
Website: www.NationalHouseOfHope.org

Family Intervention Specialists, Inc.
("P3" Preferred)

Family Intervention Specialists, Inc. is a 501(c) (3) non-profit corporation registered in the State of Georgia. We provide CORE Services to Children and Adolescents as well as CORE services to Adults. We have clinicians in 20 counties in the Metropolitan Atlanta area. We are also a provider of intensive Family Intervention. Intensive Family Intervention (IFI) is an intensive family- and community-based treatment that addresses multiple determinants of serious antisocial behavior in juvenile offenders. The approach of the intensive family intervention views individuals as being nested within a complex network of interconnected systems that encompass individual, family, peers, school, neighborhood, and indigenous support network. To facilitate change, intervention may be necessary in any one or a combination of these systems. Family Intervention Specialists, Inc. works with clients who have high acuity mental health and substance abuse issues. The focus is on co-occurring disorders. All programs are research based and outcome driven and include Multi-Systemic Therapy (MST), Brief Strategic Family Therapy (BSFT), the Matrix Model for both Adult and Adolescent substance abuse, the Nurturing Parent program, Celebrating Families, Strengthening Families and Positive Parenting with a Plan. We practice Trauma-Focused Therapy (TFT). We also have an EMDR therapist and a Certified Play Therapist.

127 Enterprise Path, Suite 402
Hiram, Georgia, 30141

Office: 1-770-222-6622
Fax: 1-770-234-4202
E-Mail: David.Anthony@fisinc.org
Website: www.fisinc.org

~Appendix H~

Great Resources to Help Find Therapeutic Boarding Schools, Group Homes, Residential Treatment Facilities, and Therapeutic Wilderness Programs

The National Association of Therapeutic Schools and Programs (NATSAP)

The National Association of Therapeutic Schools and Programs (NATSAP) was created in January of 1999 to serve as a national resource for programs and professionals assisting young people beleaguered by emotional and behavioral difficulties. The Association is governed by an elected, volunteer Board of Directors comprised of representatives from the NATSAP membership.

NATSAP publishes a directory annually to inform professionals, programs, and families about the many residential placement alternatives available to help struggling young people. Listed alphabetically, the schools and programs in the Program Directory are diverse. The directory's listings offer a wide range of programmatic types, lengths of stay, and services to meet the needs of a variety of troubled young people.

Matching the services of a particular school or program to the specific needs of a young person is arguably the most important decision that will ever be made on behalf of that young person. The NATSAP directory is not intended by itself to supply enough information to make a placement. NATSAP encourages programs, professionals, and families to have appropriate academic and psychological testing conducted and to use multiple informational resources before suggesting or pursuing a placement for any young person in any program.

Professionals and parents seeking information on placement for a young person experiencing difficulties have access to the NATSAP Directory on this website. Searching the directory will return each relevant program's basic information, including contact sources.

Website: www.NATSAP.org/search.asp

INDEPENDENT EDUCATIONAL CONSULTANTS ASSOCIATION (IECA)

Independent Educational Consultants are ethically bound to be non-biased. Some of them travel 180 days a year and visit literally hundreds of schools and therapeutic programs. They can assess your child's needs and make recommendations based on the level and type of care that will be most likely to benefit your child. Their reputation is on the line when they make recommendations. They usually only recommend programs that they have actually toured and know some of the key personnel. They can boil down the thousands of options to just a few schools or programs that they believe will be the best fit for your child.

To find members of the Independent Educational Consultants Association you can visit their website www.IECAonline.com and then search by state and area of specialty for an educational consultant. If there is not an educational consultant in your area don't be alarmed most educational consultants have national practices and will be able to help you even if you live in another state.

IECA National Office
3251 Old Lee Highway, Suite 510
Fairfax, Virginia 22030

Office: 1-703-591-4850
Website: www.iecaonline.org

THE PARENT EMPOWERMENT HANDBOOK
(A Resource of Places for Struggling Teens)

This handbook contains the information about schools and programs that range in structure from light to highly structured therapeutic and emotional growth wilderness and residential schools and programs. They generally work with students who range from mild behavioral issues to severe acute psychiatric issues. The schools selected have been voted on for inclusion by the top 100 Independent Educational Consultants in the country. This handbook also includes the contact information on the 100 Educational Consultants that received the highest ratings from the schools and programs that were included in the handbook the year before. The books can be ordered at www.strugglingteens. com this website also contains lots of useful free information about therapeutic schools and programs.

Office: 1-208-267-5550
Website: www.StrugglingTeens.com

The Greenwood Institute and The Greenwood Association Classification System (GACS)

The Greenwood Association Classification System for parents is an online learning tool that helps parents assess what level of care their son or daughter needs and whether their problems are more accurately categorized as socially maladjusted or emotionally maladjusted. The GACS system teaches you how to determine what level of care and type of program is most well suited for your child's needs. This system will help you become a better consumer of therapeutic schools and programs.

Office: 1-813-254-5303
Website: www.GreenwoodInstituteOnline.com

The Outdoor Behavioral Healthcare
Industry Council (OBHIC)

OBHIC is an organization of behavioral health providers who are committed to the utilization of outdoor modalities to assist young people and their families to make positive change. Their membership includes a number of therapeutic wilderness programs and outdoor adventure based therapeutic programs. OBHIC's mission is to unite its members and to promote the common good of our programs standards and our industry at large. This mission has been accomplished by developing and policing the standards of excellence for members.

Office: 1-541-926-7252
Website: www.obhic.com

SMALL BOARDING SCHOOL ASSOCIATION (SBSA)

When it comes to boarding schools small is better or at least that is the belief of the Small Boarding School Association. The SBSA website contains a list of member programs and educational consultants that are members of the association. According to SBSA to be a small boarding school you have to have 200 or fewer students. Remember that if you are using a boarding school as the teeth to your FAMILY Rules program you should realize that your child will likely need something more than a traditional boarding school and you should be looking for a therapeutic program or a program for special needs students. Most of the members of SBSA are traditional boarding schools that are unlikely to offer the level of therapeutic services that your child will need.

Website: www.SmallBoardingSchools.org

The Vincent-Curtis Educational Register

This is the oldest free guide to Independent Schools and Independent Camps for Families with Boys and Girls.

Office: 1-508-457-6473
Website: www.TheEducationalRegister.com

Peterson's Private Secondary Schools

Peterson's Private Secondary Schools lists more than 1,600 schools in the U.S. and Abroad. They have a reference guide you can order or you can search online.

Website: www.Petersons.com/PrivateSchools

The Association of Boarding Schools (TABS)

The TABS website and directory does a good job of laying out the advantages of boarding school and presents some research findings that highlights the benefits of a boarding school education. You can search online for the traditional boarding schools that are members of TABS or you can order their free directory. Keep in mind that none of the members of TABS work with students with significant behavioral and emotional problems. Your best resource for Therapeutic schools is the National Association of Therapeutic Schools And Programs. If your child has gotten three STRIKES and you are using my program it is very likely he or she will need a smaller, more structured, supportive, therapeutic environment.

Website: www.BoardingSchool.org

Job Corps

Job Corps is a **free** education and training program that helps young people learn a career, earn a high school diploma or GED, and find and keep a good job. For eligible youth at least 16 years of age, Job Corps provides the all-around skills needed to succeed in a career and in life. Job Corps currently trains more than 60,000 students at 122 centers nationwide. Through a nationwide network of campuses, Job Corps offers a comprehensive array of career development services to at-risk young women and men, ages 16 to 24, to prepare them for successful careers. Job Corps employs a holistic career development training approach which integrates the teaching of academic, vocational, employability skills and social competencies through a combination of classroom, practical and based learning experiences to prepare youth for stable, long-term, high-paying jobs.

Office: 1-800-733-5627
Website: www.JobCorps.gov

Focus on the Family

A Christian based organization that provides educational resources to assist parents in raising children. They also provide referral information to assist you in contacting Christian counselors in your area. When you call them, ask for the counseling department and tell them that Dr. Johnson, author of "Positive Parenting with a Plan" sent you to them.

Office: 1-800-232-6459
Website: www.Family.org

Catholic Charities USA

Catholic Charities agencies serve people of all faiths. They provide a wide range of services - housing, emergency services, health care, child care, adoption, and other critical services. For information on how you can get the help you need or to learn about local programs and services, volunteer opportunities, job openings, media contacts, and other information, please contact your local agency.

Office: 1-703-549-1390
Website: www.CatholicCharitiesUSA.org/Page.aspx?pid=292

Latter Day Saints (LDS) Family Services

The Latter Day Saints (LDS) Family Services is a private, nonprofit organization established in 1919. LDS Family Services has 62 offices throughout the United States, Canada, Great Britain, Australia, New Zealand, and Japan. The professional staff have at minimum, a masters degree in the behavioral sciences. To find a comprehensive list of LDS Family Services agencies in the United States, Canada, and abroad, please to the website listed immediately below:

Website: www.ProvidentLiving.org/ses/emotionalhealth/contact/1,12169,2128-1,00.html

Association of Jewish Family and Children's Agencies

The Association of Jewish Family and Children's Agencies is the membership organization of over 140 Jewish Family and Children's Agencies and specialized human service Agencies throughout the United States and Canada. The ASSOCIATION is a vital force in Jewish life; providing social and human services to the most vulnerable in our community. We help Jews in need here at home.

Website: www.ajfca.org

InterfaithFamily.com

InterfaithFamily.com, Inc. is the online resource for interfaith families exploring Jewish life and the grass-roots advocate for a welcoming Jewish community. This resource is for everyone touched by interfaith relationships where one partner is Jewish, on every topic of interest to them, and for everyone who works with and cares about them. InterfaithFamily.com empowers interfaith families to make Jewish choices for themselves and their children, and encourages the Jewish community to welcome interfaith families. We believe that maximizing the number of interfaith families who find fulfillment in Jewish life and raise their children as Jews is essential to the future strength and vitality of the Jewish community. Through our website, and other programs, we provide useful educational information and resources, connect interfaith families to each other and to local Jewish communities, and advocate for inclusive attitudes, policies and practices. InterfaithFamily.com produces the only Jewish resources and content in the world, either online or in print, that reach out directly to interfaith families. We deliver helpful, non-judgmental information and a warm welcome that can be accessed privately, at any time convenient to the user.

Website: www.InterfaithFamily.com

Muslim Family Services

The mission of Muslim Family Services is to assist, educate and facilitate in the success and flourishing of families based on Islamic teachings through education, counseling and liaison and supportive services. To be the best social service organization, serving the Muslims, people of Michigan and America by building strong family structures, promoting healthy marriages, helping reduce divorces, eradicating domestic violence, and providing emergency assistance.

Website: www.icnarelief.org/mfs/index.html

~Appendix I~

Funding Options for Therapeutic Treatment away from Home

How do you pay for psychological & psychiatric services? An even bigger expense is paying for residential treatment but if your child needs these services they are important enough to take out a second mortgage on your house or to use your child's college fund to pay for these services. If your child gets back on the right track, he or she can get a job and pay for his or her own college education or take out loans or get a scholarship. But they need your help now. If they don't get the help they need, they may not survive long enough to get to college or they may get locked out of college because they are locked up in jail.

Many insurance companies pay for psychiatric and psychological services. Some may pay for all or part of a child's stay in residential treatment depending on their policies, the length of stay, the level of care, and the issues your child requires services for. You may be able to get your local school district to pay for your child's residential treatment if it is clear that he or she needs residential treatment and the school district is unable to provide the type of care needed. The school district may not want to pay for these services, so it may be a battle to get them to pay for them (i.e., You may need to hire an attorney).

If you're looking for low cost psychological services for your child, you may want to check with your local community mental health center. A number of clinics offer a sliding fee scale for therapy and some of them have masters or doctorate level counseling students working there. They would be happy to provide low cost therapeutic service as part of their training. That's what they're there for. Community mental health centers are also a good place to find out about other mental health resources in your area. You may also want to contact the Department of Mental Health in your region or your County's Department of Children and Family Services. I have listed a few options for you to hopefully provide you with the funding assistance you need.

Clark Behavioral Health Financing

When faced with the challenge of paying for private healthcare, you deserve to have choices. Clark Behavioral Health Financing (CBHF) can help you find a financial solution. Let them put the pieces together so that you can focus on what's most important – the health and happiness of you and your family. They offer customized financing plans for Treatment Centers; Transitional Living Facilities; Wilderness Programs; Eating Disorder Clinics; Drug or Alcohol Rehab, Weight Loss; Inpatient and Out Patient Services and More

Office: 1-888-755-3079
Fax: 1-208-676-1702
Email: team@clarkbhf.com
Website: www.CustoMedLoans.com

Saving Teens in Crisis Collaborative

Saving Teens In Crisis Collaborative (STICC) is a 501(c)(3) non-profit organization formed in April of 2004 to assist troubled teens and their families struggling with substance abuse and other emotional issues. STICC works with health organizations, educational consultants, wilderness programs, boarding schools, rehabilitation centers and educational lawyers to fund and support these families as they complete the comprehensive therapeutic programs that they desperately need, but did not know about and could not afford. By leveraging the expertise and generosity of dedicated professionals, caring institutions, other charities, government institutions and altruistic individuals, STICC guides children and their families toward a brighter future. John D. Reuben is the Founder and President of this organization.

Office: 1-877-249-1336
Email: information@savingteens.org
Website: www.SavingTeens.org

Friends of Families with Children in Crisis

The Foundation's purpose is to provide financial assistance to families where a lack of financial resources jeopardizes a student's continued enrollment. The Foundation is focused on helping families with both parents/guardians who are committed to participating in their children's education/programs and students who are diligently progressing in those programs. The Foundation will allocate a majority of its aid in the form of collateralized loan guarantees for the benefit of families who do not qualify under conventional loan programs. The Foundation-backed loans will be granted with competitive interest rates and will not require any collateral from benefited families. The typical loan will have a 15 year repayment terms.

Office: 1-951-315-8320
Fax: 1-909-336-1942
E-Mail info@friendsoffamilies.org
Web: www.FriendsOfFamilies.org

STAR of Life Foundation

Star of Life Foundation helps families through awareness, education and support programs in communities. Since that time they have raised and provided more than $8 million in assistance and support to families. As an approved 501(c)(3) public benefits, non-profit organization, they have the ability to raise capital and assist in various ways.

Office: 1-559-822-4317
Email: info@staroflife.org
Web: www.staroflife.org

~Appendix J~
Finding Low Cost Therapeutic Treatment Options and Social Services

Low Cost Therapeutic Treatment Options

You can find many low cost therapeutic treatment options simply by using a "search engine" on your computer. Just look for "Baptist Children's Homes" in your state or neighboring state. Also, look for "Presbyterian Children's Homes", "Lutheran Children's Homes", "Catholic Children's Homes", "Jewish Children's Homes", or any other denomination you belong to or can think of typing in the search engine (i.e., "Christian Children's Homes", etc.). Many of these types of denominational children's homes will offer subsidized treatment to financially needy families because they view it as a ministry to help those who are in need.

Substance Abuse and Mental Health Services Administration (SAMHSA)

SAMHSA is part of the United States Department of Health and Human Services. Their website offers a facility locator, mental health services directory, Hispanic youth violence prevention services, state resource guides, and a state substance abuse treatment facility locator. You can also obtain lots of free information both online and in print.

Office: 1-800-729-6686
Websites: www.findtreatment.SAMHSA.gov
www.mentalhealth.SAMHSA.gov
www.oas.SAMHSA.gov

Rainbow Resources Directories (California Only)
Quickly find local shelters, places for food, health clinics, help with addictions, and many more types of California social welfare organizations. Since 1979 the Rainbow Referral Guides have been helping agencies steer needy clients to people and organizations that can help.

Office: 1-800-440-4780
Websites: www.resourcedirectory.com

Alameda County, California
The Big Blue Book is Eden I&R's Directory of Human Services for Alameda County. With it, you can find the right services, the first time. It includes listings for over 2,100 health and human service programs.

Office: 1-510-537-2710
Website: www.edenir.org

Directory of Health & Human Services Metropolitan Chicago
If you live in the Chicago area you may find this directory helpful.

Office: 1-312-491-7800
Website: www.communityresourcenetwork.org/content/home
Website: www.chicagovolunteer.net

The previous examples are just to help you get started. We obviously could not provide resources for every area in the USA. A good place to start is at a local therapist's office or at a not-for-profit community mental health center. Generally community mental health centers keep a list of services that are available in their area. You may also want to ask the school counselor at your local public school for options or ask for resources from a local church or synagogue, contact the Department of Mental Health in your region, Child

Protective Services, Juvenile Probation Department, or a local children's charity. You can also search online for information. Not all areas offer social service resource guides but if you do a search on Google for resource guides along with the name of your state you may find some helpful information.

NOTE: Please don't forget about your "Creative Teeth" option available under the letter "Y" in the acronym of FAMILY Rules. When utilizing "Creative Teeth", you're not threatening to send the child to a group home, boarding school, or residential treatment center. Rather, you're putting "reverent fear of authority" within the heart of the child by simply threatening to send him/her to a place where they absolutely do not want to go to live. Here are some examples that have worked in the past:

1. If you remember reading earlier in my book, Connie threatened to send her adolescent children, Ed and Theresa, away to live with their father if they continued to verbally and physically abuse her and/or if they refused to follow her rules. The fear of being sent away kept Ed and Theresa from being sent away. Two years later, Ed and Theresa called my office and turned in their mother, Connie, for not implementing the program "correctly and consistently" in their home (i.e., "the two 'C' words").

2. Also, if you remember reading earlier in my book, some parents in Alaska threatened to send their sixteen year old son to live with his uncle in a cabin on the Yukon River, in the middle of nowhere Alaska with the moose and grizzly bear, until he completed a home-based high school diploma program. The uncle flew in from the Bush of Alaska for the session when I explained how FAMILY Rules works to the young man. When I finished talking, he looked into my eyes and saw that I meant business. He looked into his parents eyes and saw that they meant business. Finally, he looked into his uncle's eyes and saw that he meant business. The young man chose to get off the alcohol and drugs and

actually graduated from a public high school in Anchorage, Alaska. The fear of being sent away kept him from being sent away.

3. Some parents in southern Oregon had an eighth grade daughter who dropped out of school, ran away from home, and was living on the streets, drinking, drugging, and prostituting herself. The police finally found the girl and returned her to the parents. They brought her into my office for me to explain how FAMILY Rules works to her. I informed the girl that if she doesn't follow the program and earns herself a "Strike Three" or a "Pop Fly", her parents have decided to send her to live with a missionary family in southern Mexico. Within one month, the girl earned a "Pop Fly" so her parents flew her down to southern Mexico as promised. She lived with the missionary couple who happened to run a group home for unwed teenage mothers. After two years of living with them, her life was totally changed in a majorly positive direction. She is doing very well now.

If your son or daughter ever receives a "Strike Three" or "Pop Fly" and you need to send them to a therapeutic treatment setting, please remember that there are professionals who can assist you in transporting him/her there both safely and legally (please see Appendix L).

~Appendix K~

Information about Possible Tax Deductions

I realize that in the thought process of obtaining help for your child, which is uppermost in a parent's mind, certain items may be missed. As tax filing season approaches, talk with your Certified Public Accountant (CPA) about a possible tax deduction because your child is enrolled in a therapeutic school. I have done some tax research and have located a couple of tax cases which may allow the deduction of the cost of a therapeutic boarding school or therapeutic residential program as a medical expense subject to the rules of the medical expense deduction.

There are two tax court cases which deal with the deduction of special schooling. The tax case of A. P. Grunwald, 51 TC 108 Dec 29,198: "A psychiatrically oriented boarding school recommended by a psychiatrist who diagnosed a taxpayer's child as suffering from a severe adjustment reason of adolescence. It had a residential treatment center and a staff including psychiatrists, psychologists and a psychiatric social worker, emphasized mental hygiene and psychological guidance and designed an individual program for each student."

Another case is C.F. Urbauer 63 TCM 2492. Dec 48,094 (M) TC Memo 1992-170: "Parents could deduct certain amounts spent in connection with the treatment of their son for behavioral and drug problems at a college preparatory school that addressed both the educational and emotional needs of its students. Since the son attended the school principally to benefit from its medical program and the costs of his education were incidental to the special services provided by the school, his enrollment costs were deductible as a medical expense."

The next largest expense for parents with children enrolled in a therapeutic boarding school is the transportation of the child on home visits, as well as visits during or in between parent workshops. Another case again is <u>C.F.Urbauer 63 TCM 2492. Dec 48,094 (M)</u> <u>TC Memo 1992-170</u>: "Plane fare for trips to required therapy sessions were medical expenses of parents of a student at a school for treatment of behavioral and drug problems when the school costs were allowed as medical expense"

Finally, based upon the above case, you may be able to consider the traveling of your children for home visits as a medical expense. This is an integral part of their therapy and therefore may be deductible. The costs of lodging and meals in the city where your child attends a therapeutic boarding school might be deductible because you are attending both medical workshops in dealing with your child and also attending therapy sessions with your son's therapists. You will most definitely need to talk with your CPA about the possible tax deductions mentioned above. The tax codes are constantly changing and not all CPA's would agree with the above assessment. Your CPA has the final say. I'm merely offering suggestions to explore with your CPA.

~Appendix L~

Professionals who Help Transport Children to Treatment

Association of Mediation and Transport Services (AMATS)

The members of this association of transport service providers have agreed to follow an ethical code and have strict guidelines that they have agreed to follow. The companies that are represented in this association will pick your child up and deliver him or her to a therapeutic program even if the child refuses treatment. Some of them will also help search for runaways.

Website: www.amats.org

~**Appendix M**~

How to Schedule a
FAMILY Rules Seminar

If you like what you read and would like to schedule a FAMILY Rules seminar at your agency, business, school, university, church, synagogue, or civic organization so other families in your community can benefit, please contact Dr. Matthew A. Johnson via the following options:

Office: 1-541-956-8585
Fax: 1-541-955-7165
E-Mail: DrJ@Family-Rules.com

Yes! Dr. Matthew A. Johnson does live in Grants Pass, Oregon and it may seem far, far away from where you live. Yes! I know you can't ever imagine traveling that far yourself. However, due to the modern miracle of avionics, Dr. Matthew A. Johnson is actually able to fly to your location via a jet airplane. The neighboring city of Medford, Oregon really does have an international airport. Therefore, Dr. Matthew A. Johnson can get to your community in a jiffy. Amazing, huh? So don't hesitate to contact him to schedule a FAMILY Rules seminar in your community. He really wouldn't mind traveling to your neck of the woods to present his FAMILY Rules seminar to the families in your community. Besides, where you live is probably a very nice place to visit. "Dr. J." could use an occasional change of scenery from time to time.

~Appendix N~

The FAMILY FUNctions Parenting Tool Kit

The Family FUNctions Parenting Tool Kit is the perfect way to implement the "Positive Parenting with a Plan (Grades K-12): FAMILY Rules" program by Dr. Matthew A Johnson. Each kit includes materials and a copy of Dr. Johnson's book.

So what's in the kit?

- Two (2) "Family Rules" charts

- Two (2) "Child's" Chore Charts

- One (1) "Parents'" Chore Chart

- One (1) "Rewards" Chart

- One (1) "Family Meeting Agenda" Chart

- One (1) Dry-Erase marker

- Five (5) Magnetic strips to put on backs of charts (for refrigerator)

- One (1) Refrigerator magnet with contact information on it

- One (1) Wooden box with tokens and R.A.K chips for two children

- One (1) Wooden box with a deck of Good Habit Cards

- Two (2) Small wooden boxes to put tokens in

- Set of Instructions

- One (1) "Positive Parenting with a Plan" book by Dr. Matthew A. Johnson

Contact:

Family FUNctions, LLC
P.O. Box 910
Columbia, Maryland 21044

Office: 1-443-538-1891
Fax: 1-410-992-0366

E-Mail: info@Family-Functions.com
Website: www.Family-Functions.com

NOTE: You may also buy the Parenting Tool Kit without a book, for a cheaper price, since you already bought this book.

~Appendix O~

Dr. Matthew A. Johnson

Paid Phone Consultation Provided by
Dr. Matthew A. Johnson

If you would like to schedule a paid phone consultation session with "Dr. J.", simply go to his website: www.Family-Rules.com/Store Then click on the picture of the telephone. You can schedule a twenty-five minute or fifty-minute consultation session with your debit card or credit card. Dr. Johnson's office will call you to set up the paid phone consultation appointment.

Dr. Johnson can make House Calls

If you would like to have Dr. Johnson come spend a day or two with your family to help you get FAMILY Rules up and running in your home, feel free to call or e-mail him to discuss fees and to make arrangements.

Family Rules, Inc.
PO Box 1801
Grants Pass, Oregon 97528

Office: 1-541-956-8585
Fax: 1-541-955-7165

E-Mail: DrJ@Family-Rules.com
Website: www.Family-Rules.com

~Appendix P~

"Mad Matt's Mashed Potato Salad"

During the summer of 1981, I traveled with "Athletes in Action" to Brazil, where we played twenty-seven basketball games in thirty-five days, including against some of their Olympic players. It was a whole lot of fun playing with fellow collegiate basketball players from all over the USA (e.g., Arizona State, New Mexico State, Marquette University, Florida, etc.). While playing in Brazil, my wild and crazy sense of humor earned me the nickname – "Mad Matt." No, I didn't have any anger issues. I was just a friendly laid back guy with a whole lot of wild and crazy humor mixed in. Anyway, when I returned to Anchorage, Alaska to continue to play basketball for the Seawolves, the nickname, "Mad Matt", stuck with me. While attending the University of Alaska at Anchorage, one of the inexpensive dishes that I would make that lasted a few days was "Mad Matt's Mashed Potato Salad." To this very day, my wife and children demand that I make it often or they will take hostages in our neighborhood. I wish to share my family's favorite dish with you.

The Recipe for "Mad Matt's Mashed Potato Salad"

Food Supplies needed:
12 Large Potatoes
12 Large Eggs
12 Genuine Dill Pickles
4 Cans of Large or Jumbo Black Pitted Olives
A Large Container of Real Mayonnaise
A Small Container of Yellow Mustard
Genuine Dill Pickle Juice from a Jar

Directions:

1. Peel 12 large potatoes, rinse them off, and cut them into small one or two inch chunks so they can be boiled easier in a very large pot of water.

2. Boil the potatoes in a large pot of water until they have softened enough to be mashed.

3. When the potatoes are soft and ready to be mashed, carefully drain all of the hot water into the sink.

4. Cool the hot potatoes down with cold running water. Drain the pot again into the sink.

5. Mash the potatoes in the very large pot or in a very large bowl.

6. While boiling the potatoes above, also boil 12 large eggs in a pan of water for at least 15 minutes.

7. Cool down the pan of hard-boiled eggs under cold running water in the sink for a couple of minutes.

8. Peel the eggs and place them in a large bowl and then mash them too (Hint: Hard-boiled eggs peel easier under warm running water in the sink).

9. Set the mashed potatoes and mashed hard-boiled eggs aside and allow them to cool down.

10. While the mashed potatoes and mashed hard-boiled eggs are cooling down separately, cut up the Genuine Dill Pickles into large ¼ inch to ½ inch chunks. We need good sized chunks of pickles.

11. Now open and drain the juice from the 4 cans of large or jumbo black pitted olives into the sink. Cut the olives in half. We need good sized chunks of black olives.

12. Once the mashed potatoes and mashed boiled eggs have cooled down, thoroughly mix them together in a very large bowl or very large pot.

13. Mix in the mayonnaise first until you've reached a nice mashed potato consistency that you are comfortable with.

14. Now add the yellow mustard a little bit at a time. You don't want the color to be a faint pale yellow. However, you don't want it to be a bright yellow either. You want to add enough yellow mustard to your potato salad to give it a kick.

15. Now mix in the chunky pickles and chunky black olives.

16. Last but not least, start mixing in the Genuine Dill Pickle juice from the jar a little bit at a time. This helps to add moisture to the potato salad as well as genuine dill flavor.

17. Finally, enjoy eating your "Mad Matt's Mashed Potato Salad"!!! After making and serving it, you'll understand why I've asked you to make such a big bowl full. It won't last very long. I promise. By the way, some of my family members like to microwave their "Mad Matt's Mashed Potato Salad" before they eat it.

18. When not being consumed, please always keep the potato salad refrigerated.

Note: Naturally, if you don't want to feed an army or have leftovers for a few days, simply cut the amount of the ingredients by half. Enjoy!

Now it's Your Turn

I have many books in my head that I plan to write before I kick the bucket. One of the books will include a combination of FAMILY Rules success stories along with your favorite home recipe to share with others. I've shared my FAMILY Rules success stories with you along with my family's favorite homemade recipe created by yours truly. Now it's your turn. If you're interested in submitting your FAMILY Rules success story along with your favorite homemade recipe, please e-mail both to: DrJ@Family-Rules.com

You must include a statement that the recipe you're submitting is yours and was not taken from an already published cook book. The best FAMILY Rules success stories and recipes will be added into my future book. When you send me your e-mail, please let me know if you want your full name included or just your initials along with your City and State. I want you to receive credit for your awesome recipe. I'm looking forward to sampling your recipes as well as sharing them with the larger FAMILY Rules community. Who knows? Maybe we will all get together for a big picnic or wedding feast someday.

~About the Author~

Dr. Matthew A. Johnson ("Dr. J.") is a licensed clinical psychologist. He holds degrees from the University of Alaska, Rutgers University and George Fox University. He has worked with parents and children in the mental health field since 1982 in group homes, residential treatment centers, inpatient psychiatric hospitals, and outpatient settings. Dr. Johnson was the Clinical Director for Charter North Outpatient Counseling Center in Fairbanks, Alaska. He is also the President of FAMILY Rules, Inc. He wrote "Positive Parenting with a Plan (Grades K-12): FAMILY Rules" and has taught this successful research-based behavior modification system for families in a variety of settings across the United States, Canada, and Europe. Dr. Johnson has lectured extensively on child and adolescent health issues and improving families. He has trained over 50,000 professionals. He has been featured on *The Early Show*, CNN, ESPN2, *USA Today*, and 250+ radio programs. Dr. Johnson uses his broad professional background, real-life parenting experience, and his great sense of humor to write an informative and entertaining book.

Dr. Johnson moved to Alaska in 1980 to attend the University of Alaska at Anchorage on a full-ride basketball scholarship. He is a pretty tall guy (6'9") with a sense of humor to match. He scored his first two collegiate points against North Carolina in the Great Alaska Shootout on ESPN. Also, he got half of his picture in Sports Illustrated (his silly teammate was in the way of the other half). Dr. Johnson is married to his wife, Amanda, and has four children - Levi, Hannah, Micah, and Grady. He also has two dogs - Sophie and Scout; and one cat - Harley.

Dr. Johnson loves his parents very much! As a matter of fact, his father lives with him today. Unfortunately, his mother passed away in April of 2008. Nevertheless, he grew up in a dysfunctional family and understands how the lack of organization, structure, accountability, and communication can lead to marital and family chaos in the home. He has worked with similar families in various treatment settings and has established FAMILY Rules, Inc. to combat the cancer of dysfunctional families.

Today, Dr. Johnson speaks in 80 cities per year all over the USA and Canada. He trains psychiatrists, pediatricians, psychologists, social workers, marriage and family therapists, mental health counselors, pastoral counselors, probation officers, teachers, and parents how to use "Positive Parenting with a Plan" with their families. He receives a 95% to 100% approval rating everywhere he speaks via the evaluation forms at the end of every seminar.

~Notes~

~Notes~

~Notes~

~Notes~

Intermedia Publishing Group

Publishing That Works For You

If you have a book that you would like to publish, contact Terry Whalin, Publisher, at Intermedia Publishing Group, (623) 337-8710 or email: twhalin@intermediapub.com or use the contact form at: www.intermediapub.com.